Measuring the Impact of Your Web Site

Robert W. Buchanan, Jr.
Charles Lukaszewski

Wiley Computer Publishing

John Wiley & Sons, Inc.

New York • Chichester • Weinheim • Brisbane • Singapore • Toronto

Executive Publisher: Katherine Schowalter

Editor: Marjorie Spencer

Managing Editor: Micheline Frederick

Text Design & Composition: SunCliff Graphic Productions

Illustrations: Aesthetic License/Kristine Buchanan

Designations used by companies to distinguish their products are often claimed as trademarks. In all instances where John Wiley & Sons, Inc. is aware of a claim, the product names appear in initial capital or ALL CAPITAL LETTERS. Readers, however, should contact the appropriate companies for more complete information regarding trademarks and registration.

This text is printed on acid-free paper.

This publication is designed to provide accurate and authoritative information in regard to the subject matter covered. It is sold with the understanding that the publisher is not engaged in rendering legal, accounting, or other professional service. If legal advice or other expert assistance is required, the services of a competent professional person should be sought.

Library of Congress Cataloging-in-Publication Data

Buchanan, Robert W., 1949-
    Measuring the impact of your Web site / Robert W. Buchanan, jr., Charles Lukaszewski.
        p.   cm.
    Includes bibilographical references.
    ISBN: 0-471-17249-9 (pbk. : alk. paper)
    1. Web sites--Evaluation.   I. Lukaszewski, Charles.   II. Title.
TK5105.888.B83   1997
658.8'4--dc21   96-47396
                                                                                              CIP

Printed in the United States of America
10 9 8 7 6 5 4 3 2 1

Contents

Chapter 3 Measurement Strategies and Sources 79

Chapter 4 Measurement Opportunities in Site Features 101

Chapter 9 What Do Your Measures Mean? 231

Chapter 10 Content Evolution Choices 255

Chapter 11 Strategy and Promotion Choices 277

Acknowledgments

We would like to thank all those who participated in the case studies. Their invaluable information, observations, insight, and real-life Internet and intranet experiences helped to illustrate how web site measurement is critical to site analysis, evolution, and ultimate success. Particularly, special thanks go to

- ❑ B. D. Goel and the Public Relations staff at Worldview Systems Corporation for the Travelocity web site

- ❑ Robert Hamilton, Manager, Electronic Commerce Marketing, Federal Express

- ❑ Brett Manilo, Manager, Corporate Web Systems, Silicon Graphics, Inc.

- ❑ Tom Meenan and his associates at the Senate Computer Center

- ❑ Robert Schafer, Publisher, Minneapolis and St. Paul *Star Tribune*

- ❑ Jim Wallace, Marketing Manager for Consumer Products, The Toro Company

- ❑ Barry Wegener, Communications Manager, General Mills
- ❑ Griff Wigley, New Media Manager, *Utne Reader* magazine

for their help and support in this project.

Bob & Chuck

The experience shared in this book could not have come without the willingness of eWorks! clients to embrace and experiment with this new medium. I want to thank Larry Kampa, Elgin Manhard, and Bob Seper of Campbell-Mithun-Esty Advertising; Paul Tobin of Tobin, Erdmann & Jacobsen; Joe Showalter of 3M; Alan Lederfeind of Wall Street Discount Corporation; and Craig Evans of Periscope Marketing/Communications who all jumped in early.

Finally, writing a book of this scope while managing a fast-growing Internet business has been its own challenge. All the employees at eWorks! deserve recognition for providing great service to our customers so that I could work on the book. I want to thank my brother and business partner, James Alexander, for his patience and support. To my wife, business partner, and companion, Kathy, I owe you a long vacation on your favorite island.

Chuck

I want to thank all the people at John Wiley & Sons for their faith and support in helping me write a second book, even before the ink was dry on the first book and its success measured. Also, I thank my friends Kodi and Shiloh for getting up before sunrise each morning to be my companions and lay at my feet, while I worked on this book. Thanks to my best friend, wife, and partner, Kris, for just being there, as well as creating the great illustrations which convey key messages throughout the book.

Bob

Foreword

People all over the world are beginning to realize that the Internet is a positive force in their personal and professional lives. Executives everywhere are waking up to the money-saving and time-saving power of intranets. And whole new industries are being created at unprecedented speed to grow and harness these tools. *Measuring the Impact of Your Web Site* is one of the first books to document the benefits of this incredible revolution. Even more important, this book shows you how to begin to justify funding for and measure the impact of an Internet or intranet for your organization.

While all of us an Netscape are helping to make it happen, the scope of what is happening is surprising even here. A whole new computing paradigm is being born—a world where the escalating costs of corporate desktops is giving way to less expensive server-based applications. It is a world where every home and every individual will have personal, comprehensive and fast access to whatever information, products and services we need whenever we need it. It is an age where even the notions of politics and borders are being re-evaluated.

When we named one of our products "Navigator" it was important to us to help customers find their way through the swelling seas of information and resources online. This book will help you chart a course toward creating and maintaining your own online content. The case studies of both well-known and less prominent organizations will show you what mistakes to avoid and what strategies are worth calling your own. Major users of Netscape technology including Federal Express, Silicon Graphics and Travelocity have been generous enough to provide detailed and invaluable performance information about their sites.

In sum, whether you're working with the Web or just thinking about it you need real-life lessons such as those captured so clearly in this book. Whether you're a freelance HTML developer or an MIS director, an artist or an advertising executive, a department head or a CEO you should learn the simple strategies for success presented here. And we'll be reading it here at Netscape to help make the products you need, the best they can be.

James L. Barksdale
President and Chief Executive Officer
Netscape Communications Corporation

Introduction

Are you convinced that your web site is making a difference but don't know how to prove it?

Are you worried about explaining why your site doesn't have much traffic?

Is your web site taking enough time or computing resources that it will need its own budget soon?

Do you get frustrated trying to understand raw data from web servers?

If some of these questions hit home, then this book is for you.

Web sites are still a very new endeavor for most companies. Many have rushed into sites without proper goals or planning. As a result, companies now find themselves trying to manage web sites without proper yardsticks. Continued web site funding often results in "throwing good money after bad" in the absence of an adequate understanding of web site return on investment (ROI). Today, companies are beginning to re-evaluate their initial Web involvement, modifying their sites and making decisions based on business economics and audience feedback—not just "we're on the Web, too" economics. To make these decisions requires understanding of how the site is impacting your customers, prospects, company, distribution, and many other aspects. You must also understand how your site audience is impacting the site, since it is a dual-edged sword.

Even if you aren't required to formally justify the site prior to its development and implementation, there will usually be an informal, ongoing site justification as your peers and management want to know how well the site is meeting initial expectations. Also, you'll need to be able to articulate how the site is doing in order to evolve and improve it. Satisfying these latter two requirements needs the same type of measures as a formal justification. Therefore, you need to measure and analyze the site, audience, and content both prior to implementation and during site operation to effectively manage the site. The basic facts are:

- ❏ It costs money to set up and maintain a web site; someone usually has to be convinced to spend and continue spending that money.
- ❏ Continued site measurement and analysis will improve the site's content and audience acceptance.
- ❏ Successful sites return value for the investment.
- ❏ Some sites are not providing ROI or have outlived their usefulness and need to be shut down.

This book provides a set of proven yardsticks and numerous case studies that illustrate measuring, evolving, and justifying web sites. Success or failure of a web site is rarely a black-and-white proposition. Success is often the result of properly assessing the site and making decisions on its evolution based on hard technical and business data. Failure can be demonstrable or can simply be the result of not knowing how well a web site is meeting your goals and your audience needs.

Whether you are re-evaluating an existing site, planning your first site, or trying to manage a working site, *Measuring the Impact of Your Web Site* can help you perform better. That's because the insights and tips we've gathered together here were earned the hard way. Using methodology similar to that outlined in this book, Federal Express (FedEx) justified an external Web site based on its company strategy of providing continual improvement in customer service and satisfaction through employment of new technologies. FedEx met its goal with a 90-plus percent customer acceptance and improved customer response to the two most often asked questions: "Has my package arrived?," and, if not, "Where is it?" Their measures also showed savings of over $200,000 per month on 800-number long distance charges. FedEx justified its site on well-defined goals and can continue to justify its support on measured benefits. This is just one illustration of the numerous case studies presented throughout the book.

To know if a site has met its goal of cost containment, for example, you need to be able to compare past and current costs. However, cost comparison is only the first step. To know if the site is successfully supporting your business, you need to determine customer satisfaction levels. To know if the site is performing well and has the capacity to service more users, you need site load metrics, response times, and error rates. To be valid, your information must be based on hard data, and hard data can only be acquired through measurement.

If the site is containing cost, but not meeting customer needs, you may have unhappy customers—an outcome which negates cost savings. To avoid such a misstep, you'll need to analyze both the primary measurements used to justify the site and the corollary measurements that may impact your business. If the primary goal in the previous example had been to improve customer satisfaction, then the corollary measurement may have been the cost of new services. The point is that you must measure multiple dimensions of the site to effectively determine if it is

❑ meeting the goals it was justified on,

❑ not creating negative impacts in other areas,

❑ providing unexpected benefits, and

❑ in need of improvement.

Strategy, Goals, Justification, Implementation, Measurement, Evolution

As in any project, a web site passes through many phases during its life cycle. It is rare for one phase to be entirely complete before successive ones begin; webmasters understand that the *evolution* phase is really just the beginning of a new planning and implementation cycle. While web site strategy and planning books address the early phases of the life cycle, they do not help you understand later phases or develop the critical linkage between goals and measurement needed to manage, evolve, and ensure continued support for the site.

In the pages that follow we have tried to furnish complete information on how to measure your web site to ensure its goals, and to make critical decisions on its evolution based on verifiable technical and business data. While no two organizations will use the same justification process, this book presents basic elements crucial to any successful justification process. Justification and improvement endeavors are both more effective when designed into the site from the very beginning—this begins with collecting raw data on site usage and business impact. *Measuring the Impact of Your Web Site* shows you how to measure site ROI and impact on business and customers, so you won't get tangled in the quagmire of uncertain value and spiraling costs. Many companies are beginning to recognize these needs. In September 1996, Knight-Ridder Newspapers, Inc. announced plans to build an internal traffic system to measure the way customers use content and view advertisements on 30 separate web sites developed by the newspaper chain.

Reading This Book

As Bill Krause, longtime CEO and President of 3Com Corporation, once told the people who were scheduling his appearances at product rollout shows, "time is my most precious thing; keep the rehearsals short and the time between appearances to a minimum." In today's business world, most of us would readily agree with Bill. Therefore, this book is structured to conserve your time and maximize your investment. It is divided into three parts which can be read in sequence, as standalones, or used as reference material. Here's a chapter summary to get you started.

Part I covers the justification process and measurement strategies as they pertain to and complement site planning and implementation. It describes how analyzing target audience needs and customer value requirements influence goal setting, justification strategies, and measurement requirements. An in-depth justification process and numerous case studies are presented, plus illustrations on how required measurements should be built in through the planning process to analyze audience demographics, measure the effectiveness of site content, and support the justification strategy. The concept of a hierarchy of measures—Impact, Approximated, Consolidated, and Raw Measures—is introduced. In addition, how primary, implicit, and corollary success factors affect site success and need for improvement is described. This section is designed for the site visionary, senior manager, and financial decision maker who must understand how to measure initial and ongoing site value and audience acceptance.

Part II explains the processes and tools required to accurately quantify the measures that support site justification and audience/content analysis discussed in Part I. It describes how to obtain technical site data and nontechnical measures, such as sales growth and customer satisfaction. Examples, worksheets, and flowcharts illustrate how some well-known data collection and analysis tools can be used. Of the three chapters in Part II, Chapter 5 is focused toward the same audience as Part I, while Chapters 6 and 7 present more in-depth technical information for the site manager or senior technical person.

Part III explains how to apply measures in making essential decisions about the success of the site in meeting its goals and evolutionary decisions on site content and promotion. It also reviews circumstances that would make you shut down a web site for lack of meeting its goals or other reasons. Through case studies, differences in measures and measurement between Internet and intranet sites are compared. These sections provide a method for developing actionable conclusions about the success or failure of your web site and what to do about it. This information is for the person who provides management and continued justification of the site.

Figure I.1a is a matrix of the key topics addressed in the book. It illustrates how tasks, justification, measurements, and analysis map into the life cycle of the web site. Figure I.1b shows how these various topics map into the book's chapters. Note that some topics, such as creative development, and testing and review, are not covered in this book. These topics are complex and not directly related to the focus of this book, which is site measurement and analysis. They deserve to be covered in other books dedicated to that subject.

Phases Web Site Life Cycle	Tasks Web Site Life Cycle Tasks	Justification Process		
Define need	Define need	Define need		
Planning	Set objective			
	Analyze audience	Recommend solution		
	Select content	Quantify investment		
	Choose promotion strategy			
Production	Project definition	Select justification strategies	Cost avoidance and reduction	Impact Measures
			Revenue growth	
			Customer satisfaction	
			Quality improvement	
			Other specific goals	
		Quanify ROI, cost, and risk	Consolidated measures	
			Approximations	
			Raw measures	
		Present justification		
		Approve or reject		
	Concept content and navigation	Implementation	Custom site features	
			Common site features (generic)	
	Creative and site development			
	Testing and review			
Implementation	Debut			
	Promotion			
Operation	Measurement and evolution	Ongoing measurement	How and where to gather data	
			When to gather data	
		Communicate progress		
		Evaluate whether to continue or shut down	Interpret measurements	
			Content evolution choices	
			Strategy evolution choices	

Figure I.1a Internet versus intranet Differences.

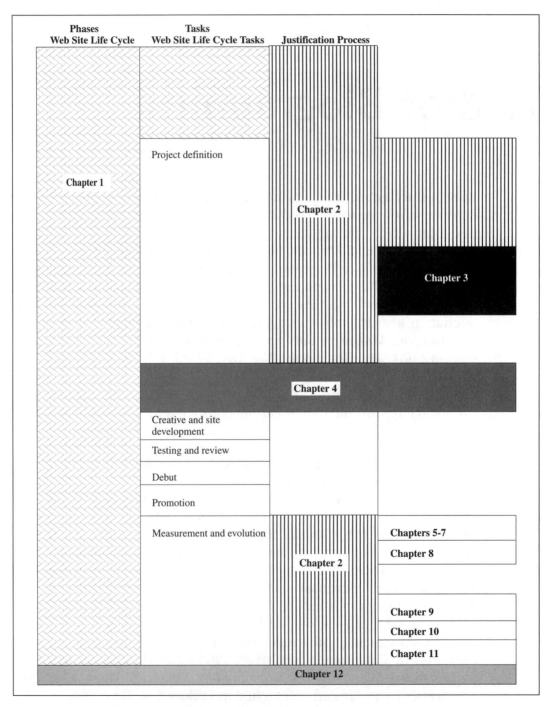

Figure I.1b Internet versus intranet Differences.

Author Biographies

Robert Buchanan, Jr. is a principal in Shiloh Associates, an independent network consulting company that provides network and Internet planning, management, and testing services to product manufacturers and Fortune 500 companies. Prior to Shiloh Associates, he was Sr. Vice President and General Manager at LANQuest, a network consulting company and independent test lab where he developed network testing procedures and testing utilities. Mr. Buchanan also spent seven years in product management at 3Com Corporation. *Measuring the Impact of Your Web Site* is Mr. Buchanan's second book. His first book, *The Art-of-Testing Network Systems*, was published by John Wiley & Sons in April, 1996. Clients include Microsoft, Novell, 3Com, NASA, NetScape, Mercury Interactive, and CommVision. Mr. Buchanan can be contacted at robtbuch@aol.com.

Charles Lukaszewski is Managing Partner of eWorks! His company provides Internet-related outsourcing services to advertising agencies, public relations firms, and systems integrators. eWorks! has created database-driven web sites for nationally recognized companies including 3M, Cargill, Toro, Jostens, Department 56, Farberware, Apple Computer, and Bayer AG. Prior to co-founding eWorks! he was Director of Advisory Services at Dataserv, a subsidiary of Wang. Dataserv purchased Mr. Lukaszewski's first company, The Network Strategies Group, in May of 1993. His consulting methodologies and client base helped launch Dataserv's own systems integration consulting business. His articles and interviews have appeared in *Communications Week*, *PR Tactics*, *Vital Speeches of the Day*, *Network World*, *Info Security Product News*, *PC Week*, *MacWeek*, and *Service News*. He can be reached at clukas@eworks.com.

Part I

Measurement Strategy and Planning

CHAPTER 1

Planning and Measurement Essentials

Successful organizations, whether in the private or public sector, know their customers, their needs, what keeps them coming back, and what would make them switch companies or products. Because customers constantly change, successful organizations must become adept at responding to new expectations for their products and services. When responsive companies are successful, their success perpetuates itself by justifying continued investment in research, product development, and customer service.

In this way, web sites are like companies. Their success is not accidental; it is based on careful preparation, thorough understanding of market needs, and a deliberate sense of timing. Success is constantly evaluated through an agreed-upon set of measures that reflect the goals of the site. When these goals are achieved, it makes sense to continue funding the site.

As a new enterprise in most organizations, web sites will be under scrutiny to determine if the business is getting value for the investment. Because of this, web sites must continuously be justified, whether formally or informally, to continue being approved and funded. Sound justifications require hard data of both a business and technical nature. Hard data can only be acquired through proactive, ongoing site and audience measurement.

Put differently, while site justification may be based on financial or other basically internal criteria, site success will be driven largely by external factors. Therefore, audience analysis and site *draw* incentives are major steps in web site planning and directly affect justification strategies and measurement requirements.

The following discussion illustrates the importance of including measurement requirements in the analysis and planning process.

Web Site Life Cycle

Figure 1.1 illustrates the life cycle of a web site, which includes four major phases—planning, production, implementation, and operation. The *steps* in the planning and operation phases show where measurement requirements and their implementation are critical to site success.

Measurement issues are included in 5 of the 10 steps which make up site planning, implementation, and operation. These steps are:

Setting an objective(s)

Analyzing the audience

Selecting appropriate content

Choosing a promotion strategy

Project definition

Concepting site content and navigation

Development and creation

Testing and review

Rollout

Site measurement and evolution

The first four items previously listed are discussed in the next section, while ongoing measurement, analysis, decision making, and site evolution are covered in Part III. The overall process shown

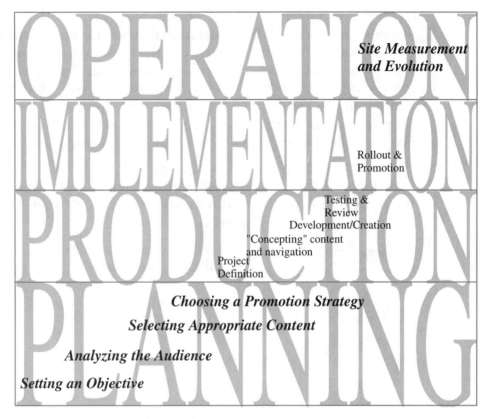

Figure 1.1 Web site life cycle.

in Figure 1.1 includes many tasks not addressed herein. You may want to buy one of the many good books on web site planning as complementary reading material. These books cover topics like site content, creative development, vendor selection, equipment and software acquisition, and project planning that are also critical to a successful site.

Case Studies Tell the Story

There is no better teacher than experience, whether it be your own or someone else's. Therefore, we believe that case studies are critical in explaining how to measure and justify your web site. Toward this end we have selected five case studies with vastly different site objectives, audiences, and organizational structure to explain some of the key points presented throughout the book. We have also taken a slightly unusual approach to presenting our studies by eliminating the typical "war story" portfolio. Instead, you will find case information and lessons learned dispersed throughout the book, as appropriate, to describe how the sites can and do evolve through planning, development, implementation, and operations stages.

We have chosen the following web sites, which are marqueed by their logo for easy reference each time they appear as examples in the book. Think of these sites as interwoven plots that will unfold as you read the book. The web sites are:

        Federal Express (FedEx)

        Toro

   Star Tribune

        Travelocity

        U.S. Senate

The following examples provide a brief introduction to the five marqueed web sites we will be touring throughout this book. Read them through to get acquainted.

CASE STUDY

 Federal Express is known to all of us as a company providing rapid and reliable movement of packages worldwide, often packages critical to our business. For 10 years, Federal Express (FedEx) has used technology to help its customers schedule shipments, and prepare shippers and labels, at the package's originating location. Initially, only customers who shipped large numbers of packages per day were automated at FedEx's expense. As technology became cheaper, FedEx's objective shifted to make that same technology offer to smaller customers. "The job of FedEx's Electronic Commerce Marketing Group," according to Robert Hamilton, Manager, Electronic Commerce Marketing, " is to implement and measure the impact of technology beyond the shipping dock." In November 1994, FedEx made a decision to use the Internet as a new means of making their technology available to the smaller (even the smallest?) customer.

CASE STUDY

TORO Toro is a leading manufacturer of home and industrial yardcare products, such as lawn mowers, snow blowers, trimmers, and sprinkler systems. Commercially, Toro is the largest supplier of irrigation systems to golf courses. Founded in 1914, Toro had sales of $919 million and net earnings of $32.4 million for the fiscal year ending 31 October 1995. The company's worldwide average employment level was 3,626.

Toro was very proactive about implementing a web site. According to Jim Wallace, Marketing Manager for Consumer Products, "We started site development in August 1995 and were the first in our industry with an online site in December 1995." This makes Toro one of the most established sites on the Net in any industry; its experiences are a valuable guide for anyone serious about the Web.

CASE STUDY

Online The *Star Tribune* serves readers throughout the Twin Cities of Minneapolis and St. Paul, Minnesota and border areas of neighboring states. It is the largest daily newspaper in the region, with a Sunday circulation of slightly less than 700,000 copies.

The *Star Tribune* started its research and development (R&D) on electronically delivered information over two years ago. The R&D

experiences significantly influenced its initial Web offering, as explained later in the discussion. After a year of evaluation and development, the *Star Tribune* launched a subscription service in June 1995 on the AT&T Interchange Network, which had been built by Ziff-Davis, then acquired. When the *Star Tribune* site went live, the Internet was beginning its rapid rise to prominence but the threat to traditional online services was only beginning to be realized. According to Publisher Robert Schafer, "We liked Interchange's financial model and after looking at their software tools, felt it was the best available electronic publishing platform." Since launch, however, subscribers uptake for this service had been low because of:

❑ Technical problems with the Interchange Network

❑ The need to distribute proprietary user-side software for Interchange Network users

❑ Customer willingness to pay

❑ Exploding use of the Internet

Recognizing that the Internet would, in fact, eclipse proprietary platforms, Schafer's team began turning their lessons into a Web-based offering. As it happened, the *Star Tribune* had, in fact, launched a web site in June 1995 along with its Interchange site, but the initial site was unpublicized and had very limited intent. In May 1996 the *Star Tribune* revamped this site into the World Wide Web edition of *Star Tribune* Online. The lessons from the Interchange Network project and the general availability of Web browsers overcame many of the previous problems and has helped to make the web site an early success story. Today the site is growing nicely and the paper is harvesting useful information from it.

CASE STUDY

Travelocity from Worldview Systems Corporation is one of the first mega-malls for travel-related products and services on the World Wide Web. Launched on 12 March 1996, the site is an exciting example of the potential of electronic commerce. Originally, it was backed by a partnership of Random House, publisher of

Fodor's Travel Guides; the SABRE Group, the information technology subsidiary of AMR Corporation; and Ameritech. In August 1996, the SABRE Group announced a letter of intent to acquire Worldview. Travelocity is an example of a *hybrid* Internet play; it sells a real-world product using the Web as a sales channel. Since many companies looking to profit from the Web need to find an effective way of selling what they already produce, this example is particularly relevant.

The Travelocity site provides two major offerings to the visitor:

❑ Up-to-date, time-sensitive information on travel destinations

❑ On-demand sales of travel-related products and services

CASE STUDY

The U.S. Senate web site was opened in October 1995 by the Senate's computer center and telecommunications divisions which are under the auspices of the Department of the Sergeant of Arms. Policy guidance, planning, and oversight of the web server are handled by the Senate Committee on Rules and Administration. A single server provides the enabling technology and support for all senator and committee home pages, but individual senators or committees are responsible for the page content, look and feel, and updates.

Based on its objectives and the structure of the relationship between the computer center, which provides site and technical support, and the Senate offices, which provide site content, the Senate web site is an illuminating hybrid of both an Internet and intranet site.

The Planning Steps

Decisions made in the following planning steps directly affect the justification strategy alternatives presented in Chapter 2 and the measurement requirements discussed in Chapters 3 and 4. Additionally, decisions made here are used as targets when analyzing how well you have done versus the plan, as discussed in Chapter 9.

Step 1: Setting an Objective

Successful Web planners typically pick one or two key objectives against which—once their site has debuted—they can judge it to be satisfactory or not. This judgment—made according to nontrivial criteria—is essential for initially justifying the site, ensuring continued funding of the site, and determining if the site is providing value and return on investment (ROI). Goals or objectives of successful sites have commonly included:

Answers to frequently asked customer questions

Resolution of customer problems

Reinforcement of a brand, product, or attitude

Education of prospective customers

Demonstration of a product or service

Creation of customer incentives to visit dealers or distributors

Sales of merchandise or services

Delivery of information to investors and shareholders

Market research

Usually it is desirable to set objectives or goals which include both financial and qualitative or quantitative measures, are reasonably attainable, and can be used to measure site progress as well as success or failure. This last point is important. As with most new undertakings, it is best to start slow and show steady progress.

CASE STUDY

 FedEx's web site objective is basically an extension of their core mission to:

❑ Provide rapid, reliable movement of packages

❑ Provide full custodial information about package status

FedEx's goal is to provide the same level of customer service for shipping and tracking through the Web as its does via 800 numbers, dedicated shipping stations at the customer's site, and PC applications.

Though not explicitly stated, a secondary objective of the site will be to sell services by expanding the site to include package shipping. In this way, the site metrics will eventually be the same as the company metrics—number of packages shipped and customer revenue per day. Another secondary objective is to take a leadership position in the shipping industry by using the Web to provide broader and deeper customer connectivity to FedEx information and applications.

Multiple measurement techniques, as discussed in Part II, are required to gather this data; it is best to include these needs during site planning, rather than trying to address them after the site is implemented, up, and running.

The other sites had vastly different objectives than those of Federal Express, as described in the following examples. But it is noteworthy that in every case, the site had explicit criteria against which to measure success or failure before it was implemented.

CASE STUDY

The Travelocity site is based on a revenue business model. In fact, this is the first site of the companies we interviewed with justification based on online sales of products and services.

A secondary objective was to create an online service in which Travelocity had control over both the content and service aspects of the business. Relationships with America Online (AOL) and others in which Travelocity provided content, but not the user interface, did not meet this second objective. With this new service, it now provides real-time access to the user through its own web site.

CASE STUDY

Online The *Star Tribune* views its site as a news and information distribution channel. The site's primary objective is a research project allowing the *Star Tribune* to quantify and qualify the market for electronic information delivery. While there has been hype about interactive television as the wave of the future, the *Star Tribune* believes that multiple forms of interactive communication will definitely be available, although most of them will take years to develop thoroughly. The *Star Tribune* wants to get in early, learn from mistakes, and be ready if it really takes off.

A secondary object is to prevent erosion of classified advertising revenues. Like most papers, the *Star Tribune* derives a substantial percentage of its revenues from classifieds. Whether they have an online news feature, Schafer and his management are convinced that other companies could start online services that could erode the *Star Tribune*'s classified advertising franchise. Therefore, they want to seize the market window in order to project their brand online first.

A longer-term objective is to evaluate selling access to databases of interest to consumers through the Internet.

The site's current focus is to provide "news as it happens" and classifieds. Whereas, the newspaper is *put to bed* at 12:45 A.M. when it goes to press for the morning edition, the web site provides updates throughout the day. Additionally, the site provides collections of articles on specific topics (neighborhood profiles, for example) and some content that is not available in the newspaper.

CASE STUDY

TORO Toro views its site as an interactive marketing program and an extension of traditional advertising programs with the objectives and requirements of:

Getting prospective buyers into existing Toro dealers

Increasing recognition of Toro in markets where dealer density is lower

Promoting the company's quality brand image

Providing accurate and convenient information about the company and products

---

CASE STUDY

The Senate site was mainly a reactive response to the requirements of several Senators to have a presence on the Internet and to general inquiries from the press and the general public about a U.S. Senate web site. The initial objective was to provide a site that drew on existing, general information resources about the Senate which were not yet available online, including the Congressional Directory and legislative background materials from the Congressional Research Service. The initial release of this service was limited to mainly *fixed* rather than *real-time* information sources.

The site's objectives are:

1. Meet the needs of the Senate offices and committees for making information available to the general public.
2. Provide external communications from the Senate to U.S. constituents, educational sites, and foreign visitors to the U.S. capital and Senate.

Future plans are underway for a more proactive site expansion based on defined requirements from Senators and committees, as discussed later in the case study.

Step 2: Analyzing Your Audience

Trying to be all things to all people (your potential audiences) will not make a site successful. In fact, it is almost a guaranteed recipe for disaster. Figure 1.2 illustrates the four predominate perspectives of most Internet users. The traditional Internet users, either *surfers* or *cool site* visitors, will probably not be the central focus audience for most business or service-oriented sites. The new type of Internet

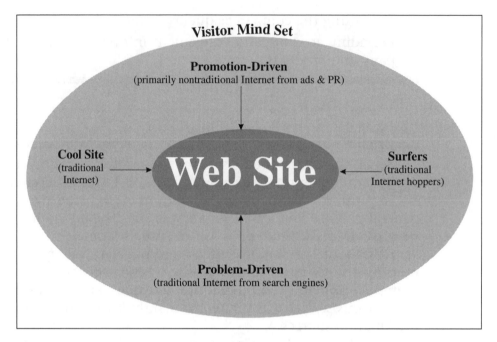

Figure 1.2 Internet visitor mind sets.

visitor, either drawn through promotional efforts, or in search of solutions, will probably be your more typical target audience. Many people are beginning to use the Internet as a reference source or replacement for the traditional yellow pages. If they have a problem, want to find information about a company, or need a product, more and more people are using the search engine capabilities on the Internet to locate applicable Web sites.

Focus is important, therefore, you must select and concentrate on a primary and secondary audience. Possible audiences who may visit your site include:

- ❏ Customers and clients
- ❏ Competitors
- ❏ Dealers and distributors
- ❏ Students
- ❏ Journalists
- ❏ Employees and vendors

□ Regulatory agencies

□ Consumer advocacy groups

□ Shareholders

The five following marqueed sites had very different audience targets, but each audience was carefully selected with specific objectives.

Case Study

 According to Christopher Lee, the Senate Webmaster, the site primarily targeted the U.S. electorate. Today, it is servicing three main audiences:

□ U.S. constituents

□ Educational sites

□ Foreign visitors to the U.S. capital and Senate.

Time limitations, organizational realities, and other factors dictated that the initial site was brought online quickly with *fixed* central data. It was realized that other potentially large audiences—reporters, lobbyists, and politically active individuals—who want more real-time information on the status of Senate proceedings would not be serviced in the first site release.

Case Study

 The site has two distinct target audiences:

Federal Express

□ **Small Business:** FedEx's objective is to be the resource of choice for small businesses by providing them accessibility and tools for shipping and tracking packages.

□ **Medium Business:** The objective is to provide resources for moderate size customers who are experimenting with new processes and technologies for improving the way they do business.

According to Hamilton, the electronic commerce marketing manager, "the research cost for a study would be higher than the experimental cost for the site, at the very beginning," since the cost of entry for the site was low. The site cost was low because FedEx leveraged the *back-office* capabilities developed for its Powership automated shipping terminals and just implemented a new web-based front-end.

Audience analysis must also consider the probability that the target audience will have the means of accessing the site. If the audience originates from business locations, as in the two previous examples, there is a good probability that it will have access to the Internet. If the target audience(s) will use the site for more personal access, then audience demographics is key to determining if potential users will have both the need and means of accessing the site.

Audiences, therefore, can be roughly divided into one of four quadrants of personal versus business use and home versus office access location, as shown in Figure 1.3. The top row includes audiences who will access the company from business locations. It is easy to determine if this target audience has Internet access. FedEx

	Primary	Secondary
Business Use	Use Internet audience analysis worksheet, Fig. 1.5	Use Internet audience analysis worksheet, Fig. 1.5
Personal Use	Use Internet audience analysis worksheet, Fig. 1.4	Use Internet audience analysis worksheet, Fig. 1.4

Figure 1.3 Internet audience use and access segmentation.

is a good example of a site with a primary and secondary audience that is most likely to access the site from a business location. The second row includes access from personal sites, but with different focuses, as discussed in the following case studies.

CASE STUDY

The *Star Tribune* joined with five other medium-size media companies to commission detailed consumer demographics in major markets around the United States. While they specifically studied online access capability in these areas, they also asked general questions so as to compare their results with other types of studies. These audience surveys verified that the demographic makeup of the Minneapolis-St. Paul area was similar to other major markets. This means that the newspaper could reliably use future studies commissioned by others without always having to fund such research as often itself.

Compared to a CNN-oriented site for national and international news, the *Star Tribune* site is more locally focused with two strongly identified audiences:

- ❑ Local households
- ❑ People outside the geographic area who need local information, such as travelers or those who have family in the Twin Cities metropolitan area

The target audience is 20 to 25 percent of the households in its distribution area who are information-hungry. It is a mass market with dozens of niche interests that the paper cannot satisfy in full today with the costs of printing and distributing a newspaper. It plans on targeting niche interests through the web site where interest and desire are revealed.

CASE STUDY

 While the information was sold to travel agents initially, the objective of the business has always been to take the time-sensitive information direct to the traveler. Internet demographics are very similar to the standard profile of people who take leisure travel. Such people:

- Are 25 to 54 years of age
- Have a medium income of $50,000 a year or more
- Frequently are "unmanaged" travelers

Analysis of the Internet audience found that Travelocity's target audience were people who were information-savvy and on the Internet. One surprising result we found echoed—from many of the site managers interviewed—was the number of older people who were also on the Internet. Therefore, the demographics of the Internet and Travelocity's target audience matched very closely.

To determine if the Internet is appropriate for your nonbusiness audience, use the Internet audience analysis worksheet shown in Figure 1.4. To determine if the Internet is appropriate for your business audience, use the Internet audience analysis worksheet shown in Figure 1.5. These worksheets can be used to rate the appropriateness of the Internet for your anticipated audience demographics.

CASE STUDY

TORO "Toro's primary audience," as defined by Wallace, the marketing manager, "is the U.S. homeowner." This, in itself, pretty much defines associated demographics of age and income. Secondarily, Toro wants to attract future customers who are moving up and about to become homeowners. Comparing its customer profile to the Internet audience demographics, shown in Figure 1.4, Toro recognized that it would be reaching a slightly younger audience than its traditional customer. This was viewed as a plus because it supported the objective of increasing recognition in new markets. It did map well to secondary target of future homeowners. Site measurements to date indicate that Toro did a good job on audience analysis.

As one of the earliest consumer products companies with a major Web presence, Toro had to be very aware of the unique culture on the Internet. Since the vast majority of Internet users were *problem-driven* rather than *promotion-driven* in selecting web sites to visit, Toro chose to create two different sites, one for each audience.

Toro's Consumer Products site (http://www.toro.com) contains complete information on its full line of mowers, snowthrowers, tractors, and handheld tools. It is attractive and offers a variety of incentives for visitors to provide information about themselves. As we will see later, it is promoted using traditional advertising methods.

By contrast, the "Ask Earl, the Yardcare Answer Guy" web site is a homeowner's dream come true. Loaded with answers to common homeowner questions, it has an irreverent Internet look. Though Toro sponsors the site and answers the questions that come from visitors, its logo is nowhere to be found. Instead, a small copyright message at the bottom of each page (which hyperlinks to the Consumer Products site) is the only credit. Woven into some of the answers, and only where appropriate, are references to Toro products. Each reference is a hyperlink that brings the visitor directly to the page for that product at the Consumer Products site.

This strategy enables Toro to provide value to both mindsets without offending either one. Traditional Internet users can stop by the "Ask Earl" site, following product links only if they choose. Shoppers can visit the Consumer Products site and link over to "Ask Earl" as an added bonus. This is also a good example of one company's solution to attracting people to their catalogue site. As you will see, Toro is very happy with its approach.

Its audience is primarily do-it-yourself gardeners, who may be both customers and non-customers of the company. While it was basically straightforward to determine the site content, the major question was whether the typical home gardener has Internet access. Today, the vast majority, over 90 percent, of their site accesses are from nonbusiness locations, with most accesses using information services, such as America Online, NECTAR, CompuServe, and Prodigy.

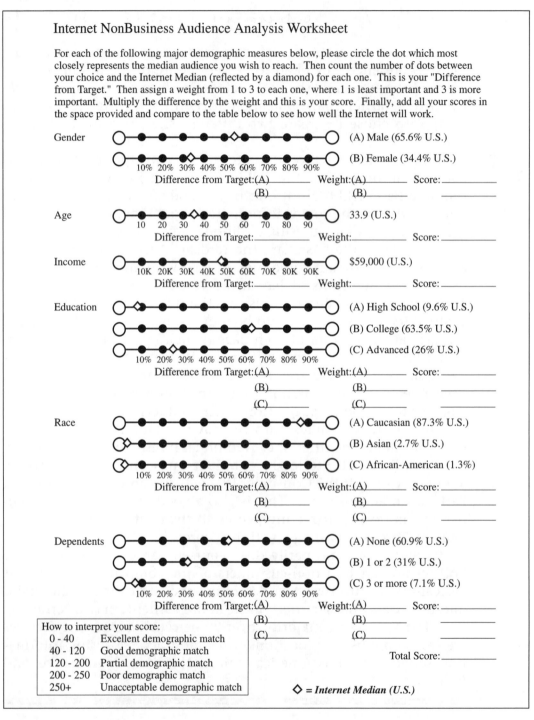

Internet NonBusiness Audience Analysis Worksheet

For each of the following major demographic measures below, please circle the dot which most closely represents the median audience you wish to reach. Then count the number of dots between your choice and the Internet Median (reflected by a diamond) for each one. This is your "Difference from Target." Then assign a weight from 1 to 3 to each one, where 1 is least important and 3 is more important. Multiply the difference by the weight and this is your score. Finally, add all your scores in the space provided and compare to the table below to see how well the Internet will work.

Gender

(A) Male (65.6% U.S.)

(B) Female (34.4% U.S.)

10% 20% 30% 40% 50% 60% 70% 80% 90%

Difference from Target:(A)_____ Weight:(A)_____ Score:_____
                        (B)_____   (B)_____   _____

Age

33.9 (U.S.)

10 20 30 40 50 60 70 80 90

Difference from Target:_____ Weight:_____ Score:_____

Income

$59,000 (U.S.)

10K 20K 30K 40K 50K 60K 70K 80K 90K

Difference from Target:_____ Weight:_____ Score:_____

Education

(A) High School (9.6% U.S.)

(B) College (63.5% U.S.)

(C) Advanced (26% U.S.)

10% 20% 30% 40% 50% 60% 70% 80% 90%

Difference from Target:(A)_____ Weight:(A)_____ Score:_____
                        (B)_____   (B)_____   _____
                        (C)_____   (C)_____   _____

Race

(A) Caucasian (87.3% U.S.)

(B) Asian (2.7% U.S.)

(C) African-American (1.3%)

10% 20% 30% 40% 50% 60% 70% 80% 90%

Difference from Target:(A)_____ Weight:(A)_____ Score:_____
                        (B)_____   (B)_____   _____
                        (C)_____   (C)_____   _____

Dependents

(A) None (60.9% U.S.)

(B) 1 or 2 (31% U.S.)

(C) 3 or more (7.1% U.S.)

10% 20% 30% 40% 50% 60% 70% 80% 90%

Difference from Target:(A)_____ Weight:(A)_____ Score:_____
                        (B)_____   (B)_____   _____
                        (C)_____   (C)_____   _____

How to interpret your score:	
0 - 40	Excellent demographic match
40 - 120	Good demographic match
120 - 200	Partial demographic match
200 - 250	Poor demographic match
250+	Unacceptable demographic match

Total Score:_____

◇ = *Internet Median (U.S.)*

Figure 1.4a Internet audience demographics for nonbusiness users.

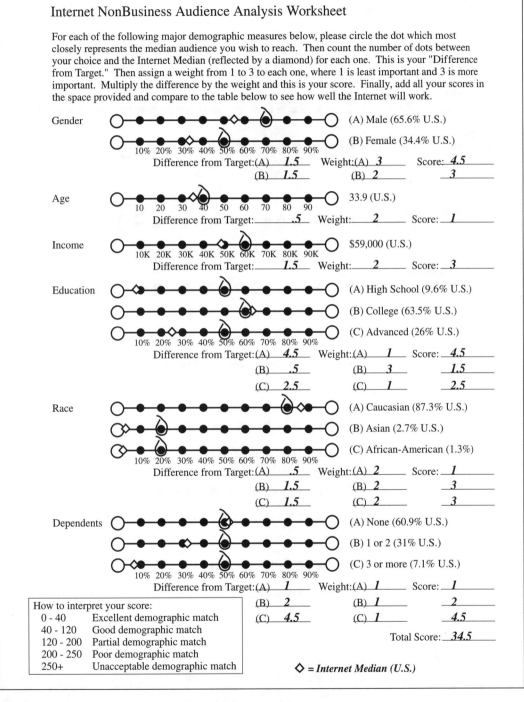

Figure 1.4b The completed worksheet.

21

Internet Business Audience Analysis Worksheet

For each of the following major demographic measures below, please circle the dot which most closely represents the median audience you wish to reach. Then count the number of dots between your choice and the Internet Median (reflected by a diamond) for each one. Each company needs to determine through research what the median number is for its online market. This is your "Difference from Target." Then assign a weight from 1 to 3 to each one, where 1 is least important and 3 is more important. Multiply the difference by the weight and this is your score. Finally, add all your scores in the space provided and compare to the table below to see how well the Internet will work.

Prospects Online

Difference from Target:_____ Weight:_____ Score:_____

Customer Online

Difference from Target:_____ Weight:_____ Score:_____

Decisionmakers Online

Difference from Target:_____ Weight:_____ Score:_____

Geographic Match

Difference from Target:_____ Weight:_____ Score:_____

Trade Press Online

Difference from Target:_____ Weight:_____ Score:_____

Other

Difference from Target:_____ Weight:_____ Score:_____

Other

Difference from Target:_____ Weight:_____ Score:_____

Total Score:_____

How to interpret your score:

0 - 20	Excellent demographic match
20 - 40	Good demographic match
40 - 80	Partial demographic match
80 - 120	Poor demographic match
120+	Unacceptable demographic match

Figure 1.5a Business Internet audience analysis worksheet.

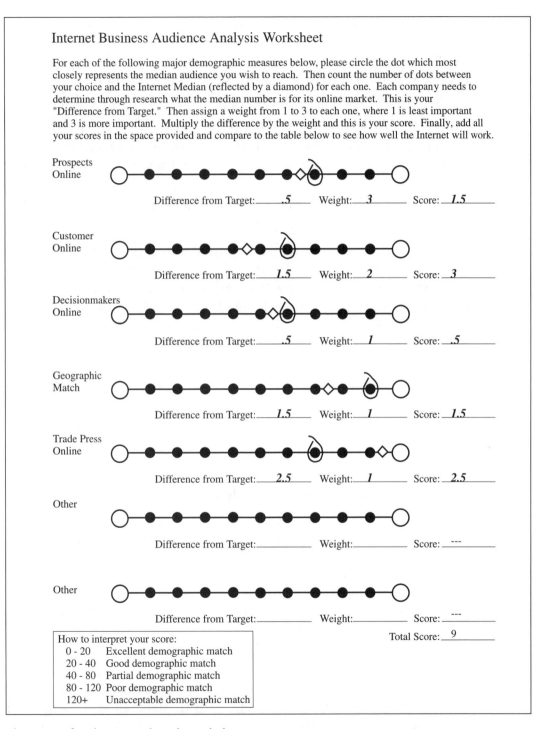

Internet Business Audience Analysis Worksheet

For each of the following major demographic measures below, please circle the dot which most closely represents the median audience you wish to reach. Then count the number of dots between your choice and the Internet Median (reflected by a diamond) for each one. Each company needs to determine through research what the median number is for its online market. This is your "Difference from Target." Then assign a weight from 1 to 3 to each one, where 1 is least important and 3 is more important. Multiply the difference by the weight and this is your score. Finally, add all your scores in the space provided and compare to the table below to see how well the Internet will work.

Prospects Online

Difference from Target: _____.5_____ Weight: ___3___ Score: __1.5__

Customer Online

Difference from Target: __1.5__ Weight: __2__ Score: __3__

Decisionmakers Online

Difference from Target: _____.5_____ Weight: __1__ Score: __.5__

Geographic Match

Difference from Target: __1.5__ Weight: __1__ Score: __1.5__

Trade Press Online

Difference from Target: __2.5__ Weight: __1__ Score: __2.5__

Other

Difference from Target: _____ Weight: _____ Score: __---__

Other

Difference from Target: _____ Weight: _____ Score: __---__

Total Score: __9__

How to interpret your score:
0 - 20	Excellent demographic match
20 - 40	Good demographic match
40 - 80	Partial demographic match
80 - 120	Poor demographic match
120+	Unacceptable demographic match

Figure 1.5b The completed worksheet.

Once the audience is defined, measurements must be included for the site that capture data pertinent to understanding

How many visitors actually use site facilities versus browsing the site?

What facilities they use and how often?

Where the visitors come from, such as visitor's domain information, links pointing to your site from other reference sites, and visitor's country of origin?

Type of browser the audience most commonly uses?

Projected versus actual audience mix.

Some data can be directly captured or consolidated from site logs. Direct questioning of the audience is another way to capture required data. Constructing site pages so that use can be inferred from the number and types of page accesses is another way of gathering information on how the site is used. Sites will tend to have different measurement requirements, but basically two types of data are significant:

❑ Measurements must be taken to collect data critical for the site justification.

❑ Data must be collected that can be used to evolve and improve site content and function.

Step 3: Selecting Appropriate Content

You must understand who will realistically visit your site in order to select content that is valuable and appropriate to their needs. Equally important as content is site presentation or graphics. Graphics provide the visualization of the site message and can include line art, illustrations, and photography. Figure 1.6 shows a typical text-oriented page. Figure 1.7 is an illustration or drawing. Figure 1.8 is a photo collage.

The site's theme is often critical to properly positioning the company and the visual aspects of the site are often key to communicating the message. To make the site easy-to-use, navigation through the site must be consistent with the level of knowledge and experience of the audience.

Figure 1.6 Typical text-oriented page.

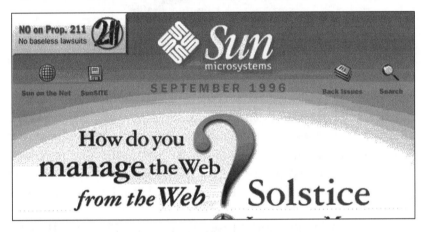

Figure 1.7 Example of an illustration.

Figure 1.8 Photo collage.

Figure 1.9 Screen shot of General Mills' home page for employment opportunities.

EXAMPLE: GENERAL MILLS BRINGS ONLINE MULTIPLE WEB SITES

A name everyone knows, General Mills, has created a very user-friendly, visually pleasing web site oriented around employment opportunities, as shown in Figure 1.9. Its target audience is Internet-based job seekers.

The home page, and subsequent pages, Figure 1.10, are designed to communicate messages and position the company to the typical, nontechnical consumer (job seeker) as well as create a simple menu for selecting topics graphically illustrated on the page. To move from the home page to the company information page, the visitor simply clicks on the company information icon or text. Page access is very fast, and there is minimal detail and text that clutter the message.

General Mills is one company that is creating multiple sites targeted to specific audiences. Another General Mills site is explicitly targeted at kids (http:// www.youruleschool.com). This allows the company to tailor content, look-and-feel, and navigation to very different audiences without making a single site overly complex.

The General Mills sites can best be described as experiments because, as Barry Wegener, Communications Manager at General Mills

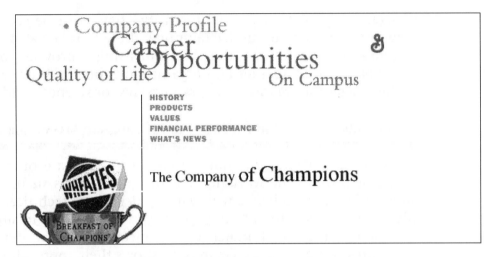

Figure 1.10 Screen shot of company information page.

puts it, "You have to be there (on the Internet) to learn first hand." These same sentiments were undoubtedly felt by most of the other company sites we interviewed. No one wants to be left out or behind, if and when the Internet takes off.

From an audience perspective, a web site visit is not unlike a visit to a store, sporting event, museum, theater, or any other outing. The audience will perceive the trip worthwhile if,

they get what they came for,

it was easy to use,

there were no problems while at the site, and

they were even a little surprised by an added benefit.

Achieving this requires that the site contain the required information (site content), that the information is persuasively presented yet "comfortable" to the audience (site graphics), and that the information is easily accessible (site navigation).

Since many visitors may be interacting with the Internet and site through relatively slow-speed interfaces, such as low baud rate modems, there is a constant trade-off in site responsiveness—speed of screen display versus visual intensity—that must be considered. One easy way to better understand how these four key elements are interrelated is by surfing the Web and using a browser to locate home pages of companies and organizations on the Internet. Look at their pages for organization, graphics, responsiveness, and flow.

EXAMPLE: MICROSOFT'S WEB SITE HAS TO BE ALL THINGS TO MANY AUDIENCES

Microsoft is a leading provider of computer software products for PCs, Macintoshes, networking, and the Internet. As such, it has a large and diverse audience with varying degrees of technical knowledge and interests. In fact, the Microsoft web site tries to support a much broader range of audience and objectives than would be recommended for most sites. Figure 1.11 shows their approach to these broad audience requirements. Across the top of the page is a menu of functions that are generic to all visitors. These can be used to search for information or go directly to subsequent pages if you are a frequent visitor. Down the left of the page are categories that pertain to:

- ❑ Subjects, such as products, support, and the Internet
- ❑ Audiences, such as developers and partners

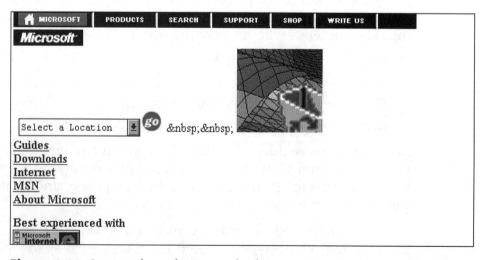

Figure 1.11 Screen shot of Microsoft's home page.

The page layout is partitioned along audience lines and experience with the site. Overall this is very effective. The only drawback is that due to the amount of graphics on the page it is slow loading across most modem lines.

Many site's content will be predicated on the business of the organization. The *Star Tribune* and FedEx are excellent examples of this.

CASE STUDY

Basic site content sections were preordained by the newspaper format. After more market research with various layouts, Schafer's team concluded that visitors were most at home with the format they already knew. The site includes metro news, national and international news, sports, leisure, weather, and other typical sections. The actual news content is the responsibility of the respective editors. Information Services (IS) developed the standard page view, layout, and databases. The pages are updated daily or as the timeliness of the news dictates. Weather, for instance, is updated every 15 minutes. Figure 1.12 shows the home page, while Figure 1.13 illustrates another popular section.

Figure 1.12 *Star Tribune* home page.

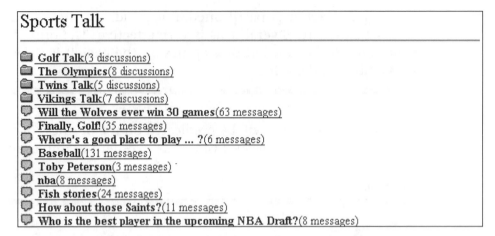

Figure 1.13 Sports section.

The site also includes interactive discussion groups, where user-generated content is shared among the participants and also contributed to by the *Star Tribune*'s editorial staff. Discussion categories can be listed using a *talk button*. When we visited the site, it included the following topics:

Community

Feedback

InfoTech

Loose Talk

News/Current Events

Sports Talk

Variety Talk

CASE STUDY

Site content was predicated on customer experience with other forms of technology. Initially, customers want to use the technology for package tracking and as an informational source as shown in Figures 1.14 and 1.15. As they become fa-

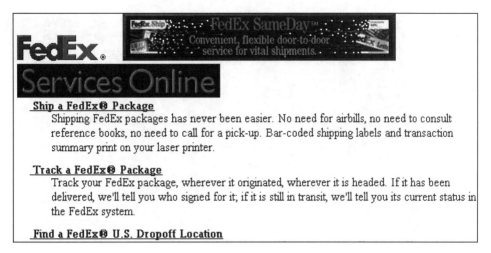

Ship a FedEx® Package

Shipping FedEx packages has never been easier. No need for airbills, no need to consult reference books, no need to call for a pick-up. Bar-coded shipping labels and transaction summary print on your laser printer.

Track a FedEx® Package

Track your FedEx package, wherever it originated, wherever it is headed. If it has been delivered, we'll tell you who signed for it; if it is still in transit, we'll tell you its current status in the FedEx system.

Find a FedEx® U.S. Dropoff Location

Figure 1.14 Information on shipping options.

miliar with the technology, some will want to be able to generate billables (send packages) from the desktop, as shown in Figure 1.16. Today, the web site provides information, package tracking, airbill-generation, and a drop-box locator service.

Figure 1.15 Tracking airbills.

PACKAGE SHIPPING INFORMATION

Recipient Information (To:)

Name:	JOHN SMITH
Company:	ABC ENTERPRISES
Address1:	123 WEST ELM STREET
Address2:	
City:	ANYCITY
State:	CA ZIP: 12345

Sender Information (From:)

Name:	CHARLES LUKASZEWSKI
Company:	EWORKS! INC
Address1:	165 WESTERN AVENUE NORT
Address2:	SUITE TWO
City:	ST. PAUL
State:	MN ZIP: 55102

Figure 1.16 Preparing airbills and package shipment.

Other site content is based on nonbusiness needs, such as for the U.S. Senate web site.

CASE STUDY

 Like the traditional organization it represents, the Senate's web site features a conservative approach, providing core functionality without glitz.

Site content is provided by individual Senators, committees, and offices. The computer center provided a generic home page for each Senator (see Figure 1.17) but most have opted to create their own tailored home page and associated pages, as shown in Figure 1.18. While the site operation and maintenance is centralized, content development is very distributed. In addition to the home directories, the site contains a press release directory which gets lots of activity. Although the Senate site is considered an Internet site, the content preparation is more typical of intranet sites we interviewed.

The best way to determine site content, graphics, and navigation is to put yourself in the visitor's shoes and answer the following questions for the primary and secondary audiences:

Figure 1.17 Web page of Senator Daniel K. Akaka, Democrat, Hawaii.

What information do I need to answer my question or solve my problem?

In what order do I need the information or am I likely to ask questions?

What is my expectation for turnaround at the site for interactive forms?

What is my expectation for turnaround of e-mail or other response information?

Figure 1.18 Web page of Senator John Ashcroft, Republican, Missouri.

Next, look at the same items from your internal viewpoint:

What are the most common requests we receive for information?

What are the most common problems our customers have?

How are we usually asked these questions (or in what order do the customers need the information)?

What tools do we use internally that may help in responding to these requests?

The answer to site content, graphics, navigation, and response time lies in the intersection of these two sets of answers. Each company, customer base, and site is different, but asking and answering these questions will get you started on developing a valuable and usable site format. The site content worksheet shown in Figure 1.19 provides an outline of key audience requirements and response information for your site.

Since FedEx and Microsoft customers are typically repeat users of their services, their sites also had to be designed to facilitate both the first time user and expedite processing for repeat users who want to skip prompts and help information. This is an important consideration that many implementations overlook. General Mills, on the other hand, probably does not have many users accessing the site over and over; therefore it does not need to provide streamlined access to specific site functions.

Once site content is defined, measurements should be defined to determine what percent of the audience is using which features and how often a feature is used. For example, if the FedEx site found that most visits were for package tracking and few customers were using the site to download software, this information may lead either to more promotion or education of the unused feature(s) or changing site content to enhance or remove the feature.

Besides basic site message content, as previously discussed, measurement requirements also help drive content needs. Requirements for audience feedback may dictate that you include surveys, e-mail, free stuff, and other content on the site. These site-specific features are listed and discussed in Chapter 4.

	Customer question	Related problem	Web Delivered Solution	User Supplied Information	Data Source
A					
B					
	Where is my package?	Package has not arrived.	Look up current status in system.	Airbill number	Package database
	Where is the nearest dropoff location and how late is it open?	Pickup deadline passed and package still needs to go tonight.	Look up store locations.	Zip code	Store database
	Can I open an account online?	Prefer direct billing.	Submit online form.	Billing contact and information.	Customer database
	How do I apply for a job?	Needs employment.	Submit online form.	Personal data and employment history.	Human resource database
	How can I reroute a package in transit?	Incorrect shipping address on the airbill.	n/a	n/a	n/a

Figure 1.19 Site content worksheet (a) and completed example (b).

Step 4: Choosing a Promotion Strategy

The Web is no *Field of Dreams*, where if you "build it, he (or they) will come." A web site is like any other business endeavor. You must attract customers; to do so you need a promotional plan targeted to the site's audience.

A site promotion plan should identify a set of specific actions that will inform a majority of the target audience that the web site exists and is worth their time to visit. Typically, the plan will include both online and off-line promotional activities that cover both the existing customer base and potential new customers. There are several basic promotional tactics that cover these objectives;

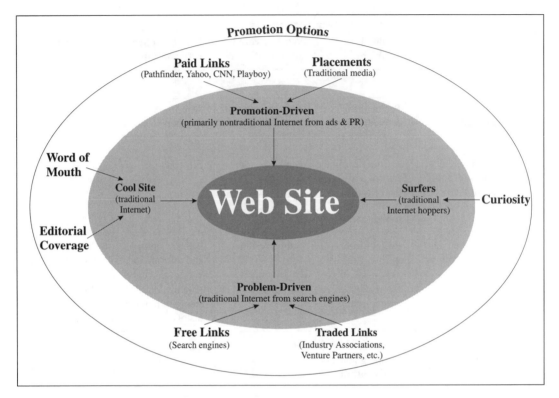

Figure 1.20 Web site promotion options.

they have been used successfully by FedEx and others, as shown in Figure 1.20. For online these are:

- ❑ **Free links:** This includes registration with online directory providers (search engines), such as Yahoo and Infoseek, and postings on relevant bulletin boards.
- ❑ **Traded links:** This is a very standard web activity wherein one web page references or points to other pages of associated information. These are called reciprocal hyperlinks and they can be established with industry trade associations, vendors, distributors, customers, and related industry groups.
- ❑ **Paid links:** This is actually an extension of online directory registration that provides the company with banners, basically paid-for advertisement, through the directory service or at related industry sites.

CASE STUDY

TORO When the site went online in December 1995, traditional media promotion in the form of news releases and media kits was used to generate initial coverage. Actual coordination of the site address with advertising did not start until April 1996. Toro has found that three promotional activities seem to work well:

- Registration through online search engines, such as Yahoo, Infoseek, and AltaVista
- Use of site addresses, called URLs, in sales collateral, advertisements, product literature, and trade show booths
- Site mention in all press activities, with samples of the site pages included in the press release

Off-line promotional activities, such as those used by the *Star Tribune* and Travelocity, leverage existing communication with the target audience. This includes:

- **Placements in traditional media and editorial coverage:** Adding the web page address and a small description of the service to printed collateral, advertisements, videos, first-response packages, and other marketing material.
- **Word of Mouth:** Adding the web page address and a small description of the service to product packages and other distributed materials.

CASE STUDY

Online The *Star Tribune* used traditional media, specialty advertising, and Internet news groups to promote the site. It believes that organizations, such as newspapers, that have daily contact with their target audience can more easily get their uniform resource locator (URL) visible. The *Star* prints its URL in the newspaper every day in many different places. This is a focused vehicle that reaches its target audience daily. The *Star Tribune* also uses locally focused advertising, such as billboards and baseball park ads.

Schafer argues, "Make the URL easy to remember. If the URL is basically the organization's name, the audience will remember it. If is it similar to the organization's name, but slightly different, the audience may remember the site, but not be able to recall the exact URL. This makes finding the site more difficult."

CASE STUDY

Travelocity had a multi-million dollar budget for first-year advertising and publicity. This budget was invested in a combination of advertising, public relations, and online promotions. For advertising, the company retained an agency which launched a campaign including a six-month run in *WIRED* Magazine, *Time, Digital, Netwide, Yahoo! Internet Life, Virtual City*, and *Interactive Week*. Also, banner ads were placed on all five major search engines. A public relations firm was hired to elicit media coverage of the venture and its progress. The company also joined Poppe Tyson's DoubleClick network, which negotiated reciprocal banner advertising between other high-volume sites.

Travelocity registered with online search engines, but did not feel that newsgroup or online service forum promotions were appropriate. Travelocity further entered into a sponsorship agreement with Infoseek for its Travel Guide. The company is studying similar arrangements with other major search engines.

Following the lead of other Internet-based services, like Digital's AltaVista search engine and Yahoo's directory, that began selling their technology to others, Travelocity has begun reselling its travel online service platform to third-party online services. For instance, the travel sections of CompuServe's web site and USA Today online are provided by Travelocity. This enables the company to put their brand in front of even more customers.

Other sites, like the Senate, can leverage the organization's general news worthiness to promote the site.

The site was not heavily promoted, but several steps were taken, including:

- ❑ A Senate floor statement announcing the release of the web site made by Senator John Warner, Chairman of the Committee on Rules and Administration, on 20 October 1995.

- ❑ Televised press conference which was later re-broadcast on C-SPAN.

- ❑ Listing the site through all the major search engines.

- ❑ Some Senators including the URL on their stationary, business cards, and other correspondence.

When you call many companies to order products, fill out warranty forms, or get product rebates, an often asked question is "Where did you hear about the company or product?" This input is used by marketing to determine the response rate for various forms of promotional activities. This same information is important for web site promotion and can be collected directly through questions asked of the audience or often interpreted from other information provided by the site, as discussed in Part II. Again, repeating the message from the prior sections, it is much easier to implement these measurements while developing the site, than after it is in operation. Therefore, as discussed further in Chapter 4, including measurement requirements in the planning process is a must.

Planning Starts with Defining a Need

The first step of the site life cycle, setting an objective, is preceded by the first two steps of virtually all successful business plans—*defining a need* and *recommending a solution* as shown in Figure 1.21. These are also the first two steps of the justification process described in Chapter 2.

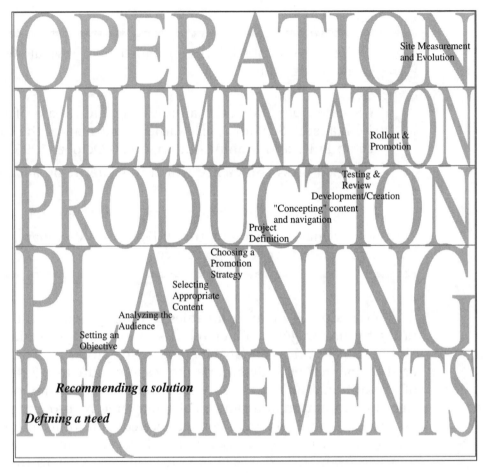

Figure 1.21 Key steps that precede putting pen to paper.

Web site objective setting, planning, justification, and measurement are interdependent tasks that are all critical to the success of the site and to understanding the financial and organizational impact of the site on the business. If you ignore any of these issues, you leave yourself open to uncertainties that can impact the site's success. *Measuring the Impact of Your Web Site* can help you better address site measurement and justification as part of the planning, ongoing support, and evolutionary activities of your web site. For further information and interactive planning worksheets, visit our web site at http://www.siteimpact.com.

The remainder of Part I discusses objective setting, justification strategies, and site measurement as they pertain to planning a new site, and managing and evolving an existing site. Chapter 2 discusses justification strategies based on customer needs and site objectives that have been used by other sites with varying degrees of success and the reasons behind their success or failure.

Measurement and Site Justification

Chances are that you didn't have to formally justify the money you spent to create your web site. Virtually all of the sites we studied began life as free-time *skunkworks* projects or were funded from general purpose budgets. But that is going to change, according to many of the managers of those sites. The staff time and computing resources needed to keep pace with the rapid growth of their sites will soon require separate approval. The key to explaining the impact of a web site is good measurements.

This chapter covers two essential aspects of justifying a web site: the justification process and basic strategies. First, we review the justification process itself, breaking it into 10 easy-to-follow steps. Second, we present six basic justification strategies for web sites. No two public or private sector organizations, or even departments, are likely to use the same justification standards or processes for approving funding or ongoing support for the web site. Each strategy requires different kinds of measurements to support the argument you are making. Additionally, you will find that the justification process will take less time and have a greater probability of success, if the web site is designed to provide relevant measurements of site hits, audience acceptance, and content usefulness from the very beginning, as described in Chapter 4.

You must be honest with yourself upfront that not all site objectives and justification strategies will lead to success. Major organizations around the world have employed different strategies with varying degrees of success, as discussed later in the chapter. However, the better you understand the needs of the site's target audience, the more prepared you are with hard facts to support the justification. The more convincingly you present the justification, the more likely you are to succeed and continue to be successful in growing and evolving the site.

Justification Process

The old adage "It takes money to make money" has a corollary: "You must usually justify what you spend or want to spend." Whether you are buying a new car for personal use, hiring new employees for your organization, or setting up a web site, the cost must be justified. Justification takes many forms, such as the simple process of mental rationalization: I deserve a new car because I worked hard for it (a typical theme in many automobile advertisements); or a more formal process where the justification must be supported by facts, figures, and a convincing argument.

The data used to justify a decision at any level must be collected, consolidated, analyzed, and presented in a fashion that makes it convincing. In personal decision making, this is often just a mental exercise, since most of the required data is already known and you are primarily trying to convince yourself, anyway. In most business environments, raw data collection, consolidation, and analysis are critical and often complex measurement processes, and the information must be visualized in an easily understood fashion to convince others.

All successful justifications, whether for a web site or for any other desired purpose, have three essential things in common, as shown in Figure 2.1a. They are:

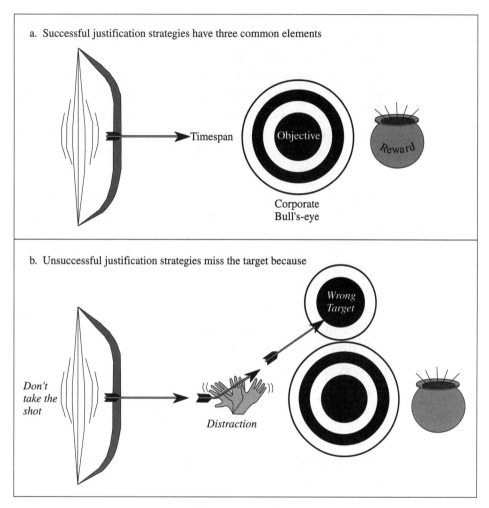

Figure 2.1 Successful (a) versus unsuccessful (b) justification strategies.

- ❑ **Target:** Base it on objective, measurable arguments.
- ❑ **Reward:** Provide an estimate of value or ROI to the organization.
- ❑ **Timeframe:** Realistically estimate the time required to achieve the stated value.

By contrast, failed justifications generally are characterized by one or more of the following, as shown in Figure 2.1b:

❑ **Distraction:** You may be dismissed with the wave of an arm by those who "know better," if you haven't done your homework on the supporting arguments.

❑ **Wrong target:** Sometimes the result is reduced credibility with management when the proposer's view of organizational priorities and finances is substantially different than management's.

❑ **Never took the shot:** When not done, it is probably the single biggest contributor to the failure of most business and personal endeavors.

The justification process is not unique to web sites. What is unique to web sites is the measurement criteria used in developing the justification, as discussed throughout the book. Evaluating whether the results achieve the site's goals, point to required changes, or even suggest shutting down unproductive sites is also unique for Internet sites.

The justification process starts when the initial need for the site is defined and ends when the site is retired, as shown in Figure 2.2. It is a 10-step iterative process that includes:

1. Defining a need.
2. Recommending a solution.
3. Quantifying the required investment.
4. Selecting appropriate ROI strategies.
5. Quantifying the return, timeline, and risks.
6. Effectively presenting the justification.
7. Receiving approval or being declined.
8. Ongoing measurements and evaluation.
9. Communication of progress toward objectives and goals.
10. Achieving objectives and continuing, or missing objectives and shutting down an unproductive activity.

The following sections highlight the critical aspects of each justification step. Following this discussion, under Justification Strategies, we explore the six basic approaches to step 4, selecting appropriate ROI strategies. Some strategies are illustrated through case studies.

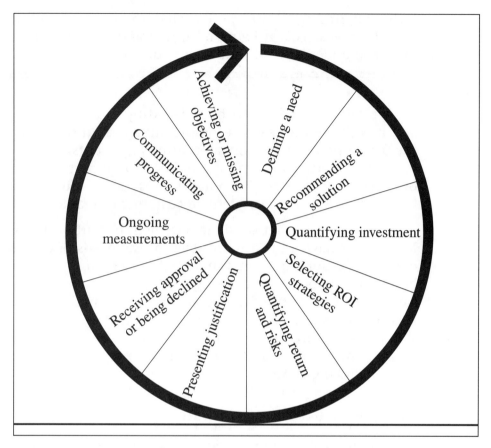

Figure 2.2 Justification is an iterative and ongoing process.

Step 1: Define a Need

The need should be a business, financial, or customer requirement that, if properly filled, will improve or advance your company's objectives. In the case of the *Star Tribune* the need was to take necessary steps to protect a source of revenue from potential erosion.

CASE STUDY

 There was a major concern surrounding how electronic commerce in general, and the web site specif-

ically, might impact and potentially erode newspaper advertising and classifieds. This is being measured and analyzed closely and is discussed under Part III, analysis and decision making.

Typically, the need can be satisfied by more than one solution and it is the second step, recommending a solution, that identifies the best approach based on supporting arguments. Many times this process is reversed and a need is defined to support a solution someone likes or wants to do, but the most successful endeavors are based on satisfying a well-defined customer or market need.

It is important that good measurement be part of needs analysis. Many of us have an instinctive feel for the needs of our customers, our organization, and our vendors. But successful justifications are built from the ground up using provable data. In this case, needs can often be quantified through the use of market research data, surveys, news articles, and even government statistics. Those who skip this step, often struggle through the entire justification process because they can't seem to bring any of the rest of their arguments to a convincing close.

Example: Web-delivered Software

There is an explosion of vendors providing free and evaluation software across the Web, which is a significant departure from traditional software sales and distribution. But the need of prospective customers to "try before they buy" in a cluttered and confusing marketplace justified early experiments by vendors. They have been pleasantly surprised to learn that by providing no-cost and no-commitment product evaluation, they often experienced shorter sales cycles and fewer customer questions and objections. These companies could have offered the software free on CD-ROM or diskette, but chose the Internet approach because it both supports their business objectives and reduces potential delays in getting the product to the customer (strike while the iron is hot).

The new trend toward electronically delivered software across the web also significantly reduces company fulfillment costs because the product and associated documentation do not always have to be shipped. Examples of companies using the Web in this fashion include Netscape (http://www.netscape.com), Microsoft (http://www.microsoft.com), and Intel (http://www.intel.com).

Step 2: Recommend a Solution

Good solutions should first, and above all, address the need. Even stronger solutions have additional value propositions that make them the most compelling approach. In the previous example, not only does the solution satisfy the need to get free evaluation software to the customer, but it does so through a timely, low-cost solution that also helps position the company in its role as an Internet provider.

CASE STUDY

 Travelocity identified three potential solutions for reaching the end user:

❑ Private network

❑ Commercial network

❑ The Internet

All three options were evaluated and the Internet was selected as the most viable solution. But, convincing the Board of Directors was a difficult process, as discussed later.

Step 3: Quantify the Investment

Unless you have done it before, it is often hard to precisely identify costs associated with implementing a particular solution. One approach, that greatly reduces some of the uncertainty of estimating costs, is to list all the expected cost items and provide a range or bracket of their estimated cost and time to implement. Figures 2.3a and b show a web site cost-estimating worksheet you can use as a guideline.

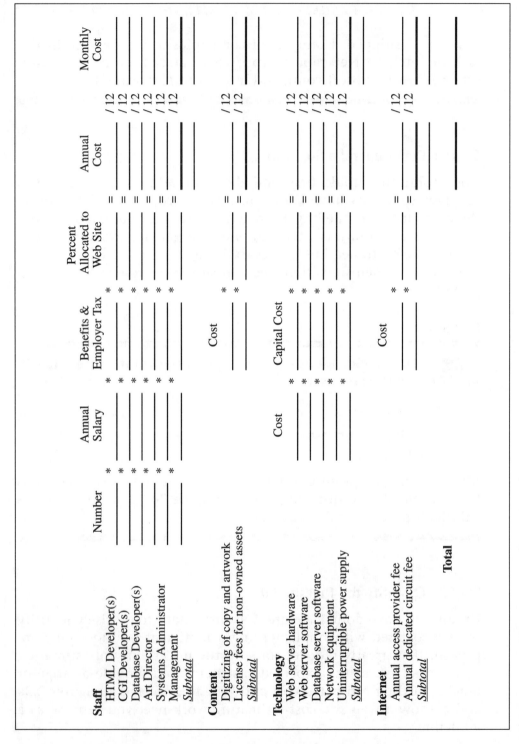

Figure 2.3a Web site cost-estimating worksheet.

Staff	Number	Annual Salary	Benefits & Employer Tax	Percent Allocated to Web Site	Annual Cost	Monthly Cost
HTML Developer(s)	1	* $30,000	* 20%	* 100% =	$36,000	/ 12	$3,000
CGI Developer(s)	1	* $35,000	* 20%	* 40% =	$16,800	/ 12	$1,400
Database Developer(s)	n/a	* n/a	* 20%	*		/ 12	
Art Director	1	* $40,000	* 20%	* 40% =	$19,200	/ 12	$1,600
Systems Administrator	1	* $45,000	* 20%	* 30% =	$16,200	/ 12	$1,350
Management	1	* $50,000	* 20%	* 20% =	$12,000	/ 12	$1,000
Subtotal					$100,200		$8,350

Content		Cost		Percent Allocated to Web Site	Annual Cost	Monthly Cost
Digitizing of copy and artwork			$2,500	* 100% =	$2,500	/ 12	$208
License fees for non-owned assets			n/a	*		/ 12	
Subtotal					$2,500		$208

Technology		Cost	Capital Cost	Percent Allocated to Web Site	Annual Cost	Monthly Cost
Web server hardware		$10,000	* 10%	* 100% =	$11,000	/ 12	$917
Web server software		$1,000	* 10%	* 100% =	$1,100	/ 12	$92
Database server software		$1,000	* 10%	* 100% =	$1,100	/ 12	$92
Network equipment		$15,000	* 10%	* 50% =	$8,250	/ 12	$688
Uninterruptible power supply		$1,000	* 10%	* 100% =	$1,100	/ 12	$92
Subtotal					$22,550		$1,879

Internet			Cost	Percent Allocated to Web Site	Annual Cost	Monthly Cost
Annual access provider fee			$18,000	* 25% =	$4,500	/ 12	$375
Annual dedicated circuit fee			$6,000	* 25% =	$1,500	/ 12	$125
Subtotal					$6,000		$500

| **Total** | | | | | $131,250 | | $10,938 |

Figure 2.3b The completed sample.

An interactive version of the worksheet shown in Figure 2.3a is available at our web site, http://www.siteimpact.com. Sites have justified varying sizes of investment based on various criteria. In some cases, they offset the site cost through other expense reductions, while other sites set aside specific funds for the site.

CASE STUDY

The *Star Tribune*'s first year one-time startup budget was in the six figure range. Ongoing costs for staffing and marketing are in line with expectations, but technology costs have proved to be higher than expected.

CASE STUDY

Budget for the site was less than $100,000. The money came from the existing technology and marketing budgets, where planned expenditures were redirected toward the Internet initiative.

There was no formal justification process at the outset, but there are ongoing weekly updates for senior management and quarterly planning cycles for new features. ROI for budgeting is calculated based on:

❑ Site traffic

❑ Online versus off-line research

❑ Online versus off-line number of packages tracked

❑ Packages shipped

❑ Software downloaded

❑ Customer satisfaction

What appears clear from our discussions with many organizations is that web site investments vary widely from around $50,000 to well over $1 million based on existing capabilities the organization can draw on, complexity of the site, and the type of content required for the target audience. We estimate that most companies can do a very good noncommercial web site for around $100,000, but commercial sites, such as Travelocity, may run into the millions to implement.

Step 4: Select the Appropriate ROI Strategy

This ties into the objective-setting phase of the planning process. For example, FedEx has a strong company policy to enhance customer services through new technology. It appeared that the Web was a good solution and would earn goodwill from customers who relied on the Internet. As discussed later in this chapter, there are many possible justification strategies you can employ; the most successful will include both quantitative and qualitative measurements.

The selected strategy dictates which measures are required to analyze the site's progress and whether it meets critical success factors, as discussed in Chapter 3, which covers measurement strategy and sources, and Chapter 9, which discusses measure analysis.

Step 5: Quantify the Expected Returns, Time Window, and Risk

This is the most difficult step in the justification process; it's where you "put your neck on the line." It can either get chopped off or you can become a decorated hero. Sometimes events you can't foresee go your way and a losing justification can be swapped for a winning one.

Most good managers on the receiving end of a funding request recognize that this is a difficult task. They will be looking as much at the rationale of how the returns were estimated, as at the actual estimated values themselves. Let's look at two possible returns and how they may be estimated.

Revenue growth is always a good, but sometimes difficult, justification strategy to quantify. When trying to estimate this, you should consider, for example:

Will the solution create new products or services?

Will the solution reach new markets or customers for our products?

Will the solution resolve a distribution problem, thereby improving unit sales?

Will the solution help overcome existing sales objections or otherwise shorten the sales cycle?

Will the solution generate more repeat business?

Answering yes isn't enough—you have to prove your claim. You need to identify how the solution will accomplish the change, then estimate how big the change will be.

CASE STUDY

 Three key risks were identified with the Internet:

- ❑ Whether the Internet would have critical mass and if consumers would accept such a service on the Internet.
- ❑ Whether the public Internet would be considered secure for commercial transactions.
- ❑ Whether the tools to create and manage an Internet-based enterprise would become commercially available or whether an investment in creating proprietary tools was needed.

Arguments that reduced the risk were based on companies like Netscape, Open Market, banks, Visa, and MasterCard all saying that the Internet could successfully use encryption for secure commercial transactions. These arguments went a long way in convincing Travelocity's board that an Internet-based service was doable and would work.

As far as tools were concerned, Travelocity reviewed available solutions and eventually settled on Netscape's technology. This was very important; otherwise, their time-to-market would have been extended and the necessary investment would have been increased.

You will probably be wrong on the quantification of the change, but the logic of why it will impact revenue growth is very important in presenting your justification. If the solution will create demand in several areas and you are conservative in your estimates, you can be wrong on individual revenue contribution, but still end up pretty close on the overall revenue impact.

Another often-used justification is improved customer satisfaction. Though ordinarily intangible and highly subjective, this can be measured quantitatively through

- improved customer survey results,
- reduced complaint levels, and
- lower return rates.

However, estimating what percentage increase or decrease you will see is the difficult part. Again, the estimating process is critical to success. First, you must quantify the need as explained in Step 1. Then, estimate how much each problem will be reduced by the web solution. Having this level of detail will show that you did your homework when you present the justification. Others may disagree on exactly how much each area will be affected by the web site solution, but in reality they won't have any better estimates than you have. The key here is to show the steps taken to make the estimate and to make sure that "all the bases were covered." In the presentation phase, this homework goes a long way toward getting both buy-in and sign-off on site funding.

Two aspects of ROI that many people overlook is timeframe and risk. Timeframe helps the decision makers understand the duration of the commitment they are making and when reviews and future decision points may be needed. Consider the case of a web site expected to cut inbound 800-number calls by $1 million. This sounds very impressive until the proposer explains that the savings occur over five years. Most managers would only treat this as a $200K benefit because they know how hard it is to predict the future. The web site is certain to be rejected if the implementation cost is over $300K, which effectively moves the break-even point too far forward to count on. Generally, stating a return without a corresponding timeframe will be rejected by the audience of reviewers as hypothetical or unreliable.

Risk analysis is the final component of a winning justification. It helps both you and the decision makers appreciate that there are potential issues that may impact the success of the project. The se-

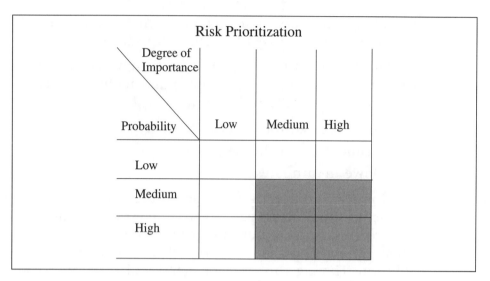

Figure 2.4 Risk impact analysis shows that the shaded quadrants are where you should focus your effort.

cret to good risk analysis is to find someone you trust and who knows your area that can honestly point out flaws. Failing that, put pride aside and draw up a list of everything you can think of that could go wrong. Then prioritize these by probability and degree of impact on the goal you've chosen. Describe in writing how you'll deal with the top three. By identifying risks upfront, you strengthen your own management credentials and improve the chances of success. You cannot focus on every imaginable risk, so prioritize the probability and magnitude of each risk and focus on those of highest impact, as shown in Figure 2.4. And, by the way, risk analysis must be a continuing task throughout the project duration, as shown in Figure 2.5.

Step 6: Presenting the Justification

This is a very important step and one that is often not given sufficient attention. This section briefly summarizes the key parts of a good justification presentation or summary report.

The justification presentation, summarized in Figure 2.6, should mirror the flow of your written document as follows.

Risk Analysis Worksheet

Revision Date: _____

Risk	Probability	Degree of Impact	Indicator	Point in project it may occur	Planned Actions	Status
1 (Description)	(Low, Medium, High)	(Low, Medium, High)	(Measure of Risk or "Trigger Point")	(Phase/Step) (Controllable/ Noncontrollable)	(Proactive or Reactive)	
2						
3						
4						
. . .						

Focus on avoiding

Tracking and escalation, as required

(a)

Risk Analysis Worksheet

Revision Date: _8/5/96_

Risk	Probability	Degree of Impact	Indicator	Point in project it may occur	Planned Actions	Status
1 Large AOL Audience	Medium	High	Browser statistics	After site enters production	Remove features that don't work with AOL Create parallel AOL compatible site	

(b)

Figure 2.5 Risk estimating worksheet (a) and completed example (b).

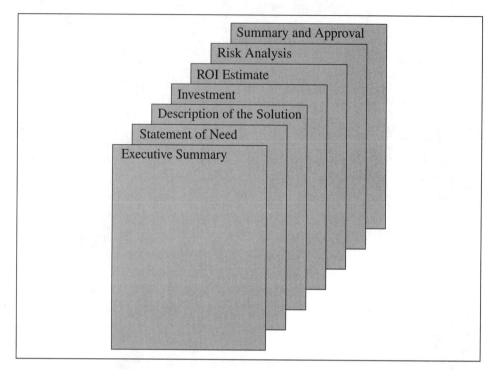

Figure 2.6 Effectively communicating your justification.

EXECUTIVE SUMMARY Your presentation should begin with a two-minute synopsis of the web initiative and the overall arguments you will use to support it. Similarly, the written document should have a cover of no more than one page which serves the same purpose.

STATEMENT OF NEED (OR PROBLEM TO BE ADDRESSED) This should be a brief overview of the needs, issues, and problems that require a solution. Use the KISS approach, "Keep it Simple, Stupid." Make it a simple list of two to four items. Focus, focus, focus will get the message across and ensure faster and greater audience understanding.

DESCRIPTION OF THE SOLUTION Describe briefly how the proposed solution addresses the general need, then show specifically how it addresses each need, issue, or problem listed in the statement of need. Be prepared to address other solutions and discuss how the proposed solution is better than the other alternatives. Have hard facts or, when they are not available, well thought-out estimates and arguments to support your conclusions.

INVESTMENT Quantify the range of time, dollars, and other resources needed to implement the proposed solution. Be prepared to answer questions on ways to reduce the investment. In your mind have a bottom line below which the project is not feasible to undertake. Often, a person gets committed to a project with a constrained set of resources that make success all but impossible. Plan ahead and know at what level of investment the project is doomed to failure.

ROI ESTIMATE As previously discussed, the logic or process behind the estimates may be as important or more important than the actual numbers. Present a clear, short summary of how the estimates were arrived at. Again, be prepared for questions on assumptions used in the estimating, and have simple, clear arguments ready to support your estimates. You may wish to refer frequently to Part II, which presents detailed calculation methods for various approaches or visit our web site at http://www.siteimpact.com for online worksheets.

RISK ANALYSIS Be upfront with the issues of risk. It is important to have the decision makers understand that you understand the risks involved, have analyzed them thoroughly, and have actions planned to mitigate or minimize their potential impact. You probably won't have a solution to every risk, but the key is to have considered the risks and have plans to address them. Nothing will kill a proposal (and your personal credibility) faster than to have the audience identify important risks that you overlooked!

SUMMARY AND APPROVAL The old adage of military training applies to virtually every form of communication: "Tell them what you are going to tell them, tell them, and tell them what you just told them." A quick summary of the problem, proposed solution, investment, return, and risk should precede your request for approval and funding. Make the request for approval and funding the last step in the presentation or report. Too many people prepare and present good justifications, but fail to "ask for the order" as the closing point. Then they find they have to go back for final approval. Don't let that happen to you.

Good presentations and reports are those that present the material from the audience's perspective. Try to predict the audience's questions and answer them in the material. Don't assume that they know the material as you do. Include a summary of all the pertinent data that supports your arguments. Everyone is very busy and a short report or presentation that clearly presents the required information will be appreciated, and read, and has the greatest chance of success.

Step 7: Approved or Denied

Only rarely are initial justifications approved. Often you'll need to "sharpen your pencil" or provide additional details for review. If your project for a web site is approved, take a second to pat your team and yourself on the back, then get on with it! However, even the best arguments don't always succeed. If the justification is not approved, ask what were the issues that influenced the no-go decision to determine if there is a chance to reverse the decision.

If the decision is based on a misunderstanding of the arguments presented, re-work the material to clarify those points. If the decision is based on unanswered questions, collect the required information and prepare an addendum to the original presentation or report for reconsideration by the decision makers. If the decision is based on other things, such as office politics, it is often difficult to successfully address these nonbusiness issues. Use this as a learning process and move on to the next project. If the decision is based on a thorough review and understanding of the arguments, then you have done your job, but perhaps a web site solution is not the best alternative to solve the problem. One site we interviewed, Travelocity, found that outside help in the form of an independent consultant was instrumental in getting the go ahead.

CASE STUDY

Like virtually every web site operator interviewed, the Travelocity team members had a strong "gut feel" that their idea was going to work. Convincing partners who didn't have the same intuitive feel to invest many millions of dollars was a critical first challenge. According to Goel, "At the time we were building our business case, there was virtually no commerce on the Internet." Proposing the Internet as a solution over a private or other commercial service was not an easy process. The only way they were able to convince the board was to evaluate 9 or 10 scenarios based on their end objectives of:

❑ Providing real-time access to content

❑ Providing transactions and/or ticketing

For each scenario they had to develop a business plan and show what types of problems they would encounter and what potential risks each held for a full five years. Through this process they were able to show that the only viable solution was the Internet because the Internet was rapidly moving toward viability and provided access to a much larger potential audience than any other alternative. Today, as commercial online networks move toward hypertext markup language (HTML)-based formats they are becoming top distribution partners for Travelocity.

To validate their assumptions, Goel's team linked the launch of the site to specific growth milestones for the Internet. "If these things happen on the Internet, we know that it is moving towards commercial viability," said Goel. The team predicted that it would take four months to reach milestone agreements within the banking and technology communities on secure commerce. It required only two months, as the adoption of new technology gained momentum faster than expected.

Finally, a three-month study with Andersen Consulting was commissioned as a second opinion. The study did not find any flaws in the business plan. In fact, it confirmed the proposed solution. The study was the final bit of convincing that upper management needed; it was much more effective than relying on other more readily available information, such as from O'Reiley or others.

Part of the process was influenced by SABRE Interactive, an investor in the project. SABRE doesn't like to make decisions like these without significant investigation and discussion which includes standard business planning practices, such as a formal justification process and business plan presentation to the executive team. The plan included a five-year projection of costs, revenue, and break-even timeframe.

In summary, the three partners collectively committed tens of millions of dollars annually to launch Travelocity. Furthermore, they committed to support the venture through a period until break-even could to be achieved. This budget covered both technology and promotion.

Step 8: Ongoing Measurement and Evaluation

While some people view the approval step as the end of the justification process, it is in reality just the beginning for a web site. Whether formally or informally, the web site will continue to be reviewed by the original decision makers, your boss, and potentially other individuals in marketing, sales, public relations, and senior management. You should take a proactive role in this review by providing ongoing measurement and analysis of how well the site is doing versus its original goals. Ongoing measurement procedures are discussed in Part II. Figure 2.7 illustrates two examples of how expected versus measured results can be summarized in a one-page chart.

Step 9: Communicate Progress toward Goals

The last thing most managers want are surprises. You should continue to keep your management and the original decision makers informed of progress, and setbacks if they occur, toward reaching the original site goals based on the measurements and analysis of hard data from Step 8.

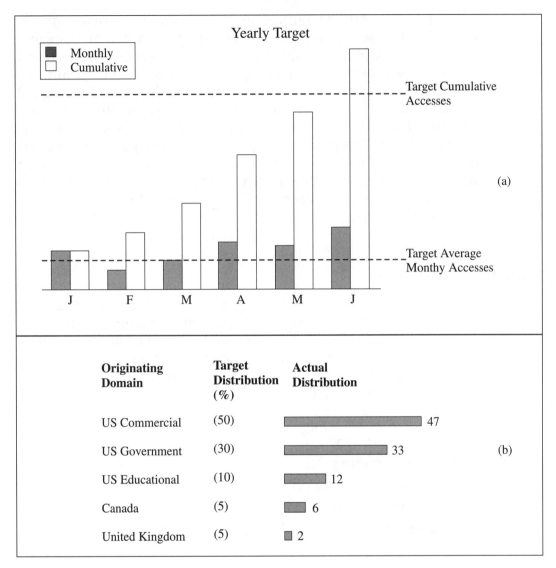

Figure 2.7 Simple methods of tracking estimated versus actual web-site access using (a) a graph or (b) a table.

Step 10: Achieving or Missing the Objective

If the original objective is achieved within the projected timeframe and budget, the site will be considered a success and ongoing funding should be easy to justify. However, few projects meet their original goals within original budget and time estimates. Usually, one or more of these (goals, budget, or timeframe) are different than presented in the original justification. When you feel that the original intent of the project has been reached, it is a good time to summarize how the actual project measurements differ from the original justification and determine if the site is a viable, ongoing endeavor. Sometimes actual measurements indicate changes that should be made in the site. They may even indicate that the site is not delivering the value its justification was based on. This may indicate that the site should be shut down. Part III discusses how to make decisions regarding site evolution and longevity based on site and audience measurements.

Justification Strategies

To successfully execute Steps 4 through 6 of the justification process, you need a strategy for quantifying, qualifying, and presenting the value statement for the proposed solution identified in Step 2. There are five or six basic strategies that have been successfully used by many organizations for any expenditure of funds, including for a web site. These are:

- ❑ Cost reduction
- ❑ Revenue growth
- ❑ Niche marketing
- ❑ Improved customer satisfaction
- ❑ Improved quality
- ❑ Addressing other critical business or customer needs

Cost Reduction

Cost reduction goals can be achieved by eliminating or containing costs, offsetting costs, and increasing productivity. Each approach has a slightly different set of detail measurements that contributes to the ROI calculation and justification argument.

Lower costs are clearly the number one benefit of Internet technology, whether used inside on an intranet or on the public Internet. Not everyone has a shot at generating revenue through the Web, but most sites can legitimately argue that they can save money. Therefore, we lead our exploration of web site justification strategies with some concrete savings approaches.

Cost Elimination or Containment

Cost elimination strategies enable an organization to largely stop major categories of expenses in exchange for a small investment that is a fraction of the overall cost savings. Such benefits usually apply at a *task* or *function* level that can be easily retooled to harness the Web.

Companies, such as Silicon Graphics, a leading provider of UNIX-based web servers and graphic workstations, and Cisco Systems, the nation's leading manufacturer of Internet routing equipment, have eliminated significant printing and distribution costs for product manuals by distributing their manuals online. They save even more money by leveraging a single set of content, for instance a manual, on both the Internet and a CD-ROM. While a printed manual may cost three to five dollars to produce, a CD-ROM costs only about a dollar and just one copy of an Internet version of the manual can be used to service hundreds to thousands of customers. These media alternatives reduce the manual costs by 70 to 98 percent or more over hard copies. It is true that there were new costs to create or convert this content into a digital form. However, these costs are so dramatically lower that the overall project meets the initial objective—cost elimination.

Other ways to eliminate costs are to maintain or reduce headcount, facilities, and other capital expenses.

Cost Offset

This strategy usually costs more upfront, but results in long-term savings to the company by making a major short-term change in how some aspect of the business is conducted. The short-term change usually requires a substantial investment that may be as much as the short-term savings from that change. Generally, cost offset strategies involve redirecting an entire *line of business* or, in some cases, *the entire organization itself.*

Productivity Increase

Productivity increases do not directly reduce costs, but allow a company to get more for its investment dollar. Increases result from reducing the time it takes an employee to complete a particular task, thus enabling the organization to produce more with limited incremental investment. Increases can also result by reducing the number of people required to get the job done. For example, if you can replace a human who is answering questions about remaining vacation time with an automated system, you have significantly cut the staff time required to respond to inquiries.

Some organizations measure productivity as dollars of revenue per employee. Cisco Systems has one of, if not the highest, productivity measures per employee. While many high tech company's productivity ratio is in the range of $250,000 of revenue per employee, Cisco Systems' ratio has been as high as $600,000 per employee. This provides more dollars for business investment, higher price per earnings ratios for its stock, higher investor equity, and, potentially, a more competitive company.

In general, intranet systems will probably provide large productivity returns. Campbell Mithun Esty, the fourteenth largest advertising agency in the United States, implemented an intranet human resources (HR) system that reduced internal costs substantially for handling regular inquiries concerning employee benefits, such as vacation and sick leave allotments, 401K plan questions, and medical coverage details. Silicon Graphics is using intranet systems extensively throughout the company to improve communication and productivity. Intranets have characteristics both like and unlike Internet sites. These differences are discussed more fully in Chapter 12.

America Online has an Internet help desk that allows a single technical support person to interface with one to three customers simultaneously, thereby reducing customer wait and response time, while minimizing the number of support staff required at America Online.

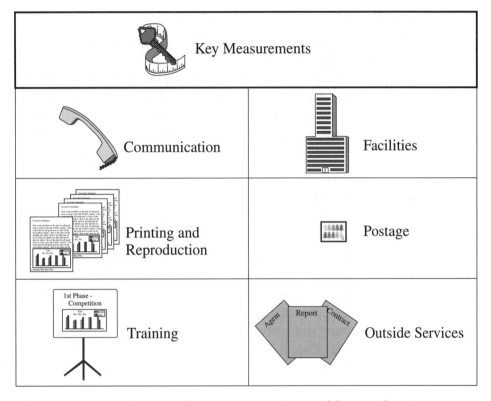

Figure 2.8 Typical cost reduction categories used for justification.

Key Measurements

Virtually all cost reduction justifications use one or more of the following expense and capital cost categories, shown in Figure 2.8, to justify their argument:

- ❏ Communication, including telephone and fax
- ❏ Headcount
- ❏ Facilities
- ❏ Printing and reproduction
- ❏ Postage
- ❏ Training
- ❏ Outside services

Cost Reduction Bottom-line Impact

The old saying, "a penny saved is a penny earned," actually has larger repercussions in today's businesses. For example, based on company gross margins and expenses, cost reduction of x dollars can have the same impact on the bottom line as a revenue increase of y, where y = several times x. When it is hard to grow revenues, most companies look for ways to reduce expenses; often, web sites can offer such reductions.

Niche Marketing

Today, probably the most common use of web sites is as a marketing tool. Companies, such as Toro, who spend hundreds of thousands to millions of dollars per year on advertising view the Internet as a relatively low-cost alternative or extension to its current marketing and communication activities. Sites are used for targeted advertising, product promotion, customer support, and product ordering at a much lower cost per prospect than other targeted or mass marketing programs. The Internet can be a conduit to other activities, such as sales programs and dealer locators, or it can be leveraged through the other media by promoting its existence and address (URL), as depicted in Figure 2.9.

CASE STUDY

TORO Based on Toro's objectives, the site was funded from general advertising dollars already in its fiscal year 1996 budget. There was no requirement or attempt to develop any specific financial justification for the site. Initial and ongoing site justification are based purely on strategic objectives (being the first in their industry on the Internet) and market-oriented measurements discussed later. Like most organizations we interviewed, Toro didn't have a good idea of what would be a good response rate for the site when they started. In this way, the site is much like a direct mail campaign. After six months of measurements (January to July 1996), Toro is well ahead of their initial estimate of about 50,000 visitor sessions in the first year. They have had 65,000 visits to the Toro site and 41,000 to the yardcare site in the six-month period.

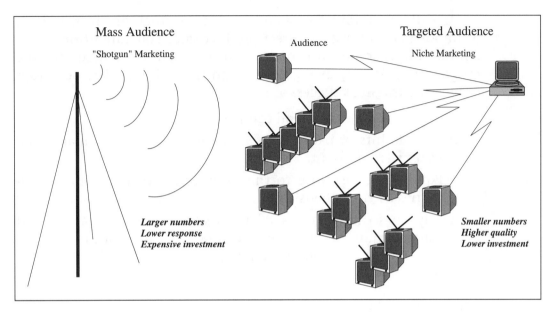

Figure 2.9 Extending marketing communications onto the Internet.

This equates to an expense of well under $1.00 per visit, which is a significantly lower cost ratio than other forms of advertising.

A web site can be developed and implemented for less than a reasonable magazine ad and for much less than television advertising. The web sites are not replacing these traditional advertising vehicles, but supplementing them. Often this is the organization's first step; it is a way to "test the waters" and provide planning input for future growth into product sales and technical support across the Internet.

Many government organizations have Internet sites that they would probably argue were implemented to improve access to their services. However, in a very real sense these sites also advertise often unknown and overlooked services that are available to the public. Through the Internet, these organizations can both serve the public and promote their services, thereby ensuring their continued budget justification in Congress and state assemblies.

As with most advertising and marketing programs, it is difficult or impossible to measure direct product sales generated from these efforts, unless some form of coupon or rebate is included for the program that is only available through the web site. The best ways to measure the site's success are:

❑ Treat it like a direct mail campaign.

❑ Use site hits or page accesses as a measure of how many *mail pieces* were sent out.

❑ Equate site response to the number of reseller database inquiries by the site visitors.

❑ Any sales that you can relate to site access (the hardest and least accurate measurement) can be used to measure the success of the promotional campaign.

Revenue Growth

Two ways of increasing revenue are to increase sales of existing products and to create sales of new products. Many companies, such as 3Com Corporation, find that their top line revenue grows faster when a high percentage (over one-third) of their products have been introduced to the market within the last 12 to 18 months. New product introductions always create a swell of orders and provide new and differential positioning which accelerates sales. Also, this often pulls along existing product sales. As an example, in the mid-1980s, 3Com introduced a dedicated network server called 3Server. Hardware sales of 3Server produced a substantial revenue stream. The new server also accelerated sales of 3Com's network operating system, electronic mail, and communications software because it provided a better platform than a generic PC for integrating these network services.

The three primary ways to grow revenue are to:

❑ Find new channels for existing products

❑ Create new products

❑ Couple these together and create new products for a new channel

Existing Products and Services

One of the most obvious examples of moving existing products through a new channel is using the Internet for catalog shopping. Companies like Hammacher-Schlemmer (available through Compuserve and Prodigy home shopping service and America Online 2Market service), that sell unique, upscale household and sporting goods, and MicroWarehouse (http://www.warehouse.com), a leading distributor of computers, peripherals, and components, have taken advantage of the Internet as a new channel for existing products.

Other companies, including WallStreet Discount Corporation (http://www.wsdc.com) and eTrade (http://www.etrade.com), are using the Internet to provide services—in this case discount brokerage trading—to the same market that has traditionally used the telephone to complete such transactions. While the services and markets are basically identical to those already serviced through other channels, the Internet channel can offer advantages, such as:

- Easier, more timely access (no waiting on hold through an 800-number)
- Lower product cost by passing savings on to the customer
- More personalized service from sites that keep track of visitor preferences
- Better record keeping of track transactions, daily closing prices, etc. (recorded on the customer's personal computer)
- No interaction with a broker (reduces time and avoids potential sales pitches)
- 24-hour access to account information and trade orders, although the trade can still only be placed during those times when the market is open

New Internet-Based Services and Products

For other companies, the Internet has created a new market for new services and products, such as online directory services like Yahoo and Infoseek. For some, such as *USA Today* and CNN, the Internet has created a new channel for new services which leverage some existing content but which have no off-line equal. For Travelocity, the Internet provided a whole new way of doing business.

CASE STUDY

Justification was based on revenue generation from a new Internet-based service business that Travelocity would provide direct to the consumer.

One of the most important success measures identified by Travelocity is the number of registered users. "The whole idea was to create a user community," said Goel. "We knew that this was going to happen and if we didn't do it, someone else would."

A second critical measure is gross sales at the site. It is interesting to note that Travelocity is a dealer not a manufacturer. Specifically, like other distributors, Travelocity makes its money from earning distribution fees on selling other companies' products. For airline tickets or merchandise, Travelocity collects a fee from the supplier for the sale. This follows the existing travel industry business model. Furthermore, it intends to be the "category killer" in online travel, sort of a Travel-R-Us. Therefore, gross sales generated by all of the participating companies at the site are a critically important metric.

A third metric is direct gross revenue from products and services it controls. For instance, with extremely high numbers of visitors streaming through every day, Travelocity has begun an online advertising program. Sponsors wanting to reach a prequalified travel audience can pay Travelocity for onscreen banners. This is a separate category of revenue. (Ironically, Travelocity probably pays a commission to an advertising broker to sell space.)

Key Measurements

Revenue growth, forecasts, sales cycle, and cost-per-sale for Internet services and product sales can be measured using the same metrics we use for conventional direct and indirect sales. These typically include:

- Revenue in dollars
- Sales out in units
- Product mix
- Sales cycle steps and duration
- Cost-per-sale

While the key measurements are the same, using the Internet as the distribution channel requires employing different methods for capturing the raw data needed to calculate these measurements, as discussed in Chapter 3 and Part II.

Improving Customer Satisfaction

When someone has a question, problem, or request, he or she typically wants fast action. Historically, customer support and service has evolved from walking back to the store where the item was purchased and getting support (possibly the fastest and certainly the most personal approach) or writing letters to phone calls, to 800-number lines, and finally to online Internet access.

Customer satisfaction can be both qualified and quantified through surveys, complaint tracking, repeat customer business, and product return levels. Customer satisfaction directly impacts revenue generation because your best prospect is almost always an existing customer. It is also important in non-revenue terms, as illustrated by the Senate web site objectives.

CASE STUDY

 There are actually two levels of customer satisfaction addressed by the Senate site. The first level relates to the computer center customers—Senators and committees. The second level relates to the Senate constituents and other interested parties.

Because the Senate is a conservative organization, there was much discussion internally concerning the site. Some Senators felt the Internet was only a passing trend, others felt frustrated by a lack of presence in the new technology, and still others were concerned about potential political abuse of a web site. This is why the initial site is very conservative.

Since the Senate was already running a gopher/ftp server onto which the web server was added, there were no cost justification requirements, as budget already existed for broadly defined central computing services which was re-allocated to the web site. The cost included site setup and administration. Senate offices fund their individual page development.

However, a technology review group is now undertaking a broad information requirements assessment for the Senate, including Internet needs. This is the first step in developing specific requirements and budgets to justify future site enhancements, which will be handled on a more proactive and formal basis.

Two ways of justifying a web site based on improved customer satisfaction are improved survey results and reduced complaint levels, as discussed in the next sections.

Improved Survey Results

CASE STUDY

FedEx
Federal Express   FedEx's objectives actually span two justification strategies. The first has to do with customer satisfaction, or as the company puts it, "to continue to enrich the site for direct use by customers." The second has to do with improving how customers work by providing them time-saving tools at their workplace for preparing, shipping, tracking, and receiving packages.

This metric seeks to quantify the number of customers that are more likely to remain loyal directly because of an Internet-related service the company provides. The previous FedEx example is designed to enhance customer loyalty. Other companies, such as Novell (http://support.novell.com) and Intel (http://www.intel.com), have also implemented various online systems to support their customers.

Reduced Complaint Levels

Another way to determine how satisfied your customers are is to measure complaint levels and severity. As a communication vehicle, the Internet can be used to remedy or communicate progress in remedying problems. Many technology and computer companies have used bulletin boards and now Internet-based systems to distribute program fixes and updates, notify users of known program problems, and provide forums for users to discuss topics of interest pertaining to various vendor products.

Companies have found that just having a forum for discussion reduces user frustration and complaint levels. Plus, users are often able to help one another find fixes or workarounds to problems.

Since the number of complaints an organization receives over time is usually easily quantified, all else being equal, it is possible to measure a decrease attributable to the web initiative, if that is the only major effort undertaken to improve customer satisfaction. Even if several activities are underway to improve customer satisfaction, the impact from the web site can be gauged through surveys, e-mails, support personnel observations, and often word-of-mouth comments.

Key Measurements

Compared to cost and revenue justifications, quality justifications are harder to quantify, but usually much easier to qualify. Besides survey results in which you should try to measure customer satisfaction through questions—"Were you satisfied with the service you received?" or, "How did you like the product during the first 90 days?"—some of the best measures of improved customer satisfaction are higher sales and lower returns.

Improving Quality

Higher customer satisfaction can be achieved without improving product or service quality. Improving quality, however, will typically improve customer satisfaction and provide other advantages to the company, such as reduced warranty costs, reduced returns, and higher product sales. Web sites can be used to help improve quality through:

❑ Providing a forum for customer comments, problem reports, and other data that can be used as input in product revisions and improvements

❑ Providing distribution of pre-release products for testing, as many software vendors are currently doing on the Internet

Don't get confused here between actions and results. The web site, per se, cannot improve product quality. It can only provide the vehicle for information exchange and customer expectation setting which will result in real or perceived quality improvement. Improved product quality can only come from improved definition, development, testing, and manufacturing. But, the web site can provide the impetus and forum to make these things happen. One way of measuring how a web site impacts quality is to track how many customer complaints result in service or product changes and how many customer suggestions are implemented. The web site can help the whole company become more market-driven by providing a forum for communication with your customers.

Addressing Other Business or Customer Needs

Any well-defined need can be analyzed and, if appropriate, an Internet-based solution can be proposed and justified just like the previously discussed strategies. The justification strategy, to be successful, must address key aspects of capability, cost, and value that differentiate it from other possible alternatives.

Some typical reasons that a web site could be implemented based on this strategy are:

❑ Create a perception of market leadership by being first on the Internet.

❑ It is believed that their customers *expect* the company to have an Internet presence.

❑ Strategically the company must create a web site because its major competitors have sites.

The *Star Tribune*'s justification for a web site is a rather unique approach, based on its forward-looking R&D approach to electronic communication mediums.

CASE STUDY

The *Star Tribune* has a very proactive and forward-looking philosophy. The newspaper previously had foreseen the need for a research and development fund to be used for evaluating various new technologies. First, the Interchange services, then the web site were justified as an R&D expense basically to ensure competitiveness into the future. Schafer's team was required to do the typical steps of business planning, budgeting, and establishing review points.

The *Star Tribune*'s justification requirements and criteria for success are linked, but slightly different. While the justification focused on R&D, success measures have rapidly evolved towards the business contribution as online information provision heats up. Success measures include:

- ❑ Number of advertisers (display ad) the site attracts
- ❑ Subscriber or user growth
- ❑ Ability to identify and develop unique content

Fortunately, one of the things not expected was profitability, at least not in the early years. The R&D-based justification provided more flexibility on this front than if the paper had chosen a different supporting argument.

Other business needs could also include revenue-neutral projects that are really specific to your particular organization or industry. For instance, many companies use sales incentive programs to motivate the sales force. An essential ingredient is the *leader board*—often a white board with current sales standings on it. An intranet version of such a board for a company with many offices is probably more expensive than the system it replaces, but offers enough morale advantages that it is worth the investment and can be used repeatedly as new programs are rolled out.

Hard Data to Support Your Justification Strategy

In the justification phase, you cannot naturally get hard data off the proposed web site, but you can and should get hard data about the systems it may be replacing or supplementing as input to your justification and planning. Once the web site project enters the planning stage, you need to consider how you are going to capture the hard data needed for ongoing site justification. To help you with both these tasks, Chapter 3 discusses measurement strategies and how they fit into the planning and operational phases of the site's life cycle.

Measurement Strategies and Sources

You've identified one or more concrete benefits that a web site will provide to your organization, but how are you going to back up your claims?

Whether you've chosen quantitative or qualitative success measures, it is rare that they can be quickly compiled. By definition, the kind of goals that managers pay attention to must span the entire range of their responsibility. The more strategic the web site, the higher you will have to go for approval and the greater your supporting justification effort will be.

This chapter is your roadmap to acquiring all of the information you'll need to demonstrate real progress on an ongoing basis. We'll show you how to decide what data is needed to support your measures, where to collect various data points, and how they relate to one another. Finally, we'll cover some good estimation and approximation methods when you can't get hard data.

Measurement Hierarchy

Chapter 2 described the pertinent data required to support specific justification strategies. We call these top-level measurements *Impact Measures* because they describe a specific benefit to your organization. However, Impact Measures can rarely be directly measured, but must instead be based on or calculated from other data that can be directly captured. This creates a hierarchy of measures, as shown in Figure 3.1.

RAW MEASURES This is data that is directly captured, estimated, or approximated from the web site or from other sources, such as phone bills or customer call logs. It forms the most basic building blocks of the Impact Measure. Raw data includes, among other things, site connections per hour, cost per minute of inbound 800-calls, number of hits per web site, number of accesses per web page, the type of browser used by the visitor, and the domain of the visitor.

CONSOLIDATED MEASURES These yardsticks are themselves roll-ups of individual pieces of raw data and used in calculating Impact Measures. A simple example is a credit card statement that rolls up many separate purchases. It is neither raw data nor the complete picture of your spending in a given month, but it's an important piece of information.

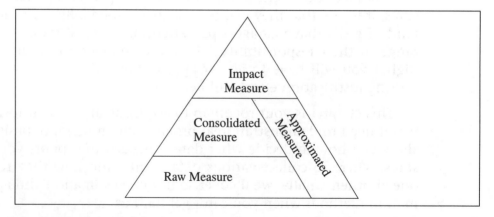

Figure 3.1 Hierarchy of measures: *Raw, Consolidated, Approximate,* and *Impact Measures.*

APPROXIMATE MEASURES These are *non-hard* quantities that are required to arrive at the Impact Measure, but for which exact data cannot be measured.

IMPACT MEASURES This is the information and data on which the justification is based. These measures create an impact on the organization and are the pertinent measures outlined in Chapter 2 for the different justification strategies.

To consider how the hierarchy of measures works, Figure 3.2 illustrates an example that you live virtually every day. Miles per hour is an important Impact Measure for almost everyone who drives a car. Through experience, it tells you if you are going at about the right speed for traffic conditions and whether you are breaking the law. You get this Impact Measure from the car's speedometer, but the speedometer does not measure the car's speed directly. Car speed is calculated from Raw Measures particular to the car. The Raw Measures include tire circumference, axle rotation speed, and the length of a mile. Depending on what country you're driving in, the Impact Measure becomes kilometers per hour and some of the Raw Measures change accordingly.

Figure 3.2 Speedometer attached to the car's axle and wheel.

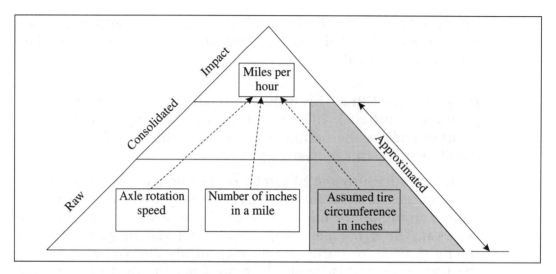

Figure 3.3 Calculating miles-per-hour Impact Measure.

If any of the Raw Measures vary, the Impact Measure changes. If any one of the Raw Measures is wrong, the Impact Measure will be off. Figure 3.3 illustrates how this hierarchy of measures is flow-charted in worksheet form. In the calculations, estimates and assumptions are often made when exact information cannot be captured or input into the formula. For example, tire circumference will vary slightly as the tire wears. Even if the tire circumference could be measured exactly, there is no description in a car's user manual on how to modify tire circumference in the formula used for calculating miles per hour. Therefore, tire circumference is actually an Approximated Measure in these calculations.

Sometimes there is more than one method of calculating a particular consolidated or Impact Measure. In place of the standard car speedometer, a wind velocity gauge, similar to that used on an airplane, could be substituted to calculate miles per hour. These gauges measure airspeed, typically in knots, and this data could be converted to miles per hour, as shown in Figure 3.4. This method eliminates the need to know the tire circumference (and assume it is correct) and the axle rotation (and any mechanical problems that could affect it).

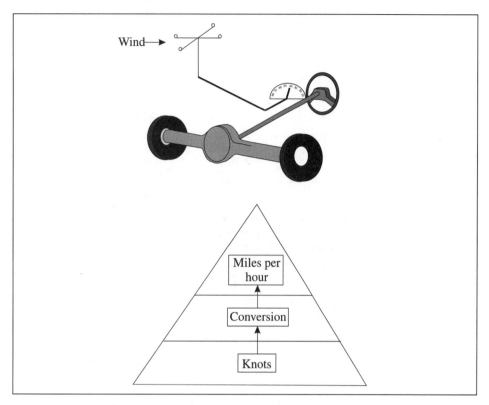

Figure 3.4 Alternative method of calculating miles per hour.

This example should help you to visualize Impact, Approximated, Consolidated, and Raw Measures, as well as the relationships between them. Of course, since the speedometer does all the work for you, it's not necessary to actually do the work yourself. However, with a web site, there's no dashboard that you can consult to instantly provide the hard-hitting measures you need to see, to avoid getting pulled over. So let's consider some web-specific examples of the measurement hierarchy.

CASE STUDY

 A great example of a site not justified on the basis of cost savings, but in which substantial cost savings were

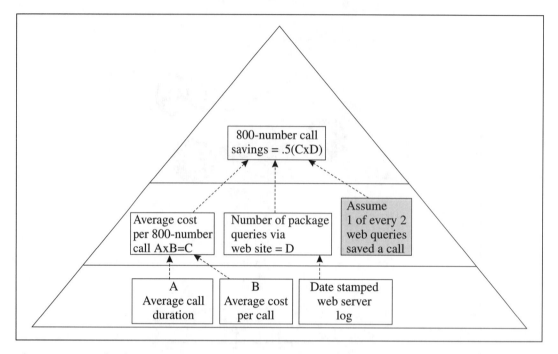

Figure 3.5 Calculating savings in 800-number telephone costs.

realized, is Federal Express (FedEx). If we apply this measurement hierarchy to the 800-number cost justification used by FedEx for its web site, the resulting worksheet looks like Figure 3.5. This formula only measures the savings achieved by reducing 800-number calls, not other potential savings from such things as lower hiring rates and costs, and reduced facility costs.

In Figure 3.5, the Raw Measures collected by the web server will be in electronic logs that can be scanned to extract pertinent data. Other data sources, such as call logs in customer support, may be automated or manual, depending on how the individual systems and tracking are implemented.

For FedEx, cost elimination justification is calculated based on the immediate net expense difference resulting from implementing the site. While cost reduction was not the explicit primary objective, it was certainly a corollary objective, based on the expectations of some percentage of customers using the site versus the 800-number.

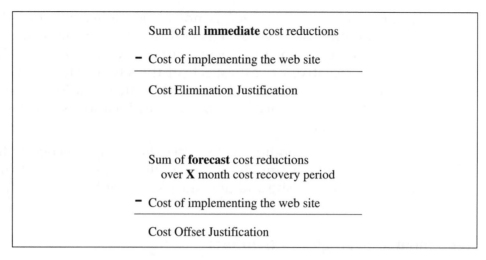

Sum of all **immediate** cost reductions

− Cost of implementing the web site
_____

Cost Elimination Justification

Sum of **forecast** cost reductions
over **X** month cost recovery period

− Cost of implementing the web site
_____

Cost Offset Justification

Figure 3.6 Cost elimination and cost offset justification formulas.

On the other hand, cost offset justification can be thought of as having two distinct aspects: a cost recovery period and an ongoing operating cost reduction. For any cost-based justification, the argument must be based on the sum of all savings minus the cost of implementing the site and its ongoing costs. For FedEx, potential Impact Measures could have reduced long distance costs, reduced headcount, lowered capital equipment depreciation, reduced facilities, and reduced training costs. For cost elimination and cost offset justification strategies, the equations are shown in Figure 3.6. In general, for any justification strategy the equation is shown in Figure 3.7.

If the strategy is cost-based, then the calculation is predominately cost-oriented. If the justification is quality- or customer satisfaction-based, then the calculations are more qualitative. The

Sum of all contributing Impact Measures

− Cost or other impacts of implementing the web site
_____

Justification Strategy

Figure 3.7 General justification strategy equation.

primary message, however, is not to be fooled into thinking that there are only positive or plus contributions to implementing the site. A well-developed site plan must also consider and address the potential negative or cost aspects of the site development. Detailed methods for calculating the contribution of various quantitative and qualitative Impact Measures for justification strategies are discussed in Part II.

The next section briefly discusses the need to recognize both explicit and implicit site objectives, while the remainder of the chapter discusses both site and non-site sources of Raw Measures.

Recognizing Strategy Implications

As mentioned in the Federal Express Case Study on page 83, justification strategies usually represent both primary and corollary objectives that are explicitly stated and understood. Often, there is a third type of objective called an *implicit objective*. These objectives are always interrelated as illustrated by the following case study.

CASE STUDY

FedEx **Federal Express** FedEx's objectives actually span two justification strategies. The first has to do with customer satisfaction or as the company puts it, "to continue to enrich the resources for the customer." The second has to do with improving how customers work by providing them time-saving tools at their workplace for preparing, shipping, tracking, and receiving packages.

FedEx wants to measure how many visitors the site has and what services each one uses. Because FedEx offers customers ways of accessing the company's services online, site metrics are the same as business metrics:

- Packages shipped
- Packages tracked
- Software downloaded
- Package drop-off searches completed
- Customer satisfaction

Note that these measures are the same measures discussed previously as they are used in site ROI analysis.

Most justification strategies will include similar implicit and corollary objectives to the primary objective. It is important that you measure, analyze, and communicate progress on these objectives as well as the primary objective. Part III discusses how to analyze justification measures and covers corollary and implicit measures you should also review.

Defining the Data

Required measurements are a function of the justification strategy(ies) (explicit primary and corollary objectives, and implicit objectives) used to support the web site. In Figure 3.6, Raw and Consolidated Measures are required to calculate the Impact Measure.

For each Impact Measure used in the justification, a worksheet similar to Figure 3.6 must be developed to help you determine what specific data is required to calculate the Impact Measure. We will get you started by providing flowcharts for each of the Impact Measures defined in Chapter 2. The flowcharts can be found in Chapter 5. If you have other Impact Measures, you should develop a corresponding flowchart. Usually data will have to be collected from four sources:

- ❑ Business measures
- ❑ Existing systems
- ❑ The web site
- ❑ The web site audience

Business measures are required to add the critical cost component to usage information collected from the servers and existing systems. You may need access to gross sales, net sales, unit copy costs, unit shipping costs, per-minute long-distance costs, and so forth. Depending on the scope of your organization, this information may originate in your business unit. Otherwise, you may have to find contacts throughout the organization to assemble a credible package.

Data from existing systems, such as 800-number operations, manual production and printing processes, advertising and promotional programs, and other activities that may be supplemented or replaced by the web site must usually be collected as part of getting information together for the justification process. Data from existing system(s) is required to establish a baseline against which to compare the success of the web site, and calculate percentage differences between existing and site access rates, costs, and customer satisfaction, as illustrated in Figure 3.5.

Data from the site is used to quantitatively measure utilization, response, errors, and services used. Data collected from the audience, such as through user surveys and e-mail, measures qualitative aspects of the site and audience acceptance of the site. Together these four data sources and approximations are rolled into the Impact Measure calculations.

As you define the Impact Measures and identify the raw data required to calculate each measure, the first step is to select one or more of these sources for the raw data. It is likely, however, that you will identify the need for certain raw data that doesn't exist or cannot be directly captured. For instance, because of the way the Internet works internally, you can measure the number of hits on the site, but not the number of people visiting the site. Hits can tell you how many times a given element of the site was requested in a specified period. However, each hit does not equate to a unique and individual visitor.

If, instead, you measure the number of page views (the difference between these two measurements is explained more thoroughly in Part II), you can measure the number of accesses of a given page, which may represent the information on a particular product or service offered through the site. This is a closer approximation of "people" than hits. However, there is still no direct way to measure the number of visitors to the site. You cannot tell if one visitor accessed the same page multiple times, or if several visitors accessed the page.

CASE STUDY

To measure their progress toward stated goals requires both site- and nonsite-generated measures. With the *Star Tribune*'s early online endeavors using the Interchange Network, users had to be registered subscribers. This allowed more specific audience measurement than is possible via the Web.

With the Internet, the Star Tribune is finding audience measurement more difficult. They are measuring:

- ❏ Site hits to establish activity trendlines
- ❏ Unique hosts to estimate daily traffic
- ❏ Page hits to measure access to specific stories or pages on the site
- ❏ Advertiser interest, as a nonsite measure, through traditional channels

From the first two measures they are estimating the number of pages seen per user. We will discuss their results to date and what they may mean in Part III.

In this you will have to make an educated guess if your measurement hierarchy demands a count of "people." You might choose an indirect measure, such as the number of people requesting the very first page at the site. If this is the most publicized URL you have, chances are that this quantity is the best approximation you will get. Another method would be to take some other concrete number, such as the total number of e-mails sent in, and multiply it by an arbitrary factor. You would need to supply a clear rationale for your choice of the factor, but this, too, might meet your justification needs.

The following section discusses the need to identify data sources early in the site planning process so that you can integrate these into the development and operations plan. While sources for external raw data may already exist in current systems, they must be delineated and methods must be planned to access them on a regular basis for comparisons and calculations with the web site data. Since the web site is new, its raw data sources must be planned for and implemented as part of the web site project.

Identifying the Data Source

Once you have defined the required Raw Measures, you need to define the source or determine methods for estimating or approximating the Raw Measures. Many sites, such as Toro, use both quantitative and qualitative measures.

CASE STUDY

TORO Toro measures its site both quantitatively and qualitatively, as shown in Figure 3.8. Quantitative measurements include hits, page views, originating visitor domain, and browser type. The objective is to track the number of visitors, what they saw, and where they came from. Toro does not attempt to track sales related to site visits at this time. However, one obvious measurement that equates to direct sales was made during the East coast blizzards in 1996. Use of the dealer locator (already one of the most heavily used features) increased dramatically during this period. It turned out that snowed-in homeowners in the East couldn't get snow throwers because the local stores were all sold out. So many turned to the Web and proceeded to have them shipped in from Toro dealers in the midwest.

Qualitatively, Toro uses informal feedback from their dealers and distributors, e-mail, and internal comments to measure the acceptance of the site. The company has received e-mails from visitors that:

- ❏ Tell them they have a nice site
- ❏ Thank them for prompt service and feedback through the site
- ❏ Tell them that they were expecting to find, and glad to have found, Toro on the Internet

Product complaints also occur from time to time, but constitute an extremely low percentage of e-mails. So far the site has per-

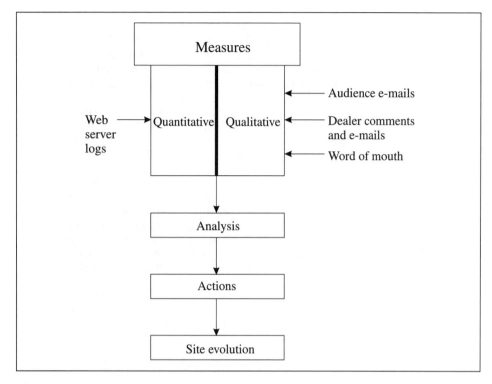

Figure 3.8 Toro site measurement strategy.

formed above expectations both quantitatively and qualitatively, but there is still room for improvement as discussed in Part III.

The following sections outline sources for both quantitative and qualitative data.

Web Site Raw Measures

The most raw form of information available to you will likely be the logs from your web server. In the next few paragraphs, we'll introduce you to how a web server records events. Though you will almost certainly want to apply a more sophisticated analysis tool, it's vital to understand the capabilities and limits of the web server itself.

```
pm1-16.inetnow.net - - [26/May/1996:13:51:46  -0500]
    "GET /icons/TTUE.GIF HTTP/1.0" 200 1544
pm1-16.inetnow.net - - [26/May/1996:13:51:51  -0500]
    "GET /images/None.GIF HTTP/1.0" 200 820
pm1-16.inetnow.net - - [26/May/1996:13:51:57  -0500]
    "GET /grasses.html /HTTP/1.0" 200 782
schaller.cnsnet.com - - [26/May/1996:13:52:02  -0500]
    "GET /grasses/faq.thinning.html HTTP/1.0" 200 1743
pm1-16.inetnow.net - - [26/May/1996:13:52:07  -0500]
    "GET /grasses/faq.dying.html HTTP/1.0" 200 6182
schaller.cnsnet.com - - [26/May/1996:13:52:48  -0500]
    "GET /grasses/faq.mowing.html HTTP/1.0" 200 15473
pm1-16.inetnow.net - - [26/May/1996:13:53:10  -0500]
    "GET /images/None.GIF HTTP/1.0" 200 820
schaller.cnsnet.com - - [26/May/1996:13:54:10  -0500]
    "GET /grasses/faq.watering.html HTTP/1.0" 200 10380
schaller.cnsnet.com - - [26/May/1996:13:56:39  -0500]
    "GET /grasses/faq.soils.html HTTP/1.0" 200 17223
schaller.cnsnet.com - - [26/May/1996:13:59:10  -0500]
    "GET /grasses/faq.temperature.html HTTP/1.0" 200 1910
schaller.cnsnet.com - - [26/May/1996:13:59:39  -0500]
    "GET /icons/WeedsT.GIF HTTP/1.0" 200 1182
```

Figure 3.9 The access log records date, time, user id, and request information.

Web servers usually provide a log or logs in which site accesses and events are stored. The following sample logs are the standard format from a Netscape Commerce Server. Figure 3.9 shows a sample access log, Figure 3.10 shows a referral log, and Figure 3.11 shows an error log.

```
[26/May/1996:13:56:39 -500] /grasses/faq.soils.html schaller.cnsnet.com -
    Mozilla/2.0 (Win95; I) http://WWW.yardcare.com/grasses.html
[26/May/1996:13:59:10 -500] /grasses/faq.temperature.html schaller.cnsnet.com -
    Mozilla/2.0 (Win95;I) http://WWW.yardcare.com/grasses
[26/May/1996:13:59:39 -500] /icons/WeedsT.GIF schaller.cnsnet.com -
    Mozilla/2.0 (Win95; I) http://WWW.yardcare.com/
[26/May/1996:14:02:09 -500] /toro.shtml schaller.cnsnet.com -
    Mozilla/2.0 (Win95; I) http://WWW.conline.com/txmall/garden.html
```

Figure 3.10 The referral log records browser type and previous URL.

```
[24/May/1996:11:57:01]  info: successful server startup
[24/May/1996:12:02:12]  info: growing process pool from 1 to 5
[24/May/1996:12:02:24]  info: growing process pool from 4 to 8
[24/May/1996:12:02:32]  info: growing process pool from 4 to 8
[24/May/1996:12:02:34]  info: growing process pool from 5 to 8
[24/May/1996:13:00:52]  info: I/O to 198.161.109.6 timed out
[24/May/1996:13:01:56]  info: for host slr6.ccinet.ab.ca, handle-request reports:
     read from 198.161.109.6 failed, error is Connection refused
[24/May/1996:13:10:51]  info: for host pm205.westol.com, handle-request reports:
     read from 204.171.146.70 failed, error is Connection refused
[24/May/1996:13:41:06]  info: I/O to 204.171.146.70 timed out
[24/May/1996:13:41:40]  warning:  for host krech.cray.com, http-parse-request reports:
     while scanning HTTP headers, read failed
[24/May/1996:14:02:29]  info:  for host mddevaul.b25.ingr.com, handle request reports:
     read from 129.135.238.18 failed, error is Connection refused
```

Figure 3.11 The error log records significant events and problems.

The format of these logs varies somewhat from server to server. Netscape's format is different from NCSA, and both of these differ from Microsoft. Regardless of format, data from these logs provides:

❑ **Date and time stamps:** This allows you to determine the most common access times and days.

❑ **Visitor domain:** This details where your visitors are originating, whether through commercial online services, such as America Online (http://www.aol.com) and NETCOM (http://www.netcom.com) or from organization domains, such as the University of Michigan (http://www.umich.edu/), Fidelity Investments (http://www.fid-inv.com:8080/), or McDonnell Douglas Corporation (http://www.dac.mdc.com/).

❑ **Files requested:** These are the raw elements that make up a web page. The server has no knowledge of the relationship between a page and the items on it, such as images. Therefore, the web browser must interpret the page layout and make multiple requests for images, sounds, Java applets, and other elements until the page is complete. The server records every single request. Each request constitutes one *hit*.

- **Browser type:** This identifies the most common browser types used by visitors, since different browsers may or may not handle various page attributes. You may find that having two sites (a universal page and an optimized page for one or two browsers) best meets your audience needs.

- **Referring links:** An increasing number of browsers will tell you the URL where the visitor came from immediately prior to coming to your page. This is vital information if you want to determine who is linking to your site or what path a visitor takes through your own site.

- **Server errors:** This gives data on how the web server is performing, particularly at high loads, and its reliability.

- **Server changes:** This tracks how the site is changing, such as increasing the number of processes or threads because of heavier loads.

Non-Site Raw Measures

Non-site Raw Measures, which are often needed to calculate cost comparisons between the existing process and the web site, must be gathered from throughout the organization. Often, estimates or averages are used for this data. An average is a calculation based entirely on hard data, such as adding 50 numbers together and dividing by 50 to get their average. An estimate uses hard data and non-hard data in its calculation. For example, if you use the number of pages copied per day (hard data) times a factor to represent the number of pages that were used for customer responses, the resulting estimate is a combination of hard data and *non-hard* or approximated data. Estimate, as defined in the dictionary, is "to make an approximate calculation of (value, amount, size, etc.)." Typical examples include:

- 800-number phone charges
- Postage, printing, and reproduction costs
- Facility charges
- Overhead costs
- Training costs

Site development costs should be tracked closely by the project team, as these details are needed in the justification strategy calculations for initial site payback. Also, site operational costs need to be tracked to determine ongoing cost offset, if that was part of the original justification strategy.

Qualitative Measures

Three primary data sources for qualitative data are surveys, e-mails, and informal comments from peers, managers, and others. Surveys are the most formal process and should be constructed to collect information for answering specific questions about how easy, useful, and informative the site is. E-mail is an excellent source of immediate feedback on the site. It is less structured than a survey and you may be surprised how often people will include comments in an e-mail that they would not tell you in person. Informal comments provide good information. Comments from people in the organization who have tried the site provide company perspective on the site, but comments from sales and marketing are often a better indication of customer perspective of the site. These methods and others are discussed in more detail in Chapter 4.

Approximated Measures

Approximations may need to be made for both site and non-site data. As noted previously, estimates and averages are generally based on actual data, but approximations are derived conclusions (often subjective) using estimated, averaged, or raw data measurements. Approximate is defined as "to come near to in quantity, quality, or condition, nearly exact." *The major caution concerning approximations is that bias, whether conscious or unconscious, can skew results.*

For example, many web browser and server software vendors use market share as a potent competitive weapon. To measure market share, they approximate their installed base of customers from the number of downloads of the software measured through their web site. While an accurate measurement can be made of the number of times software is downloaded, an accurate measure of how the software is used cannot be gathered. Consider the following scenarios:

❑ One person can make several downloads but have only one computer.

❑ One person can make a download to upgrade or replace a damaged version, which does not actually increase share.

❑ A download may never be installed.

❑ One person can make a download and install the software on several nodes, resulting in higher share.

With this level of uncertainly, how can the vendors determine how their software is being used? They cannot, so they often approximate their installed base in the most favorable light possible.

Another important approximation that all sites must make is "how many people visit the web site." Because the underlying connection between the web server and any given visitor is called, in technical terms, *stateless*, the system cannot track the series of requests made by an individual node. The server looks at each request as a *new* connection. The server software can track the number and type of requests, but it cannot relate individual requests back to a particular visitor or track how many and what type of requests an individual makes. The bottom line is that you, as the web site manager, can measure site hits and page requests, but not visitors. Therefore, for the time being the actual number of site visitors can only be an approximated number.

The two reasons you may need to approximate a key piece of raw data are:

❑ There is not a readily available source for the data.

❑ Sources can be identified, but you do not have the time or resources to acquire the data at this time.

Storage Approaches that Minimize Analysis Work

The web server log file is the source of most raw data for the site, but since a typical log can grow to be 40 to 50 megabytes in length, it can be difficult to process if some thought is not given beforehand to its management. If a site experiences 250,000 hits per day and each hit generates a one line (80 character) entry, the daily log will be 20 megabytes in size. If logs are only restarted once a week, the weekly log could be over 100 megabytes. To facilitate log handling, Microsoft's and Netscape's web servers, for example, provide several options for controlling the location and size of the log, as well as how often a new log file is started—daily, weekly, or monthly.

As illustrated in Figures 3.9 through 3.11, log file entries are not typically easy to read and certainly do not lend themselves to providing Consolidated Measures or other useful data. Most logs have to be scanned and key data extracted and summarized to provide meaningful information. Figures 3.12 through 3.15 illustrate some forms of useful measurements that can be consolidated from the raw log data.

Figure 3.12 shows summarized access by page, which is often equated to specific features or information contained on the web site. This allows you to measure site use compared to initial projections and plan site modifications to improve access in the future.

Figure 3.13 shows access by the hour of the day. This information is important in understanding what periods of the day the site is used most heavily and in determining required site capacity. By

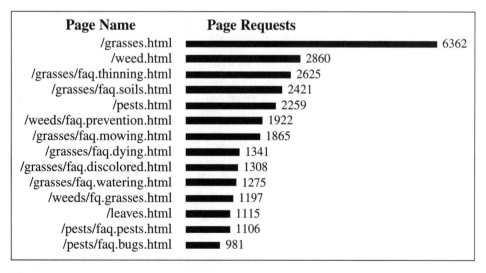

Figure 3.12 Statistics on page accesses.

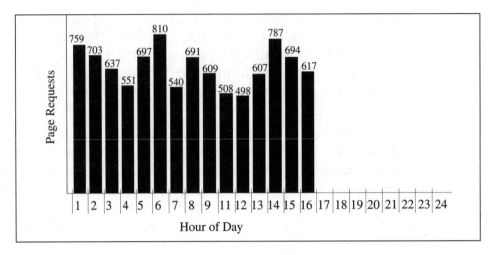

Figure 3.13 Statistics on access by time of day.

extrapolating these numbers, you can also get some approximation of the access distribution by geographic region of the country. For a West coast site, early A.M. access will probably be from the East coast, while late P.M. access will most likely represent West coast access. Nine A.M. to 1:00 P.M. access will be distributed across the entire country. If you calculate the percentage between the A.M. and P.M. access rates and apply it to the 9:00 A.M. to 1:00 P.M. access totals, you can get a first order (rough) estimate of the distribution of access across the entire country.

Figures 3.14 and 3.15 show further accumulation of access statistics to show access by day of the week in Figure 3.14, and a trendline by month for the first nine months of the year in Figure 3.15. This can help you track the success of the site and also to determine trends, such as high weekend access or seasonal access of the site.

To scan the web server logs and extract information into reports or graphs, such as previously shown, or into consolidated databases for further analysis, you need to either develop data reduction programs or use commercially available programs. These tools and programs are discussed briefly in Part II.

Once you have a firm foundation in the fundamentals of measurement strategy and implementation from Parts I and II, Chapters 8 and 9 discuss when and how to analyze site measures. Chapters 10

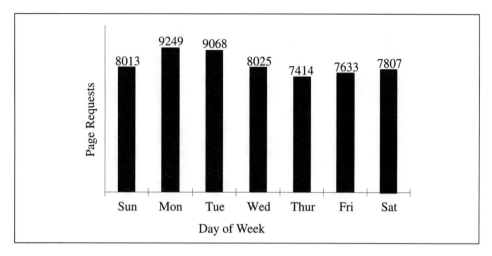

Figure 3.14 Statistics on access by day of week.

and 11 then enumerate ways to proceed based on your measurements, analysis, and conclusions. You may be surprised by some of our case studies' experiences and decisions.

Raw site data, however, cannot tell you much about audience preferences, satisfaction, or acceptance of the site. Other data collection methods need to be planned for and used as outlined in Chapter 4, so that you have sufficient data to conduct a thorough analysis.

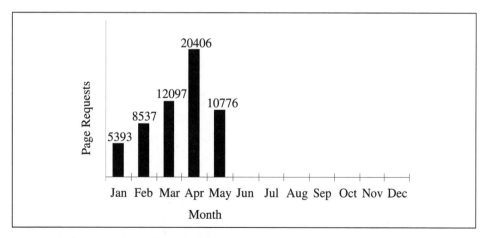

Figure 3.15 Statistics on access by month.

Measurement Opportunities in Site Features

You've seen the importance of planning and setting clear objectives for continued justification and management of the site. In the last chapter, you saw the different types of measures and how they relate to one another. In this chapter, we will discuss how to implement generic and specific web site feature-oriented measurements. Generic measurements, typically server statistics, are the best way to monitor overall site activity, performance, and reliability. Site-specific features, on the other hand, are your best bet for building a one-on-one relationship with visitors because they generally require visitors to make choices, offer comments, and expose preferences.

In the first part of this chapter, we cover generic server statistics. The second part of the chapter covers some of the most common site-specific features including e-mail replies, survey forms, and ordering. Collectively, these measures are required to validate your objectives and analyze site effectiveness. There are also two other categories of measurements which are important to consider:

❑ **Non-site Raw Measures:** Often, to calculate or complete analysis of the Impact Measure, you will need to collect data that is not site-based. This has already been discussed in the previous chapter and includes information, such as outgoing phone charges, facility costs, and so forth. As you read the following sections, consider for each measure what non-site information you will need to complete your Impact Measure calculation and make note of it. This will provide you with a complete list of the Raw Measures that need to be collected. Armed with this, Part II describes how to collect these Raw Measures and calculate corresponding Impact Measures.

❑ **Business-specific measures:** These are unique to the site, such as most common keywords accessed for search engine sites or order form types accessed from commercial sites. Either special tools are needed to measure these for the former measure or they can often be measured as page hits for the latter category. Since these measures tend to be very specific to the business, they are not discussed further herein, but you can use the guidelines discussed in this chapter to develop business-specific measures you require for your site.

Non-site Raw Measures are discussed further in Part II. Business-specific measures are very unique to the individual site and therefore are not pursued further in this book.

Measures are required to confirm your assumptions and make changes based on site usage to better accommodate your audience. During planning, design, and development you make critical decisions that influence the site which should be confirmed or modified based on actual site use. Decisions are made during four phases of the planning process which require corresponding measurements to be designed into the site. The four phases discussed in Chapter 1 that influence site measurement requirements are:

❑ Setting your objective(s)
❑ Analyzing your audience
❑ Selecting appropriate content
❑ Choosing a promotion strategy

Measurements identified in the Setting-your-objective phase are required to support your site justification strategy. These must be captured to provide the hard data you need to support ongoing site

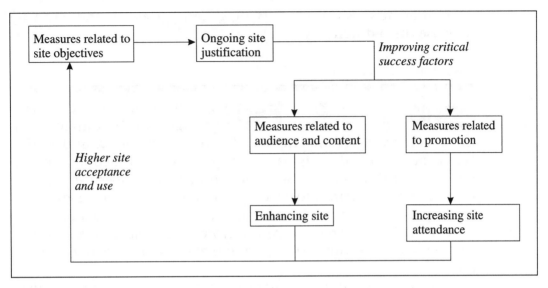

Figure 4.1 Interrelationship of site measures and goals.

justification. Measurements identified in the other three phases are used more to understand site activity and audience, and to provide data on which to base site enhancements. Subsequently, changes based on these measurements should improve the measurements used for site justification, as shown in Figure 4.1.

Other non-quantitative measures, such as e-mails, survey forms, and responses to coupons or free giveaways, can provide direct visitor feedback about the site. However, to be effective, you must capture the critical information contained in these responses as well as understand what percent of the total visitors the respondents represent. The following sections describe proven and effective methods of measuring the site.

General Site Measures

These Raw Measures are gathered directly from the site, usually through access or error logs. These are generic measures that are appropriate to virtually all sites, even when the sites have very different justification strategies. The following three case studies show why different sites capture varying generic measures and also why they use them differently.

CASE STUDY

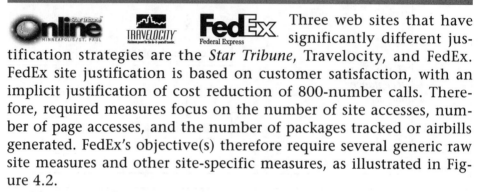 Three web sites that have significantly different justification strategies are the *Star Tribune*, Travelocity, and FedEx. FedEx site justification is based on customer satisfaction, with an implicit justification of cost reduction of 800-number calls. Therefore, required measures focus on the number of site accesses, number of page accesses, and the number of packages tracked or airbills generated. FedEx's objective(s) therefore require several generic raw site measures and other site-specific measures, as illustrated in Figure 4.2.

The *Star Tribune* has a somewhat unique justification strategy, which is based on an R&D model as shown in Figure 4.3. The paper wants to learn from the site so that it can be prepared to jump in, if online Internet services take off. Therefore, its measures are less exact and cover a much broader spectrum. To justify the site, the *Star Tribune* must:

❑ Measure site growth rates
❑ Identify niche markets that can be satisfied through the site
❑ Learn about online classified ads handling
❑ Measure impact on advertisers and advertising dollars

The first objective can be met by collecting generic site measures of site and page hits, but the other objectives require that the *Star*

Generic measures:
    Site accesses

Site-specific measures:
    Number of packages tracked
    Number of package airbills generated
    Number of downloads

Figure 4.2 FedEx site justification measures.

Generic measures
    Page hits

Site-specific measures:
    Click throughs (advertising sales)
    E-mails
    Classified ad sales

Figure 4.3 *Star Tribune* uses the web site as an information communications R&D lab.

Tribune collect and analyze content, audience, and promotion-related measures, as discussed in a later section.

Travelocity can also use general site measures to monitor and show growth trends for number of visitors, but it, too, needs site-specific measures, such as number of bookings and audience demographics, to really understand its business and consumer base.

Generic site measures are used to determine:

❑ **Site and page hits:** General site activity and growth; time of day, day of week; and month/season of year use statistics
❑ **Errors and alerts:** Site reliability
❑ **Date/time stamps:** Site activity and responsiveness by hour, day, and week
❑ **Other accesses:** Number of search engines (spiders) attempting to index the site
❑ **Page hit sequence:** Navigation through the site

One generic measure that is vital to the success of the site is navigation, or specifically easy-to-use, effective navigation, as discussed in the next section.

Site Navigation Measures

Site navigation defines the method by which users move around the web site. In developing the site there are often questions that need to be answered, such as:

In what order should the information be displayed to the visitor and what selections should each page provide?

Should the site be hierarchical or flat?

Can you use HTML 3.0 features like frames which can flatten a site but which not all browsers support?

Some common measures that will help you understand site navigation and determine if the previous decisions were the right ones include:

- ❑ Average number of pages retrieved per visitor
- ❑ Most common pages retrieved by visitors
- ❑ Most common path through the site
- ❑ Number of visitors who just view the splash screen
- ❑ Number of spiders attempting to index the site
- ❑ Average duration of visitor session

These measures are extracted from logs by scanning the logs and combining data from multiple entries for a single visitor. Many browsers now include the last prior location that the user visited before coming to your site and the last page accessed prior to the current page. Analyzing this information can help you understand how visitors transverse you site and how long they spend on each page. Since the activity (and path) of a single visitor will be spread across many entries in the log, you have to scan or order the log by visitor identifier to extract the required information. This is too large a chore to be done manually. Either a program has to be developed or you have to use an outside service for this analysis. Consider Toro's experience with site navigation.

CASE STUDY

TORO. Toro did not initially establish any measures directed toward analyzing how visitors navigate through the site or access information. Like most web site implementors, the company made assumptions on how the data should be presented and how the visitor would interact with the site. Unfortunately, you cannot control and cannot even accurately predict how the audience will interact with the site and what will be most comfortable and efficient for them. Toro found out that requiring a visitor to navigate through several selections and pages before getting to specific product information was in effect "hiding" the information. Feedback they received through e-mails and other informal comments, brought this to their attention. Based on these measures, the company plans on changing the site to provide more information upfront and more lists of items to select from, which should reduce key strokes and improve site responsiveness.

Figures 4.4 through 4.6 illustrate how log entries can be extracted for a single visitor and related to the visitor's path through the site. Generally, you will be more interested in the *average* path through the site for most visitors, which can be developed by analyzing many individual paths or by analyzing the ratio of page hits for specific site features. For an individual user, this analysis is usually reserved for debugging.

Developing navigation through a site is very similar to developing the pathways through a city park. Some park planners believe in laying out the walkways, then putting in barriers or other incentives, as necessary, to keep people from straying off the paths. Others believe in putting in the grass, scrubs, and trees, then adding pathways to facilitate where people naturally walk. Neither approach really works on a web site. You can't force people to adhere to your paths if these do not seem natural and efficient to them, and you can't have a site without some structure. Therefore, as experienced by both Toro and the *Star Tribune*, you need to:

Take your best shot at designing a responsive, quick path to the core information on the site.

Measure how people are using the site.

Be prepared to modify the site, as required, to better facilitate visitor navigation.

```
pm1-16.inetnow.net - - "GET /images/Weeds.GIF HTTP/1.0" 200 1073
pm1-16.inetnow.net - - "GET icons/WedsT.GIF HTTP/1.0" 200 1182
schaller.cnsnet.com - - "Post /faqsearch.cgi HTTP/1.0: 200 22795
atl-ga6-19.ix.netcom.com - - "GET / HTTP/1.0" 200 2978
atl-ga6-19.ix.netcom.com - - "GET /images/Grass.GIF HTTP/1.0:" 200 210
schaller.cnsnet.com - - "GET /images/Leaf.GIF HTTP/1.0" 200 1598
pm1-16.inetnow.net - - "GET /images/Leaf.GIF HTTP/1.0" 200 1598
atl-ga6-19.ix.netcom.com - - "GET /icons/grassT.GIF HTTP/1.0" 200 1123
pm1-16.inetnow.net - - "GET /icons/LeafT.GIF HTTP/1.0" 200 1145
pm1-16.inetnow.net - - "GET /images/Pests.GIF HTTP/1.0" 200 2204
pm1-16.inetnow.net - - "GET /icons/PestsT.GIF HTTP/1.0" 200 1105
pm1-16.inetnow.net - - "GET /icons/TTU.GIF HTTP/1.0" 200 367
pm1-16.inetnow.net - - "GET /icons/TTU.GIF HTTP/1.0" 200 367
atl-ga6-19.ix.netcom.com - - "GET /images/earl top.gif THTTP/1.0" 200 8551
atl-ga6-19.ix.netcom.com - - "GET /images/earl left.gif HTTP/1.0" 200 700
atl-ga6-19.ix.netcom.com - - "GET /images/earlanim4f101.gif HTTP/1.0" 200 930
atl-ga6-19.ix.netcom.com - - "GET /images/earlright.gif HTTP/1.0" 200 1327
atl-ga6-19.ix.netcom.com - - "GET /images/earlnoyyom.hig HTTP/1.0" 200 3427
atl-ga6-19.ix.netcom.com - - "GET /images/Weeds.GIF HTTP/1.0" 200 1073
atl-ga6-19.ix.netcom.com - - "GET /icons/WeedsT.GIF HTTP/1.0" 200 1182
pm1-16.inetnow.net - - "GET icons/TTUE.GIF HTTP/1.0" 200 1544
pm1-16.inetnow.net - - "GET /images/None.GIF HTTP/1.0" 200 820
pm1-16.inetnow.net - - "GET /grasses.html HTTP/1.0" 200 782
atl-ga6-19.ix.netcom.com - - "GET /images/Leaf.GIF HTTP/1.0" 200 1598
schaller.cnsnet.com - - "GET /grasses/faq.thinning.html HTTP/1.0" 200 1743
pm1-16.inetnow.net - - "GET /grasses/faq.dying html HTTP/1.0" 200 6182
schaller.cnsnet.com - - "GET /grasses/faq.mowing.html HTTP/1.0" 200 15473
atl-ga6-19.ix.netcom.com - - "GET /icons/LeafT.GIF HTTP/1.0" 200 1145
atl-ga6-19.ix.netcom.com - - "GET /images/Pests.GIF HTTP/1.0" 200 2204
atl-ga6-19.ix.netcom.com - - "GET /icons/PestsT.GIF HTTP/1.0" 200 1105
```

Figure 4.4 Log entries.

```
wod-ga6-19.ix.netcom.com - - "GET / HTTP/1.0" 200 2978
wod-ga6-19.ix.netcom.com - - "GET /images/Grass.GIF HTTP/1.0:" 200 210
wod-ga6-19.ix.netcom.com - - "GET /icons/grassT.GIF HTTP/1.0" 200 1123
wod-ga6-19.ix.netcom.com - - "GET /images/earl top.gif THTTP/1.0" 200 8551
wod-ga6-19.ix.netcom.com - - "GET /images/earl left.gif HTTP/1.0" 200 700
wod-ga6-19.ix.netcom.com - - "GET /images/earlanim4f101.gif HTTP/1.0" 200 930
wod-ga6-19.ix.netcom.com - - "GET /images/earlright.gif HTTP/1.0" 200 1327
wod-ga6-19.ix.netcom.com - - "GET /images/earlnoyyom.hig HTTP/1.0" 200 3427
wod-ga6-19.ix.netcom.com - - "GET /images/Weeds.GIF HTTP/1.0" 200 1073
wod-ga6-19.ix.netcom.com - - "GET /icons/WeedsT.GIF HTTP/1.0" 200 1182
wod-ga6-19.ix.netcom.com - - "GET /images/Leaf.GIF HTTP/1.0" 200 1598
wod-ga6-19.ix.netcom.com - - "GET /icons/LeafT.GIF HTTP/1.0" 200 1145
wod-ga6-19.ix.netcom.com - - "GET /images/Pests.GIF HTTP/1.0" 200 2204
wod-ga6-19.ix.netcom.com - - "GET /icons/PestsT.GIF HTTP/1.0" 200 1105
```

Figure 4.5 Single visitor extracted records.

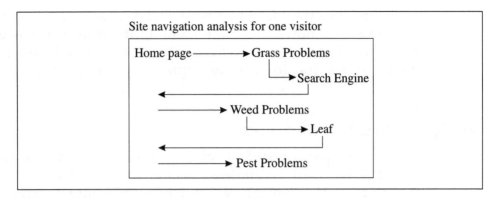

Figure 4.6 Visitor's navigation through the site.

Using Generic Site Measures

Part II discusses the Raw and Consolidated Measures typically collected for the justification strategies discussed in Chapter 2. For cost reduction and revenue enhancement strategies you can probably use portions of or all of the measures and calculations presented. For other strategies you can use the flowcharts as your guideline for defining your own set of measures as they pertain to your organization.

Once the measures are identified, the next step is to supplement the plan with requirements and time to implement the processes needed to collect and consolidate the data. For the site-based measures there are two basic steps:

❑ Ensure that the log files collect the needed Raw Measures.

❑ Develop the tools or use a service to extract the log data and create consolidated results. Part II discusses a few of the more common tools and services available.

For non-site measures, create procedures to collect the required data on a systematic basis. Usually, this will be on a monthly or quarterly basis. While many companies start by tracking site measures daily, they soon discover that there is little variance once a pattern is established. Most organizations will end up tracking measures at most weekly and often only monthly.

A simple method for identifying measures and sources is to flow-chart the collection and consolidation of the data. The concept of a hierarchy of measures flowchart was introduced in Chapter 3; Part II presents specific, in-depth examples for you to review.

Site-Specific Feature Measures

As discussed previously, web site logs do not collect Raw Measures that directly relate to audience comments, preferences, or acceptance of the site. Therefore, audience and content measures are some of the most difficult measures to implement.

Audience information measures, as illustrated in Figure 4.7, are generally captured:

Formally through surveys

Informally through e-mails

Motivationally through site incentives

Indirectly through estimates and assumptions

Therefore, planning for and capturing these measures requires both site and non-site activities. These tasks should be incorporated into the site plan to ensure that they are completed and incorporated into ongoing site analysis and evolution. The *Star Tribune's* measuring procedures provide an example.

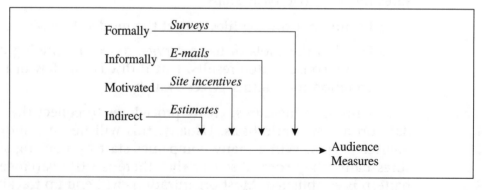

Figure 4.7 Audience measure sources.

CASE STUDY

To measure their progress toward stated goals requires both site- and non-site-generated measures. With the *Star Tribune*'s early online endeavors using the Interchange Network, users had to be registered subscribers. This allowed more specific audience measurement than is possible via the Web.

With the Internet, the *Star Tribune* is finding audience measurement more difficult. The paper is measuring:

- ❏ Site hits to establish activity trendlines.
- ❏ Page hits to measure access to specific stories or pages on the site.
- ❏ Advertiser interest, as a non-site measure, through traditional channels.

From the first two measures the paper estimates the number of pages seen per user. It also used surveys to determine initial market need and is using reader surveys to determine site acceptance and use.

As with the *Star Tribune*, surveys are often used both pre- and post-site implementation to assist planning and to measure results. There is nothing unique about conducting a web site survey. They can basically be handled like traditional marketing or customer service surveys.

E-mail input is not unlike traditional customer letters, except for the fact that you are likely to also get words of praise as well as complaints. This informal measure of audience acceptance of the site can be useful in judging how people use the site and which features they like best about the site. The major drawback with e-mail is that you cannot proactively collect the measures; you must wait for visitors to send them to you. Therefore, this should not be considered as a primary source of measures, but only as an opportunistic measure. Other approaches, described later in this chapter, including survey forms and free giveaways, are a more proactive method of soliciting audience input.

Many times audience measures must be estimated. Often, audience characteristics or segmentation can be assumed based on more exact measures, such as page hits or visitor domains. For instance, the *Star Tribune* receives a significant number of page hits on its sports pages. Since historically, sports pages are read by males much more than females, the paper assumes that these page hits indicate a predominance of male visitors to their site.

The key is to identify what information is important to you in understanding how the site is used, then determine what is the most effective measure for collecting the raw data needed to provide that information. While there are numerous examples throughout the book and in the case studies, most web sites, like most networks, will be unique and the requirements for individual measures will vary. Also, realize that once the site is up and running, initial decisions on measurements often must be tuned. Be persistent and continue to modify the collection process until you get the required audience information.

The following feature-specific techniques will help you deal with these issues and others about your site:

E-mail response pages
Survey forms
Quizzes
Free stuff incentive or giveaways
Coupons
Online order forms
Downloads
Multimedia elements and Java applets
Ad banners
Chat rooms
Bulletin boards

E-mail Response Page

An e-mail is a preaddressed electronic letter with a space or spaces for a message to be added by a visitor to the web site. Two examples of e-mail systems on web sites that you may want to look at are (http://www.toro.com/consumer)—then **click** on "Talk to Us"—and (http://www.mmm.com)—then **click** on "Comments" at the bottom of the screen.

There are two basic methods of letting visitors send you e-mail from your web site. The first is to insert a hyperlink that triggers the built-in e-mail program in the visitor's browser. Instead of the link pointing at a web page, such as (http://www.xyz.com/page2.html), it specifies the e-mail address where comments are to be sent (mailto:webmaster@xyz.com.). The resulting screen looks like the one in Figure 4.8.

This approach is the most common and it involves very little programming work, so it is cheap. However, the company is also creating much more work than necessary to reply to visitors' requests. Sites that use this technique are missing several important measurement opportunities.

Number of nonpostmarked e-mails: The number of people who request the page but don't send an e-mail is lost. Because the "mail to" instruction is handled by the browser, your web site only knows when people send an e-mail. You have no idea how many

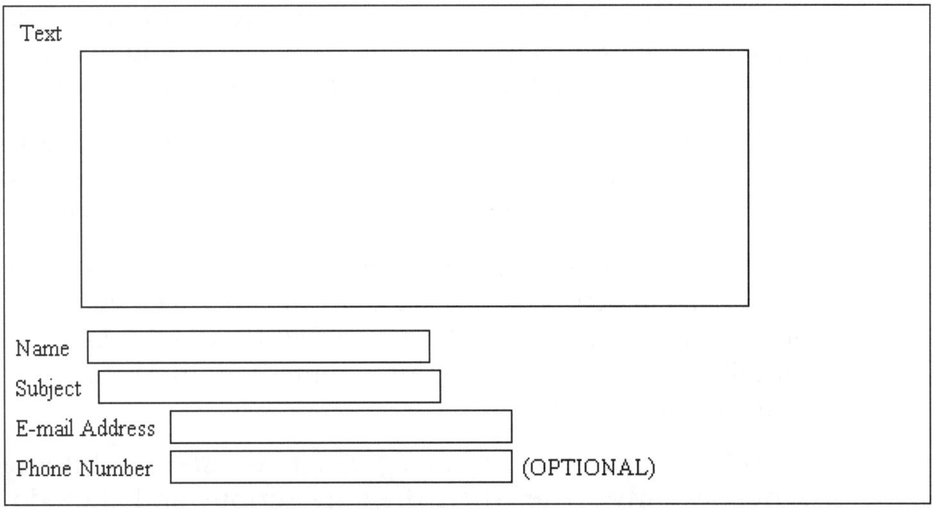

Figure 4.8 3M web site audience comment form.

people clicked on the hyperlink, but then never followed through. This *attrition factor* is important to know when making changes to site content.

Unfocused input: The standard browser e-mail window is a blank slate—the visitor can write whatever he or she wants. While there can be value in this, most web site operators we interviewed are interested in getting answers to specific questions. There is no way to do this with the mail to tag.

Expensive responses: Visitors expect to have questions answered quickly. Another downside to unfocused e-mail is that you never know what you're going to have to answer. This can become very expensive in terms of staff time, not to mention increasing your turnaround when you have to find the right person for an answer.

An alternative being used at an increasing number of sites is to create an actual web page to receive the e-mail information. The mail page is a form which requires additional Common Gateway Interface (CGI) or Application Program Interface (API) programming to implement. Because the e-mail response mechanism is now part of the site, you can measure attrition. Much more important, however, is that you can pose specific questions, thereby focusing the input and cutting your response costs.

Before you decide to use e-mail as a response mechanism, there are several questions that must be answered or you may find that the e-mail system doesn't provide input and can even become a liability.

Who is going to handle replies? You can generally start with one person. If the site contains specialized content (such as technical answers to specific questions), you may need a certain type of person.

How much of an employee's time should be allocated to answering e-mail? This depends on the scale of the site. Average sites by a large or very large company will draw a few hundred e-mails per month initially. Over time your e-mail volumes will increase by 5 to 20 percent per month.

What is your goal for turning around a response? Internet visitors generally only write when they are serious and they do expect a prompt answer. Twenty-four hours is good; 12 hours is great; more than 72 hours is unacceptable.

Will you use a real company employee or a fictional person? Some companies have a *marketing contact name* like John Smith to maintain a constant presence to the outside world through turnover or to avoid having to identify particular employees in national advertising where it might bring undesirable personal contacts. If this practice will be extended to the web site, you will need to set up an e-mail address for the fictitious person.

What are you going to do with the e-mail addresses? If your plans include future contacts with those who send you e-mail, be sure to establish a database upfront so you don't lose any names.

E-mail is a great source for measurement opportunities. Through e-mail you can typically measure:

- ☐ If using CGI or API program-generated e-mail forms, the number of requests for mail page.
- ☐ If using CGI or API program-generated e-mail forms, the percentage of visitors requesting e-mail page.
- ☐ How many times visitors access the e-mail page. This measure is useful for establishing a percentage of response, similar to the "how many cards were returned" analogy in a direct mail campaign.
- ☐ Number of e-mails received.
- ☐ Percentage of visitors sending e-mail. This is useful for measuring attrition; that is, 1,000 people came to the site, 100 looked at the e-mail page, and 10 actually sent e-mails. If your attrition is high, how can you modify the web site to improve it? See Part III for helpful approaches.
- ☐ Size of e-mail mailing list.
- ☐ Rate of growth of e-mail list.
- ☐ Cost-per-name. Cost-per-name is a common direct marketing benchmark—how much did it cost you on average to add one name to your mailing list? How does it compare on the Internet when you factor in site construction and ongoing costs to your traditional media cost?
- ☐ Percentage of frivolous e-mails. How many e-mails do you receive which are pranks, not serious questions, mistakes, and so on. These ought to be low. If they are high, what can you do to improve? Again, see Part III for ideas.

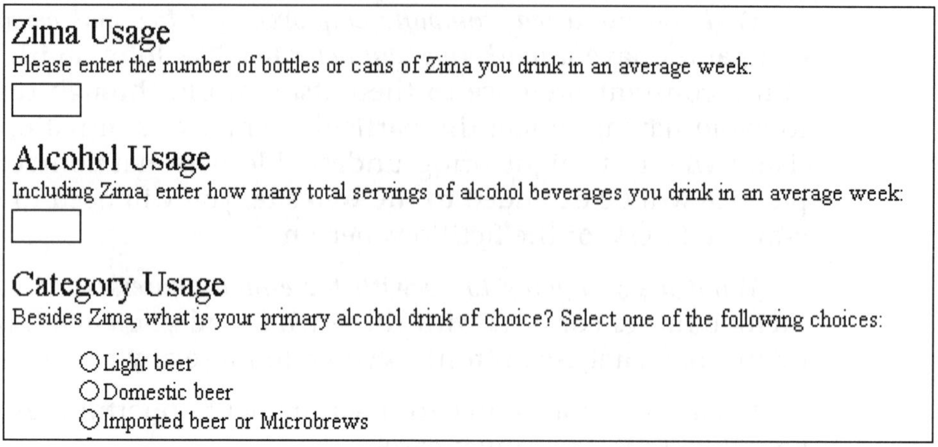

Zima Usage
Please enter the number of bottles or cans of Zima you drink in an average week:

[   ]

Alcohol Usage
Including Zima, enter how many total servings of alcohol beverages you drink in an average week:

[   ]

Category Usage
Besides Zima, what is your primary alcohol drink of choice? Select one of the following choices:

    ○ Light beer
    ○ Domestic beer
    ○ Imported beer or Microbrews

Figure 4.9 Zima web site survey form for joining Tribe Z.

Survey Form

Internet survey forms are interactive questionnaires for gathering background information from a web site visitor. Often incorporated into a *Free Stuff* page or some other giveaway designed to appeal to the visitors and motivate them to fill-in the form. Figure 4.9 shows a typical survey from Zima Corporation.

Before deciding to include survey forms on your web site consider the following:

❑ *Frequency of reporting.* How often will you need to take action on the information? If you are just creating reports, weekly or monthly is probably sufficient.

❑ *Format of reporting.* Will you need it exported to a spreadsheet, database, or word processor? Or, can your web hosting service or IS department provide online roll-ups?

❑ *Integration with other market research data.* How will you compare it to and/or combine it with market research from traditional sources? If the Internet demographics are at odds with your demographics from traditional sources, it probably has to be compared.

❑ *Demographics of audience versus business demographics.* Precisely how does the Internet differ and what implication does this have for the questions you want to ask?

By answering these questions before implementing the survey process, you will ensure that the form asks the right questions, and that the collected information will be valuable and integrate with other existing measures.

Survey forms provide several measurement opportunities, some of which overlap e-mail and several of which can provide additional data. These include:

- Number of requests for survey page.
- Percentage of visitors requesting survey page. As with e-mail forms, this measure is useful for measuring response rates and attrition.
- Number of surveys received. Comparing this to the number requested shows the attrition and also provides the overall percentage of visitors submitting a survey form. Again, the number of people submitting a form is generally less than those requesting the form. The trick is to design the site and/or payoff in such a way that minimizes the difference in requests versus submittals.
- Percentage of *trusted* submissions. This measures how many submitted forms have accurate information. You can probably clearly exclude some that are obviously garbage, but what provision will you make for those more difficult to differentiate.
- Demographic roll-ups of answers. This is the real goal: summarizing all answers to your questions in a way that gives you a better idea of how to market to or communicate with the online audience.

Quiz

An online quiz with some type of reward for visitors is becoming a more common draw all over the Web. This can be a fun way to make points about your product or service. You can use a quiz to test how much your audience really knows about you. Quizzes have other applications as well, such as screening tests for job applicants. Personal development consulting firms are racing to create Internet-based versions of popular personality tests such as the Myers-Briggs.

Typically, a quiz consists of a series of questions with multiple choice answers. Some quizzes allow you to retry a question if you get it wrong, while others make you keep going. The most basic tests revolve around a single web page with hyperlinks to each answer. The most sophisticated quizzes, such as on 3M's home page (http://www.mmm.com/quiz) using technology from *e*Works! keep track of each visitor's score and allow visitors to answer questions over a period of many visits.

If you think a quiz or test of some type is appropriate for your site, think through the following issues:

What is the reward for successful completion? What will be truly meaningful enough to bring more visitors and give them the incentive to play?

If a reward is involved, how will you handle fulfillment? (Review the shipping and international issues for Free Stuff previously discussed.)

Will you permit retries?

Do you want to individually score visitors?

Should all players receive the same questions in the same order?

Can the same player win more than once?

A quiz provides many valuable measurement opportunities:

- Number of players per month.
- Number of winners per month.
- Number of completed visitor records.
- Average number of players who correctly answer each individual question. This measure can tell you how successful you have been in educating players. Also, you may wish to make easy questions harder.
- Average number of players who incorrectly answer each individual question. This may tell you where you have been unsuccessful in educating players. Difficult questions may need to be made easier.
- Average number of questions answered by players. Not all players will finish the quiz. If you are using software such as

*e*Works! WebQuiz that allows you to track individual players, you will find that some players drop out. A high drop-out rate early on means you should rethink your questions.

Free Stuff Incentive

As the name implies, free stuff doesn't cost anything, but there is a price the visitor must pay in the form of information. Free stuff is accessed off a page at the site where the visitor can receive some type of useful "gift" in exchange for responding to a survey form or taking some other kind of action. A good example of a free stuff page is shown in Figure 4.10 a and b.

Even free stuff can't just be given away. To get value, and to cover yourself, you must plan ahead to determine the following:

What are you going to give away? What kind of inexpensive items can you give away as gifts that will be viewed by the online community positively enough to get its members to answer your questions? Do you have leftover giveaways from past promotions? Can you cheaply produce something? What about giving away a smaller number of more expensive items, such as in a scavenger hunt or other contest?

Figure 4.10a Toro page for free stuff giveaways.

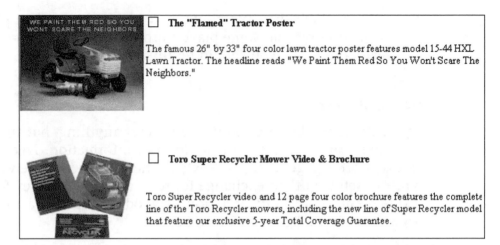

Figure 4.10b Toro page for free stuff giveaways.

Are there legal issues with the nature of your giveaway? If it's a contest, you may have to meet certain state or federal guidelines. If it's really valuable, you may create a tax implication.

Will you give away to people outside your country? Don't forget the postage and shipping cost for the free stuff. Going international will increase the overall cost of your promotion; remember that the Internet is worldwide.

What are the most successful items in terms of improving attrition rate? Unfortunately, no one really knows. What you can try is rotating through many kinds of items to determine which ones produce the best response numbers?

Fulfillment turnaround goal (12 hours, 24 hours, 1 week, etc.). How quickly you send out the free stuff affects two key visitor attributes. First, it affects how long you get visitor share-of-mind. Second, it affects your perceived responsiveness to visitor needs. An effective program must balance between these two issues to create the right perception. In fact, you can even split the giveaway into two mailings to extend the share-of-mind and improve response perception.

Fulfillment method. Will you handle fulfillment yourself, or hire an outside firm? How will information submitted by the visitor be communicated to whomever is handling the fulfillment? Typical options are e-mail, fax, or some kind of online transmission.

Measures provided by giving away gifts are basically the same as those collected by survey forms. In fact, often survey forms use free giveaways as incentives for the visitor to complete the form and provide accurate information.

Coupons

Coupons are promised discounts off a real-world purchase delivered via your web site instead of on paper. Alternatively, they can be for a rebate or for a "gift" to be redeemed at the time of purchase (i.e., buy this tractor and receive a certificate worth $50 off your Internet access this month). Coupons have not been used extensively on the Web. With coupons, in general, there are several issues that can make a coupon program financially unfavorable for a company, so usually coupons end up representing only a small potential dollar value or there are such stringent controls that the program becomes a hassle for the recipient. If you are considering a coupon program, think about the following issues before implementing it.

Can one person redeem multiple coupons?

How will you identify abusers?

How will you repay merchants who accept the coupons?

Is there a redemption limit at which you would discontinue the coupon?

How long are the coupons good for?

Coupons provide site measures similar to survey forms or free giveaways. When using coupons, it is also a good idea to measure coupon-related items, such as:

- ❑ Number of downloads
- ❑ Number of redemptions and response rate
- ❑ Most effective coupons online; least effective coupons in terms of redemptions

- ❑ Average time from download to redemption
- ❑ Where redemptions occur (mail order, in store, etc.)

Collecting content and audience measures through effective surveys or simple giveaways, we believe, is preferable to coupons because of the reasons previously noted.

Online Order Form

Think of an online order form as an automated clerk and cash register. The visitor specifies a product or service he or she wishes to purchase and provides the information necessary to complete payment.

Many of the issues associated with online order processing are similar to the issues associated with mail-order processing. Online systems offer some potential new advantages for both the payment method, such as Cybercash or First Virtual, and order fulfillment, such as automatic shipping through an electronic link to a shipper's site, such as FedEx. Generally, you must consider:

What methods of payment will you accept? This could include traditional credit cards and new online payment methods, such as Cybercash and First Virtual.

How will you confirm receipt of the order?

How will you confirm shipping of the order?

How will you obtain approval or decline of the payment method?

Who will handle fulfillment?

What is your fulfillment turnaround goal?

Measures of online transactions are also very similar to traditional measures for mail order:

What are the most popular types of items bought online?

What is the most popular price point by item category?

What is the most popular payment method?

What is your average transaction size?

How frequently do your transactions occur?

What is the overall revenue growth?

Figure 4.11 Intel web page for software download.

Downloads

Downloading allows a site visitor a place from which he or she can access software, screen savers, or other electronic data needed or desired for his or her system. Many software vendors provide the capability for visitors to download evaluation versions of software, software upgrades, software patches, documentation, and other related items, such as adapter drivers. Companies like FedEx allow visitors to download software tools and utilities for package airbill preparation and shipment scheduling. Downloads provide a convenient method for timely and low-cost distribution of software, updates, and other electronic data, as shown in Figure 4.11.

In planning a download capability for your site, you should consider:

What software, documentation, or other content will you offer for downloading?

What software, documentation, or other content will you not offer for downloading?

How will you explain what is available and not available to site visitors when they ask?

What hardware platforms will you support?

What operating systems will you support?

If application-specific, what application version will you support?

Are there mirror sites you can use to provide alternatives if your site is bogged down or the intervening links are congested. Are there better sites visitors can use if they are in another country?

If the software is offered on a trial basis, how will you limit access?

If the download contains content or code that could be argued to be someone else's property, do you have permission in writing to distribute it?

Download measures are oriented toward collecting data that can be used to improve the download process and focus your attention on the content most desired by the audience. These measures include:

❑ Number of downloads per hour, day, or week.

❑ Average download speed (measured as duration of download divided by size of downloads). This will help you understand what type of communication links your visitors are using. If download time is too long, you may want to take steps to compress the content to improve transfer rates or segment the content to allow the users to have a finer selection criteria.

❑ Most popular download.

❑ Most popular hardware platform and operating system.

❑ Most popular version to download.

Multimedia Elements and Java Applets

These items include animation, audio files, video files, or Java applets that provide special attraction at your web site. Multimedia elements and Java applets can add real sizzle to your site, but you have to carefully consider what formats to support and how large to make the associated files. These selections influence responsiveness and appeal of the content to the audience. Be sure to review the following points prior to making any decision:

❑ What format will you use for the element? For each data type, you will want to support the one or two most popular formats. For audio files, you probably want a Windows .WAV file and RealAudio, possibly followed by AIFF. For movies, it's the Apple Quicktime and Windows AVI format. For animation, use Shockwave or animated GIFs.

❑ Do you need to support multiple formats?

❑ What is the maximum size in bytes of a multimedia element or applet at the site? As with downloads, this significantly influences site responsiveness, particularly when the visitor is on a slow-speed link.

❑ Do you want to force a download whenever a visitor comes to the page or allow him or her to choose? The first provides ease-of-use, but may impact response. The second requires the user to make one additional request, but can save time, if he or she chooses not to initiate the download and moves on to another page.

❑ Do you want to place multimedia elements on their own server so as not to degrade requests for standard pages?

Ad Banners

Ad banners are paid advertisements you place at your site for which you are compensated by another party. The ad is typically *hot*, so that clicking on it brings the visitor to the site of the sponsor.

In preparing for an ad banner you need to consider many of the same issues you would when placing your own promotional banner on the site, plus other issues such as pricing and auditing:

How will you display the ad?

What pages will you display ads on?

Will you customize the ad that is displayed based on information you know about the visitor?

How will you provide independent third-party auditing of the traffic statistics your pricing is based on?

What will you charge for your ads? How long does that cover?

Will you give "make-goods," or additional ad time if your site is down or otherwise unreachable?

Measuring key aspects of advertising that impact the amount you can charge for the ad and the type of advertisers you are likely to attract is key to successful advertising on a site or in any other medium. These measures include:

- Number of click-throughs per ad to the advertiser's site. This measures how effective the ad is in generating visitor interest.
- Most popular types of ads (in terms of click-throughs) appearing at your site. This measures audience interest or possibly the quality of the ad.
- Number of click-throughs versus total number of ads displayed (the overall click-through rate).

Chat Rooms

Chat rooms provide a two-way or multi-way communication medium between visitors and you. One of the most notable chat room systems is America Online's technical support forum, where users interact with technical support personnel through a chat room. Usually, the technical support person handles 2 to 3 discussions simultaneously, but many users, up to 15 or more, can listen-in on the conversations. Often the user can get his or her problem resolved by listening to these other conversations. If you have access to AOL, you can reach the technical support chat rooms through the following procedure:

1. Select **Go to Keyword** from menu bar.
2. Enter keyword **Help**.
3. Select **Tech Support Live** from menu choices.

Chat room support issues are similar to e-mail considerations, but with three notable additions:

- Chat rooms require a person to be online during the total time the chat room is open. With an e-mail system, the responsible person can usually be doing other tasks and checking the mail periodically.
- The person supporting the chat room needs to be knowledgeable about all the topics that are likely to be encountered. Vis-

itors will expect a high degree of interaction in the chat room and immediate response to most questions.

❏ It is very important that you establish a protocol in the chat room to maintain control or you may find that too many people try to "speak" at once. In the AOL example, each new person entering the chat room is "greeted" by the technical support person and told that he or she will be serviced on a first come, first served basis and asked to please wait his or her turn.

Chat room measures should include:

❏ Number of visitors to the room.

❏ Average, minimum, and maximum duration of stay in the room.

❏ Subjective measure of parting comments on the value, quality, or other aspects of the chat room. Many visitors, as they leave, will have a parting message, such as:

"Thanks, you have been very helpful."

"I have to get off now, but I'll be back."

"This isn't getting me anywhere, I'm leaving."

Collecting the intent, if not the actual message, will help you understand how effective the chat room is to the audience.

Bulletin Boards

This is an electronic form of the bulletin board you are familiar with at your club, grocery store, or local bus stop. It's a place where site visitors can leave messages for others to see and respond to if they desire. In planning a bulletin board, you should consider:

How will you display bulletin board messages?

Will you provide visitors a means of searching for messages on the bulletin board by topic, key word content, and so on, or will messages just be listed chronologically?

How long will you keep a message on the bulletin board? This impacts disk storage requirements.

How often will you review new messages for suitability? What is your criteria for accepting or rejecting messages?

Bulletin board measures focus on understanding how the system is being used and planning for growth as required. This includes:

- How many messages are entered per day, week , or month.
- The average number of messages on the bulletin board per day, week, or month.
- The average duration of a message before it is removed. You can ask the person who places the message to remove it when it has expired, but most often you will end up removing it after a preset duration.

Tying Measures into Your Promotion Plan

The previous sections have outlined numerous methods of measuring site content appeal and collecting audience feedback from your site visitors. The remaining question you need to answer is where your audience is coming from. It is great that they got to your site, and hopefully found it valuable, but to attract more visitors you need to know what promotional efforts are "drawing the crowd."

There are two ways of gathering these measures. The first is to simply ask. Using the previous techniques, you can often ask the visitors how they heard about the site. This is typical of a question we often see on survey forms, rebate coupons, and warranty cards. Most visitors will fill in the question, if they use the form. But, as previously noted, visitors may start, but never complete the form due to attrition. All is not lost, because there are ways of collecting this critical information.

If the visitors are linking to your site from another site, or if they are accessing your site directly, you can measure which promotional activity brought them to your site, by using different site addresses (URLs) in different promotional campaigns. This allows you to measure the source of the audience by the URL they used to access the site and thereby determine which promotional campaign reached that audience.

For visitors who access your site based on seeing or hearing about it from a non-Internet source, such as a TV ad, product collateral, or newspaper ad, you can list a different URL in each media and track visitor rates based on the URL they use.

Likewise, for online ad click-throughs and referring links you can have each point to a different URL and also track where each visitor originates. Tracking visitor draw by promotional activity will help you determine where to spend additional time, money, and resources to reach more of your target audience.

Planning Completed, Let's Get to Work

Part I, Chapters 1 through 4, have laid the groundwork for defining, developing, and implementing a justification, measurement, and management strategy and tasks for your web site. Once the site goes into production, however, all this upfront work will only be valuable if you collect and analyze the site measures you have identified as critical to your success. Therefore, Part II explains techniques and tools for collecting and consolidating our site measures.

Part II

Measurements and Consolidation

5

Impact Measures

B ased on the discussions in Part I, case study input, and client experiences, we have compiled a long, but probably not all-inclusive, list of significant Impact, Approximated, Consolidated, and Raw Measures, as outlined in the Measurement Hierarchy presented in Chapter 3. You should use these as a baseline for your measurement planning and implementation, but we suspect that you will want to tailor some of them to your unique environment.

Part II is composed of three chapters. Chapter 5 covers the top 11 or so Impact and Approximated Measures. Chapter 6 covers over 20 Consolidated Measures and Chapter 7 defines about 50 Raw Measures and lists common sources for each. Since Part II is a "How to capture and calculate the measures" section, you will not find the extensive reference to case studies included in Part I. We will pick up the case study plots again in Part III as we discuss what the organizations learned from these measurements and how they are modifying their sites based on the measures.

For the formulas and calculations presented throughout Part II, it is very important to understand when a measure is used and what type of measure it is. Therefore, each time a measure appears, it is followed by a letter in parenthesis which denotes its level in the hierarchy:

❑ Impact Measures are shown with an (I).

❑ Approximated Measures are shown with an (A).

❑ Consolidated Measures are shown with a (C).

❑ Raw Measures are shown with an (R).

You should also note that we use a standard one-year timeframe for most calculations, except for items like collateral printing which are often a one time charge associated with a product launch, or budgeted once or twice per year. Just be aware that as you review then apply these formulas, you must maintain a consistent timeframe based on the duration of the effort or accepted practices within your organization. Also, the calculations do not include issues relating to current value, tax increases, and other standard financial accounting practices that are applied differently through various organizations. Again, use your organization's standard practices for these items. You can probably get required instructions from your finance department.

The remainder of this chapter discusses how to calculate the Impact Measures typically used in site justifications, as outlined in Chapter 2.

Cost Reduction

As discussed in Chapter 2, cost reduction can be justified through cost elimination or cost offset. As a refresher, cost elimination strategies enable the organization to rapidly and completely stop major categories of expenses in exchange for a small investment that is a fraction of the overall cost savings. In these cases, the web site investment has a break-even window of less than six months. Cost offset strategies result in long-term savings to the organization by making a major short-term change in how some aspect of the business is conducted. The investment will not break even for 12 to 24 months.

The following sections discuss the process and issues in calculating Impact Measures associated with cost reduction, including:

❑ Printing and postage cost avoidance or reduction

❑ Communication cost, including long distance, 800-number, and fax avoidance or reduction

❑ Headcount avoidance or reduction, which often includes training

❑ Facilities and capital expense avoidance or reduction

❑ Tax avoidance or reduction

Other potential savings can be realized through reductions in outside services, taxes, and other organization-specific expenses. If you think you can justify an expense reduction not discussed, you can use the outlined processes to calculate the savings for that expense.

Printing and Postage Avoidance (I)

Calculation: Average per piece cost (C) * Pieces avoided (A) - Web site cost (C)

Figure 5.1 illustrates the calculations for printing and postage expense avoidance, including a key assumption concerning the number of pieces avoided (A). There are two measures for approximating the pieces avoided (A).

Method 1

Estimate the number of brochures or other collateral that didn't have to be sent because visitors found what they were looking for at the web site. As with all approximations, you want some kind of reasonably concrete standard for arriving at your number, which can be gathered from generic site measures as shown in the following examples.

EXAMPLE 1 For a marketing web site, a good standard is: How many sessions (C) included at least six page views (R)? This tends to eliminate *surfers* and those who come but aren't interested. (Be sure to exclude spider visits (R) from automated indexing engines as these will inflate your count.) Alternatively, if there is a particular page that is important to telling your story (such as a page of customer testimonials), you could just count the page views (R) of that document.

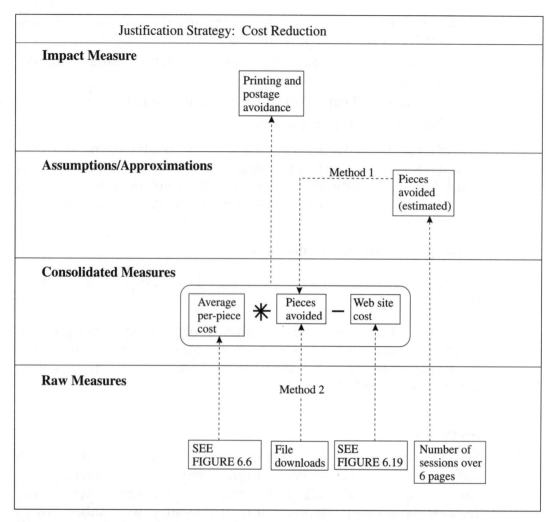

Figure 5.1 Calculating printing and postage expense (I) avoidance.

EXAMPLE 2 For a reference web site, you could measure how many sessions (C) looked at online product manuals, then make a provision for repeat visitors (A).

Method 2

Precisely measure the number of downloads (R) or hits (R) on specific files as illustrated in the following example.

EXAMPLE For instance, if you operate a stock brokerage, you send out many copies of your new account application. With the Web, you could convert it to Adobe PDF format and measure downloads (R). It is pretty safe to assume that each download (R) equals one piece avoided (A).

Communication Expense Avoidance (I)

Calculation: Average per call cost (C) * Calls avoided (A) - Web site cost (C)

All forms of electronic communication expenses can be calculated using the flowchart shown in Figure 5.2.

In the previous calculation, calls avoided (A) cannot be accurately measured; therefore, the calculation is usually arrived at through other measures that can be easily defended. To arrive at a number you can easily defend, you need the number of web site sessions (C) during your justification window (A) multiplied by an avoidance percentage (A). You have probably noticed that two of the three measures you need are also assumptions, but these can be derived by the following process.

The justification window (A) is the amount of time over which you are estimating your savings due to the web site (typically one, two, or three years using accepted financial standards for your organization). The most difficult number to estimate is the avoidance percentage (A), which is the number of visitors that didn't call because they got what they needed at the site. There are several ways of approximating this.

Method 1: Arbitrary Selection

You choose a percentage based on a gut feeling.

Method 2: Visitor Surveys

Federal Express has performed extensive surveys of its web site users to arrive at a very accurate avoidance percentage (A). It has used

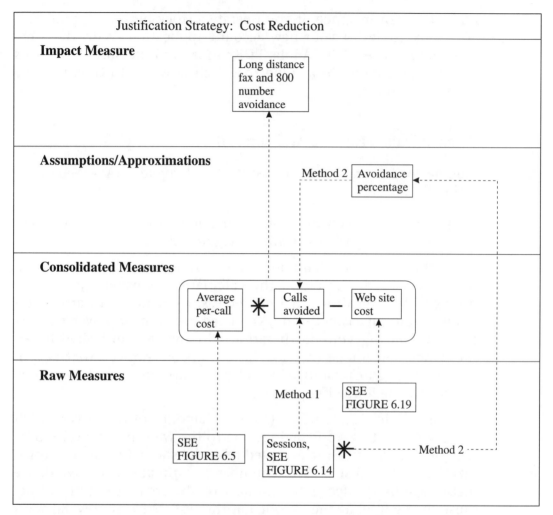

Figure 5.2 Communication expense (I) avoidance calculations.

both online surveys and telephone-based random sample surveys. While FedEx started with an arbitrary number, it now knows that the actual percentage is much higher than originally estimated.

Method 3: Measure Overall Difference

If your call volumes have grown at a predictable rate and all of a sudden grow more slowly when the web site debuts, you can reasonably take credit for the amount of decrease due to web site use.

Method 4: Measure Customer-by-customer Difference

If you keep records of calls, you should know which customers you interact with by telephone. If you can require customers to identify themselves at the web site, you can go back and measure a decrease in telephone traffic. With enough customers, you should be able to reach an overall avoidance percentage (A) that can be extrapolated to your entire customer base.

Headcount Expense Avoidance (I)

Calculation: Average annual salary (C) * Positions avoided (A) - Web site cost (C)

Reduction or avoidance of headcount expenses can be calculated using the flowchart shown in Figure 5.3.

This Impact Measure attempts to quantify productivity increase in your workforce as a result of a web site. Productivity increases result from reducing the time it takes an employee to complete a particular task, enabling the organization to produce more with a limited incremental investment. Savings can also result from eliminating tasks altogether, freeing that person up to take on new duties. There are many ways to arrive at a defensible estimate of positions avoided (A); the exact method will depend greatly on your site and your organization. Following are two widely accepted methods.

Method 1: Measuring Decrease in Workload

To use the FedEx call center example, if you know that the average call takes 5 minutes and you will reduce call volumes by 80 calls per day, then you have effectively avoided one position ($5 * 12 * 80 = 8$ hours per day). Don't forget to include your ratio of managers to subordinates as you may be able to save on managers if you decrease enough direct reporting positions.

Method 2: Measuring Position Avoidance or Reduction

If you can convert an entire area of your operation to the Web and there is no residual work, you can count the cost of all positions in

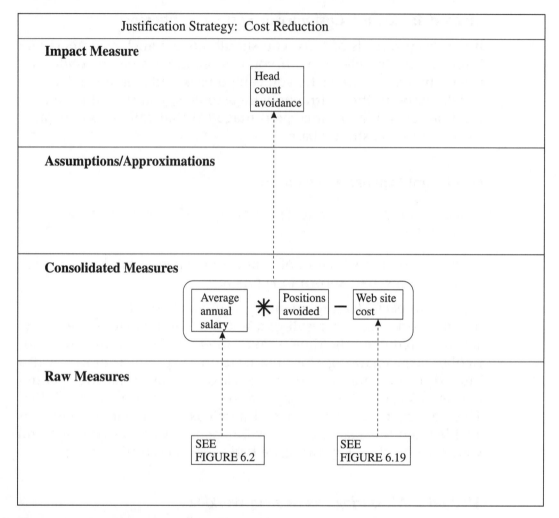

Figure 5.3 Headcount expense (I) avoidance.

that area. For instance, if you operate a brokerage and you switch to all web-based orders, you can now automate the placement of trades at exchanges. This may result in eliminating positions in your trading department.

Facilities and Capital Expense Avoidance (I)

Calculation: Investment avoided (A) + Cost of capital (R) - Web site cost (C)

Reduction or avoidance of facilities and capital equipment expenses can be calculated using the flowchart shown in Figure 5.4.

Organizations that can shift a majority of their functions online stand to reap tremendous savings in facilities and capital expenditures (I). Even moderate headcount savings can result in significant facility savings by avoiding office space, furniture, computers, and telephones. The following four methods indicate ways to approximate the amount of facilities and capital investment avoided (A).

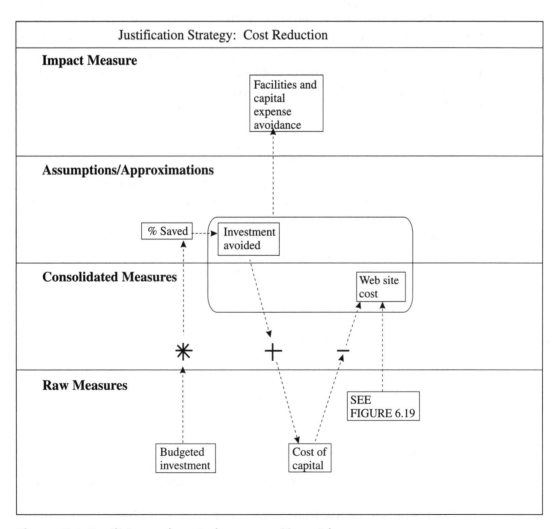

Figure 5.4 Facilities and capital expense (I) avoidance.

Method 1: Measure Headcount Decrease

If you allocate a specific sum for facilities to each staff position to cover telephone, computer, and other expenses, then you can count a facilities credit for each position you save. (Make sure not to count twice if you've already built this allocation into your salary cost!)

Method 2: Specific Improvement or Purchase Avoidance

Let's say your organization buys a new copier for every 100,000 copies per year. Let's further assume that by creating an intranet with electronic versions of commonly used documents (telephone list at 5,000 copies per month, organization chart at 1,000 copies per month, etc.) you have avoided purchasing some number of copiers. These savings represent specific cost avoidance measures based on the intranet.

Method 3: Warehouse Reduction

If you operate a hardgoods company and are able to shift 10 percent of your orders online in the first year, you probably can reduce your warehouse space needs. Since the orders must be fulfilled anyway, you may be able to negotiate fulfillment directly from the manufacturer. By computerizing your inventory system, you may also be able to reduce the amount of time inventory sits on the shelf through more accurate management.

Method 4: Branch Elimination

As banks convert from teller-based transactions to ATM and online transactions, the need for extensive branch networks decreases. In this case, you can sell entire facilities.

Tax Avoidance or Reduction (I)

Calculation: Company-by-company tax change (C) - Web site cost (C)

Tax reduction or avoidance can be represented by:

❑ Lower income taxes

❑ Reduced employer taxes, such as for Social Security, disability, and unemployment

❑ Reduced sales or value-added tax, including collection and tracking costs

❑ Off-shore import taxes on manufactured goods

These are just some of the taxes, because, as you know, the list of taxes goes on and on.

Because the area of taxes is so complex we have not tried to explicitly address it in this book. But you should be aware that this is an area to evaluate as you analyze web impact on your business, products, distribution, and bottom line.

Revenue Growth

Revenue growth was the third major site justification strategy discussed in Chapter 2. It includes increased sales, investment, or contributions to your organization as a direct result of your web site. Revenue can either come from moving an existing product or service in a new distribution channel (the Internet) or from creating entirely new products and services that exist only on the Web.

Increased Sales of Existing Products or Services (I)

Gross Income Calculation: Product price (C) * Number of web sales (A)

Net Income Calculation: Product price (C) * Number of web sales (A) - Product cost (C) - Web site cost (C)

At this stage of the Internet's evolution, accurate sales forecasts are as much an oxymoron as "military intelligence". Your best bet is to break down all of the individual products or services you have to offer and develop specific targets for each one. Then use the flow-charts shown in Figures 5.5 and 5.6 to calculate gross sales (I) and net revenue (I), respectively.

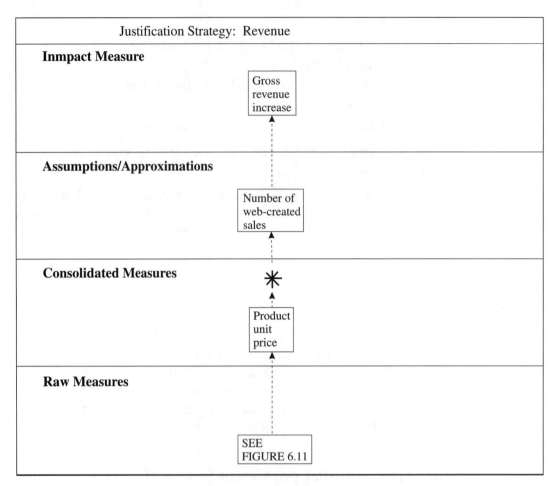

Figure 5.5 Calculating gross sales revenue from web site sales.

Early results from some of our case studies indicate that online promotion plays a critical role in resulting sales levels. If you are not actually selling online but are using the Internet as an extra promotional tool, then the problem is even more difficult because you have to track how many real-world sales are attributable to the web site (i.e., Toro). Even if you are selling online, customers may not buy the first time they come to the site. You may also wish to track preferences in payment method, depending on terms you receive from credit providers. Therefore, it is essential to develop a

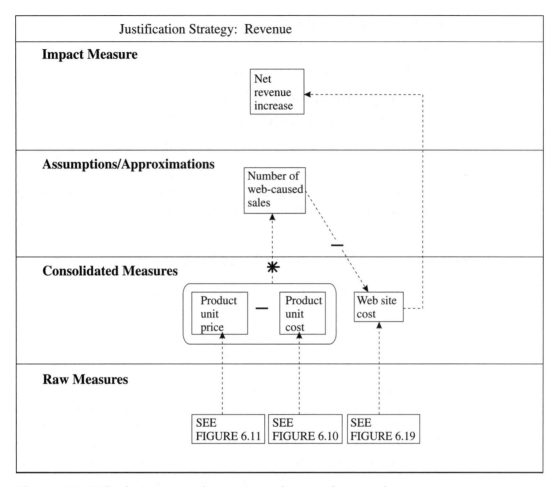

Figure 5.6 Calculating net sales revenue from web site sales.

similar set of metrics as in real-world sales to help pinpoint your forecasting ability:

Percentage of buying visitors (C)

Average visits preceding sale (C)

Ratio of sales volume to site depth (C)

Top payment methods (C)

Top shipping methods (C)

Typical purchaser profile (C)

Return and exchange rate (C)

Ratio of online to real-world volume (C)

Top visit-generating promotions (C)

Average annual per-customer spending (C)

Average annual per-customer purchases (C)

These measures are Consolidated Measures, many of which can be calculated based on hard web site data. Approaches for calculating or approximating these measures are discussed in Chapter 6.

Increased Sales of New Internet-based Products or Services (I)

Gross Income Calculation: Product price (C)* Number of web sales (A)

Net Income Calculation: Product price (C) * Number of web sales (A) - Product cost (C) - Web site cost (C)

The calculations for gross and net revenue are the same as for existing products delivered across the Internet. Often, this product category includes Internet-delivered products and services which are sold in the real world as well as those sold over the Internet. Yahoo is an example of a product existing only on the Internet, but which depends totally on advertising that is sold by people using telephones. Travelocity is using these financial measures to determine the success of its site, just as every company does to determine the success of its product lines.

Improved Customer Satisfaction

This metric seeks to quantify the number of customers of a given organization that are more likely to remain loyal because of some Internet-related service it provides, including general communication and problem resolution. The first section discusses improved evaluations or survey results; the second section covers lower complaint levels.

Improved Surveys or Customer Evaluations

Calculation: Net satisfaction change (C) * Internet contribution (A)

Use Figure 5.7 to calculate customer satisfaction changes due to the web site.

Most customer evaluations or surveys use a numbered scale to assess satisfaction. Often times you'll hear, "we were rated 4.7 out of 5" or "8 out of 10." Sometimes, it will be expressed as a percentage

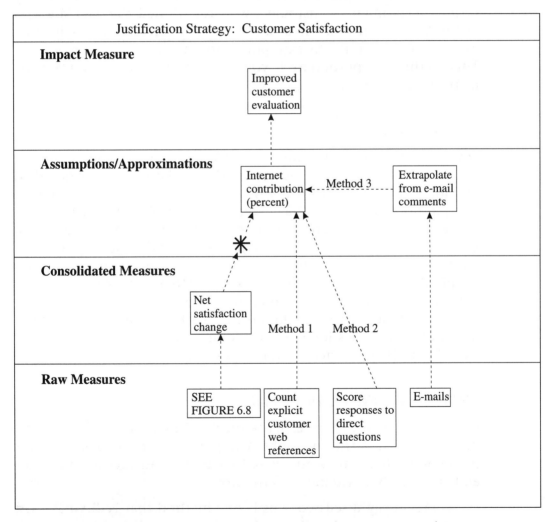

Figure 5.7 Calculating customer satisfaction based on survey results.

of customers choosing different rankings, such as, "73.8 percent rated us excellent with only 10.2 percent rating our service as poor." Regardless of the method you use, you must decide how much of future changes can be credited to the web site. This involves approximating the Internet contribution (A). Following are three possible methods for doing this.

Method 1: Score Explicit Comments

If your surveys include a free-form essay area, you could simply count the number of customers who mentioned the web site as a factor. Since such essay areas are used only rarely, you would then have to select a ratio to extrapolate to your entire customer base. This method is appropriate if you don't want to bias the result by mentioning the site.

Method 2: Direct Query

You can include one or more questions in the survey itself about the web site and its impact. Questions should be carefully drafted to provide defensible estimates of impact on satisfaction. For instance, the question, "How often have you used our web site?" with a number scale is very objective. You could also try, "Has our web site made it easier to do business with us (yes or no)?" These approaches do have the potential to bias your answers since you are reminding people that you have a web site. On the other hand, you could try something innocuous like "Have any of the following new service programs made it easier to do business with us?" and list a number of options. This question could be done as an essay instead, but that would most likely decrease your responses.

Method 3: Positive Internet E-mail

If you include an e-mail response mechanism at your web site, you may wish to track the levels of e-mail praise (R). These measures can be incorporated into your overall customer satisfaction measures and are directly attributable to the site.

As previously discussed, this is one method that FedEx has used extensively to measure the success of its site relative to overall customer satisfaction with the company. This is a good method of determining if the site is providing the same quality as other areas of the company.

Changes in Complaint Levels

Calculation: Net complaint change (C) * Internet contribution (A)

Figure 5.8 illustrates how to calculate customer satisfaction based on reduced complaint levels.

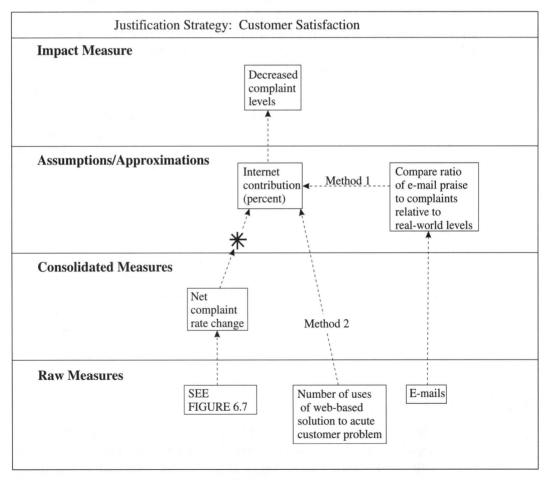

Figure 5.8 Calculating customer satisfaction based on complaint levels.

There are two distinctly different aspects to complaints when a web site is involved. Fortunately, both are easier to measure than customer satisfaction and to approximate the Internet contribution (A) in the reduction in complaint levels.

Method 1

The first aspect, which you will notice immediately, is that complaints will often increase (sometimes dramatically), but that your customer satisfaction will also climb. How is this possible? The web site gives unhappy customers a convenient way to vent frustration; they often feel that e-mails and surveys will be read by a real person instead of the public relations department. The bottom line is that the number of unhappy customers hasn't changed, but you've made it easier to hear from them. In this you have an accurate measurement—e-mail complaints (R).

You also have the opportunity to respond to and/or correct their problem if you act promptly. This results in increased satisfaction because you are perceived in a new positive light. Many of our case studies have experienced follow-up e-mails praising the organization for its responsiveness. You can also measure these e-mail resolutions (R) as another raw data point on customer satisfaction.

Method 2

The second approach involves reducing real-world complaints by solving specific problems via the web site. For instance, if you are a software company and your number one complaint is that a certain bug is causing system crashes, you can place a fixed version at your web site for download. You can then measure downloads (R) to quantify the improvement.

Quality Improvement

A web site that doesn't provide obvious financial benefits or product promotion may still make sense if it can noticeably improve the quality of the products or services you provide. For real-world products this is likely to take the form of an intranet that is used by your workforce to make a better product through decreased defects (I) or an Internet site that provides improved communications and product feedback from your customers. The customer input is then used in future product development to provide needed features, which doesn't precisely decrease defects, but does provide a strong customer perception of product improvement.

Calculation: Net defect change (C) * Internet contribution (A)

Figure 5.9 illustrates how to calculate product quality changes. Again, note the approximation for Internet contribution (A) as seen

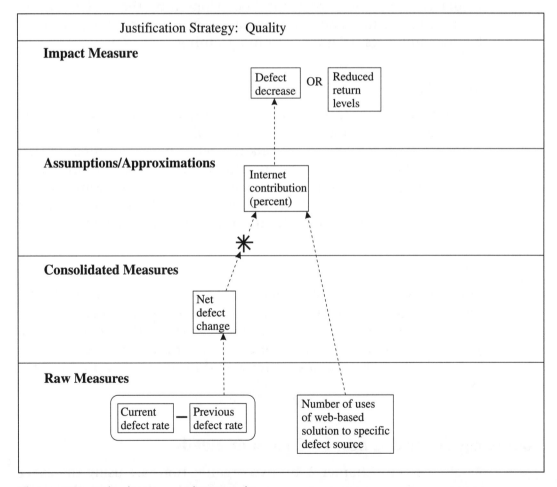

Figure 5.9 Calculating product quality.

in many of the prior figures and discussions. For quality increases this approximation can be done on a defect-by-defect basis or across the board as shown in the following methods.

Method 1

As with reduced complaint levels (I), an Internet or intranet web site can be the best tool to provide a solution to a common problem that results in known defects. For example, if you are an auto maker and incorrectly secured radiator hoses are a significant source of defects, you could place intranet kiosks on the shop floor, using multimedia to teach the correct method. Hopefully, that defect would reduce significantly and you may have saved significant dollars over taking employees off-line for formal training.

Method 2

Intranets can lead to overall defect reductions through enhanced communication. Using bulletin boards (also known as *threaded discussions*), your employees can talk to each other about many different subjects. You can create specific *quality forums* to talk about ways to improve products. To measure the Intranet contribution (A), you would have to pay attention to the actions that come out of such discussions, then tie them to specific defect reductions.

Method 3

Bulletin boards on a public Internet site or via the Internet's USENet area can provide incredibly valuable feedback on products and services. By encouraging your customers to share their experiences, you may learn of defects you were unaware of or enhancements being made by some customers that would improve your products for everyone.

Addressing Other Business or Customer Needs

As discussed in Chapter 2, no two organizations are using the exact same justification strategy or combination of strategies for their web sites. Beyond the more general justifications and measures presented in Chapter 2 and this chapter, many companies are finding business- and customer-specific reasons for implementing a web site. All sites, however, must be measured to determine both return on investment and ways to evolve the site to better meet audience needs. If you have strategies or needs other than those presented here, you can still develop effective measurement techniques by using the concepts and approaches presented in this chapter and in Chapters 6 and 7.

Case studies, like Toro, *Star Tribune*, the U.S. Senate, and Silicon Graphics, show how each organization develops a specific rationale and justification for its site and develops a corresponding set of measures to track the site's progress. Each organization can still use the hierarchy of measures by substituting appropriate measures at each level for its unique justification and measurement requirements.

CHAPTER 6

Consolidated Measures

A s discussed in Chapter 5, Impact Measures are calculated from Consolidated and Approximated Measures. Approximated Measures, as discussed in Chapter 5, are based on non-hard data and are often difficult to determine. Consolidated Measures, on the other hand, are based on a combination of site and non-site hard data which is usually easy to collect, if you have planned in advance, as discussed in Chapters 3 and 4.

Examples of Consolidated Measures

This chapter briefly discusses 22 Consolidated Measures which will be useful to you in measuring your site. For each measure, we present a short definition and a formula and/or flowchart. Many of the case studies interviewed used similar calculations in their site measurements. The Consolidated Measures discussed in this chapter are:

Average annual per-customer purchases (C)

Average annual per-customer spending (C)

Average annual salary (C)

Annual hosting cost (C)

Average per-call cost (C)

Average per-piece cost for collateral (C)

Average visits preceding sale (C)

Net complaint change (C)

Net satisfaction change (C)

Percentage of buying visitors (C)

"Person" (C)

Product cost (C)

Product price (C)

Ratio of online to real-world volume (C)

Ratio of sales volume to site depth (C)

Return and exchange rate (C)

Session and average length (C)

Top payment methods (C)

Top shipping methods (C)

Top visit-generating promotions (C)

Typical purchaser profile (C)

Web site cost (C)

Average Annual Per-Customer Purchases

This is the total number of individual products or services bought by an average customer in one year from your web site, as shown in Figure 6.1.

Calculation: Total web items sold (R) / Total web customers (R)

Average Annual Per-Customer Spending

Average annual per-customer spending (C) is the sum of all dollars spent on products and services at your web site in one year by the average customer.

Calculation: Total web item revenue (R) / Total web customers (R)

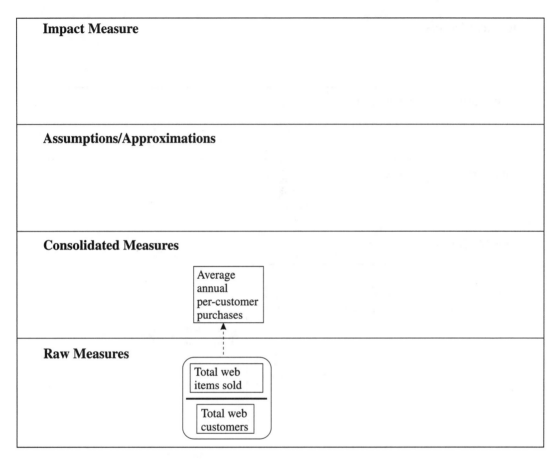

Figure 6.1 Calculation for average annual per-customer purchases (C).

Average Annual Salary

The *fully loaded* or *fully burdened* cost to an organization of a particular position for one year is the average annual salary (C), as shown in Figure 6.2.

Calculation: (Base salary midpoint (R) + Bonus potential (R) + Facilities allocation (R)) * Benefits percentage (R) * Employer tax percentage (R)

Annual Hosting Cost

Annual hosting cost (C) is how much it costs to connect and serve your web site for a period of one year, whether insourced or out-

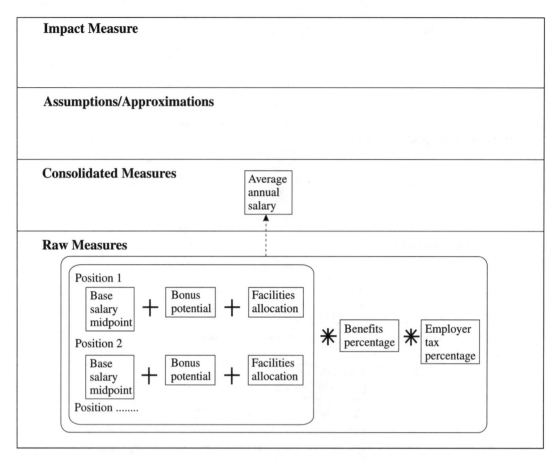

Figure 6.2 Calculation for average annual salary (C).

sourced. Depending on the method, the calculation for the Consolidated Measure is significantly different, as shown in the following methods.

Method 1: Calculating Insource Costs

((Server hardware cost (R)+ Server software cost (R)+ Network equipment cost (R)) / Depreciation period (months) (R))

+ Monthly Internet access fee (R)

+ Monthly local loop fee (R)) * 12

+ Systems administrator salary (R)

+ Annual maintenance agreements (R)

Method 2: Calculating Outsource Costs

(Monthly Hosting fee (R)+ Volume surcharges (R)) * 12

As you can see, insourcing has many more components to consider, plus more upfront capital costs for hardware. Calculations for these two methods are shown in Figures 6.3 and 6.4, respectively.

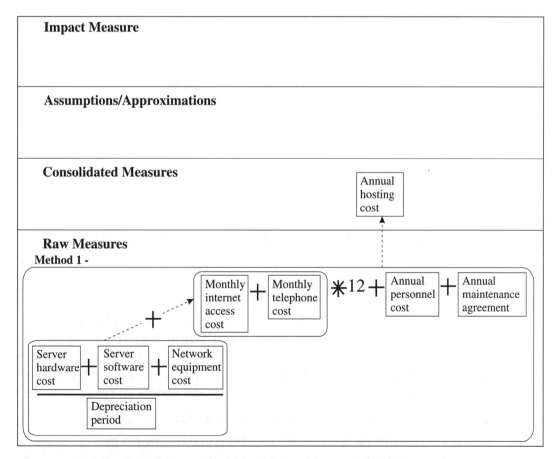

Figure 6.3 Calculation for Method 1, insource annual hosting cost (C).

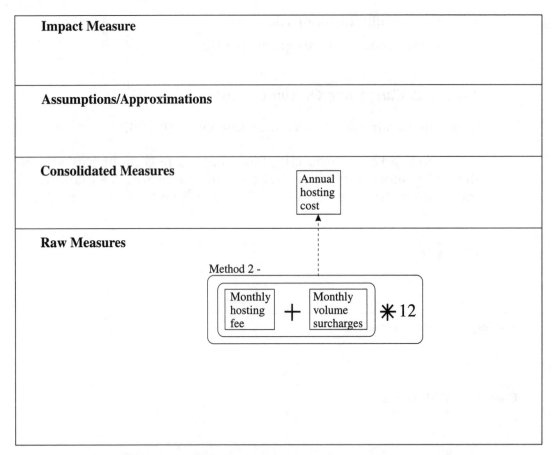

Figure 6.4 Calculation for Method 2, outsource annual hosting cost (C).

Average Per-Call Cost

The average per-call cost (R) will depend on how much a particular type of telephone call costs your organization and the percent volume of each type of call. Most telephone switches and services can provide you average call cost and volume, which is usually tracked by a telecommunications or IS department. Common call types include:

- ❑ Outbound local metered call (voice, data, or fax)
- ❑ Outbound long-distance call (voice, data, or fax)
- ❑ Inbound 800-number call (voice, data, or fax)

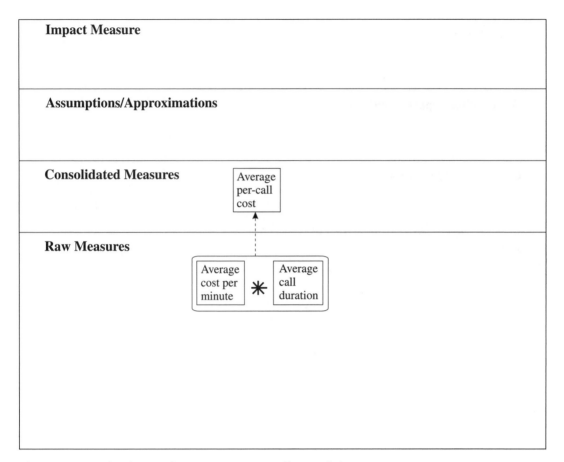

Figure 6.5 Calculation for average per-call cost (C).

The basic calculation for all calls, as shown in Figure 6.5, is:

Calculation: Average cost per minute (R)* Average call duration (R)

Average Per-Piece Cost for Collateral

Calculation: (Total creative cost (R)+ Total production cost (R)) / Run size (R) + Per-piece shipping cost (R)

This represents the actual cost to create, produce, and ship a specific collateral piece as shown in Figure 6.6.

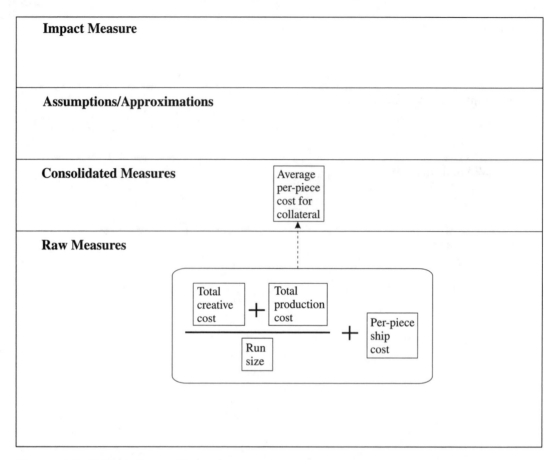

Figure 6.6 Calculating collateral costs.

Average Visits Preceding Sale

This measures the number of times a specific person visits a commerce web site prior to making the decision to purchase a specific item there.

Calculation: Sessions (C) per person (C) including a product page view (R) prior to purchase (R) of that product via the site.

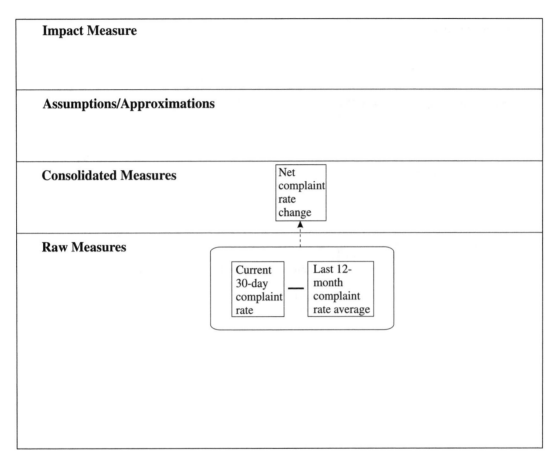

Figure 6.7 Net complaint change (C) calculation.

Net Complaint Change

This is the increase or decrease in the rate of complaints received by your organization per time period (usually one month). The following calculation and Figure 6.7 should be used for this Consolidated Measure.

Calculation: Mail complaints per month (R) + Telephone complaints per month (R) + e-mail complaints per month (R).

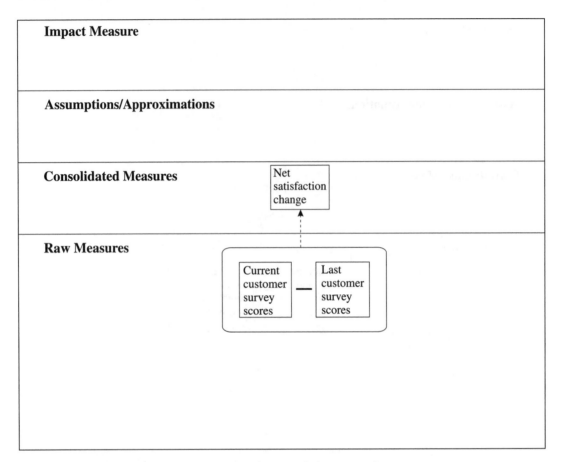

Figure 6.8 Calculating customer satisfaction (C) rating change.

Net Satisfaction Change

This is the increase or decrease in the satisfaction rating your customers express towards your organization as measured by a survey comparison, as shown in Figure 6.8.

Calculation: Current survey scores (R) - Last customer survey scores (R)

Percentage of Buying Visitors

Percentage of buying visitors (C) is the ratio of overall web site traffic to those visitors who actually make a purchase at the site, as shown in Figure 6.9.

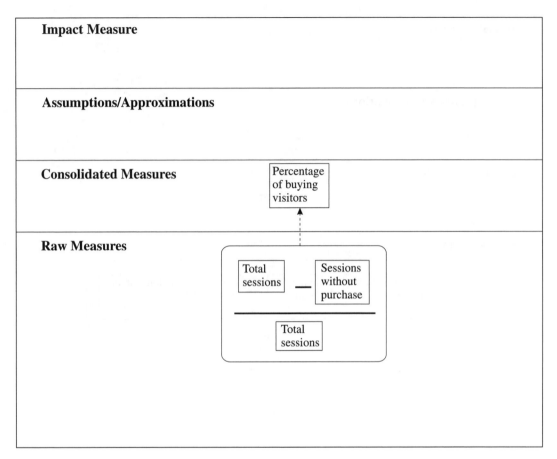

Figure 6.9 Calculating percentage of buying visitors (C).

Calculation: (Sessions (R) including at least one purchase (R)) / sessions (R)

"Person"

A single individual visiting your web site, regardless of the number of sessions is considered a *person* (C). Person measures are achieved through unique cookies (R) or unique user id (R) measurements.

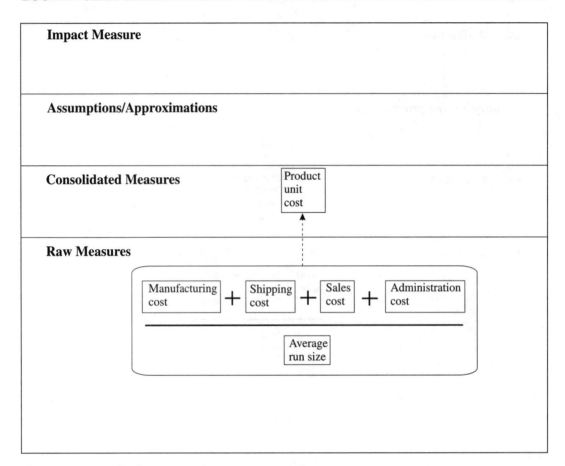

Figure 6.10 Calculating product unit cost (C).

Product Cost

Product cost (C) is the total cost to produce a product or provide a service amortized into a single unit. For Web-sold goods and services, this must also include any shipping or travel costs. This information should be available from a product manager or your accounting department and is generally company-confidential. This is typically calculated as product unit cost, as in Figure 6.10.

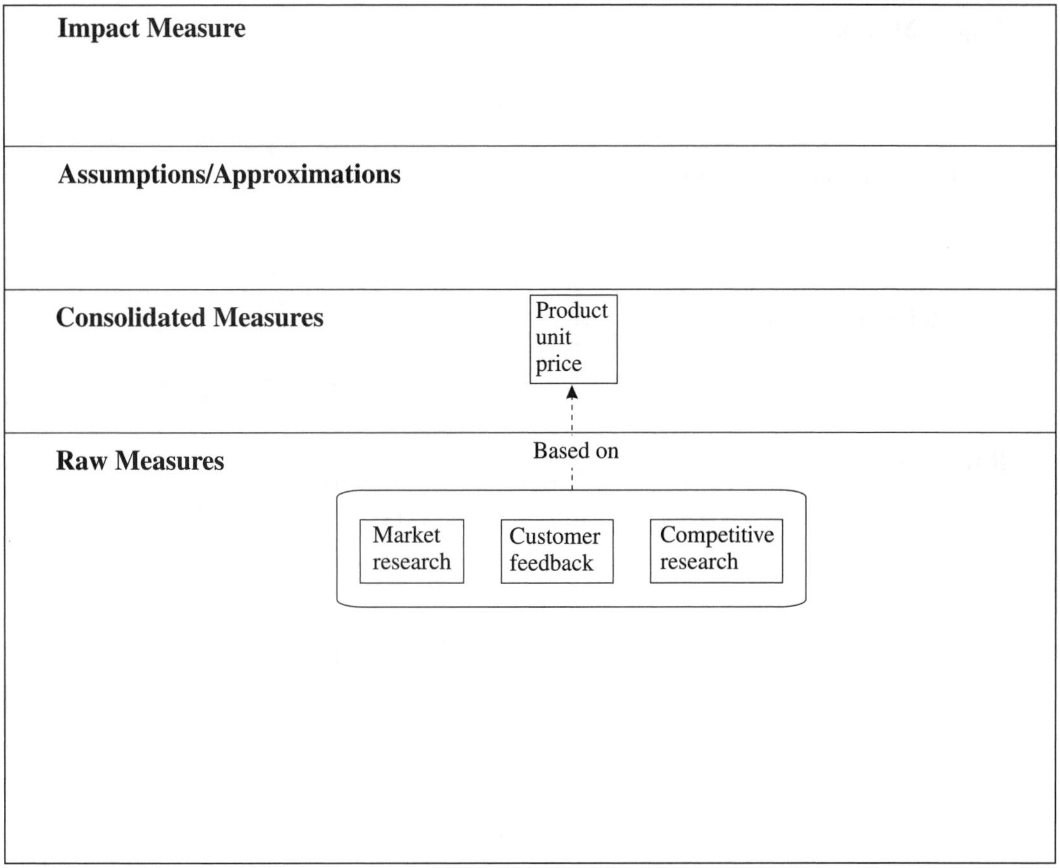

Impact Measure	
Assumptions/Approximations	
Consolidated Measures	Product unit price
Raw Measures	Based on Market research Customer feedback Competitive research

Figure 6.11 Calculating product unit price (C).

Product Price

This is the typical or average selling price of a product or service offered by your organization through a web site. Again, this information should be available from a product manager, product price lists, or your accounting department. This is typically calculated as product unit price, as in Figure 6.11.

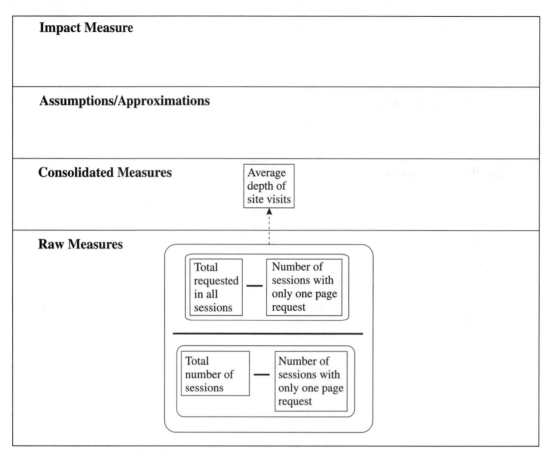

Figure 6.12 Calculating site depth.

Ratio of Online to Real-World Volume

The ratio of gross dollar sales at your web site for a given product to the gross dollar off-line sales provides volume comparisons.

Calculation: (Online product purchases (R) * Product price (C)) / Gross off-line revenue (C)

Ratio of Sales Volume to Site Depth

This represents the gross dollar volume of sales at your web site for a specific product as a function of how many clicks (R) a visitor

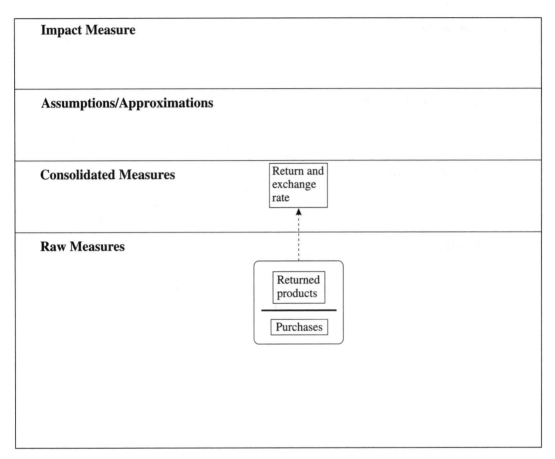

Figure 6.13 Calculating product return or exchange rate.

must make to first encounter it. You vary the depth of a product over time to have apples-to-apples comparisons. Figure 6.12 illustrates how to calculate site depth.

Calculation: Product purchases (R) per Day at X clicks (R)/ Product purchases (R) per day at 1 click (R)

Return and Exchange Rate

This is the percentage of purchases (R) which are subsequently returned for credit or refund or exchanged for another product, as calculated in Figure 6.13.

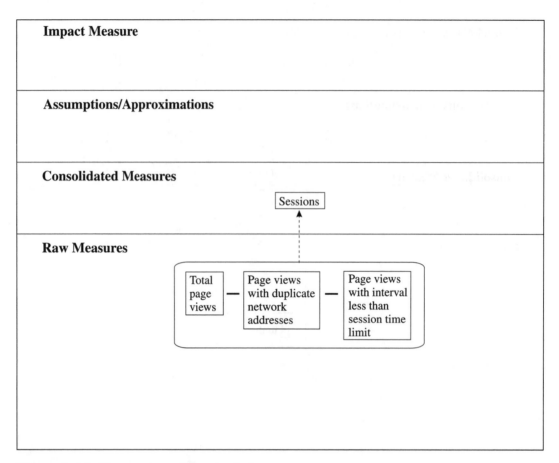

Figure 6.14 Site sessions (C) calculation.

Calculation: Returned products (R) / purchases (R)

Session and Average Length

Sessions are the total number of individual visits to a web site, regardless of the number of pages viewed. Session length is the sum of all page intervals during an individual session. These calculations are shown in Figures 6.14 and 6.15, as well as in the following statements.

Session calculation: All page views (R) from the same network address (R) occurring within a session time limit (R) of one another.

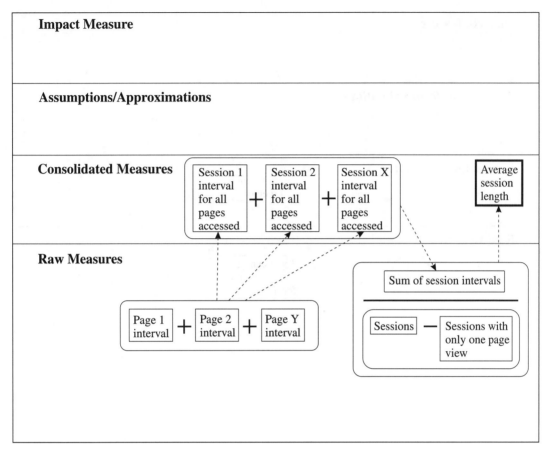

Figure 6.15 Session length (C) calculation.

Session length calculation: Sum of all page views (R) from all session / (Sessions (R) -sessions with only one page view).

Top Payment Methods

The preferred payment methods selected by purchasers as measured by their choice at the time of sale can be recorded by the online order form during the purchase (R).

You should track the top five payment methods (R), as shown in Figure 6.16.

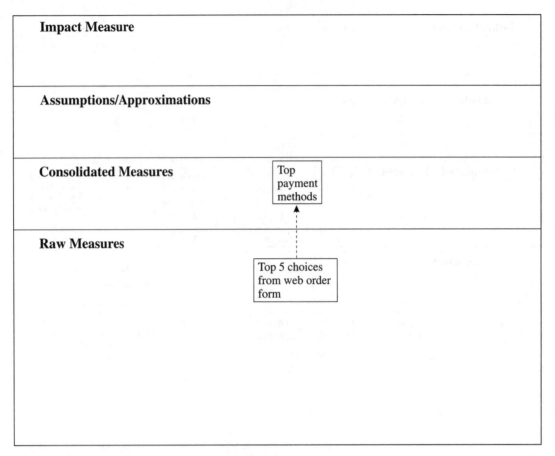

Figure 6.16 Top five payment methods (C) per order form.

Top Shipping Methods

These are the preferred shipping methods selected by purchasers as measured by their choice at the time of sale, as in Figure 6.17. Measure the top five shipping methods (C) as recorded by the online order form during purchase (R).

Top Visit-Generating Promotions

These are the most successful methods of bringing visitors (R) to the web site as measured by the point of origination or the URL they

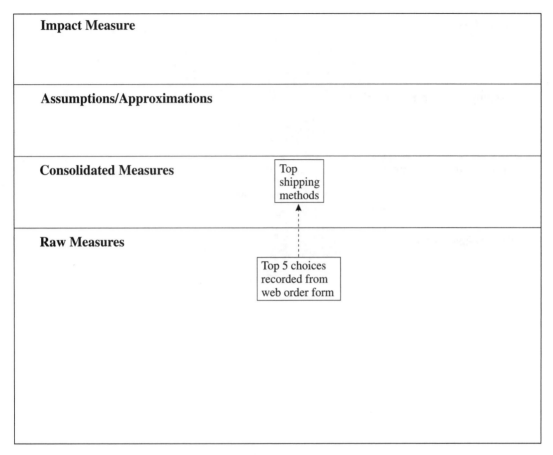

Figure 6.17 Top five shipping methods (C) per order form.

use to access the site. Measure the top five referring links (R) over a given time period, as shown in Figure 6.18.

Typical Purchaser Profile

This is the demographic profile of a given person (R) as expressed in responding to an online survey and/or via database clickstream data. Look at average (R) data over a statistically representative sample.

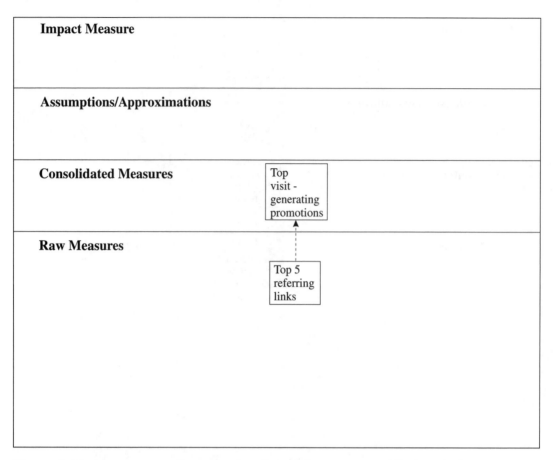

Figure 6.18 Measure top five referring links (C) over a specified period.

Web Site Cost

This represents the total investment required to create, maintain, and update a web site over its first year. Figure 6.19 and the following calculation show how to determine this critical Consolidated Measure.

Calculation: Site Creative Fee (R) + Site Programming Fee (R) + Annual Hosting Cost (C)+ Site Annual Update Budget (R)

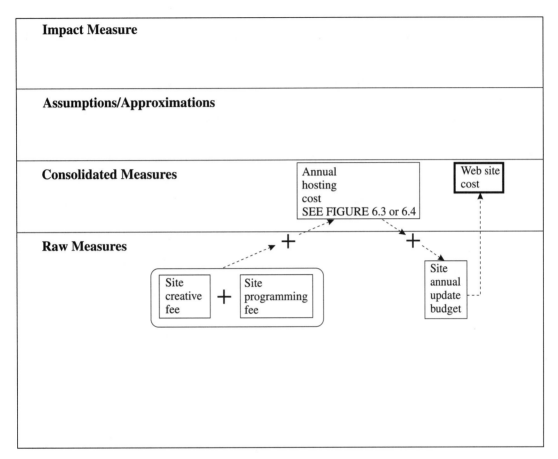

Figure 6.19 Calculating web site cost (C) over a one-year period.

CHAPTER 7

Raw Measures

As discussed in Chapter 6, Consolidated Measures are based on a combination of site and non-site hard data, which is usually easy to collect, if you have planned in advance. This chapter defines the 50 or so most common Raw Measures, gives common sources for this data, and discusses analysis tools and approaches used to extract Raw Measures from the web server logs.

Scanning site logs to reduce individual entries into meaningful consolidated information requires data reduction methods. The first part of this chapter discusses products and services available for site log and visit analysis.

Web Server Log Analysis Tools

The search for better understanding of web site traffic has led to an explosion of software programs which analyze web server logs and site visits. Our research has indicated that most web site managers are as confused about the differences between these products as they are about what the actual data means. It's not the site managers' fault—neither the trade press nor the vendors of analysis products have done a good job of differentiating their offerings. The analysis vendors are squeezed between site managers who are starving for more information about their site attendees and web server vendors who are adding so many new features every month that the analysis tools vendors can't keep up.

Types of Analysis Tools

Part of the reason there's so much confusion about web server log analyzers is that no one has bothered to point out that there are several distinct types of products. We've identified three major categories, each of which is discussed in detail shortly. Trying to compare the market leaders in two different categories can be really frustrating. While virtually all of these software tools try to answer at least a common set of questions, no two packages get there the same way.

As shown in Figure 7.1, we've coined terms for the three major server log analysis categories in the marketplace today: local server analysis, remote server analysis, and standalone desktop analysis.

LOCAL SERVER ANALYSIS These software programs are installed on the same machine as the web server. They automatically process web server log data several times per day and make their reports available via a special web site.

REMOTE SERVER ANALYSIS These are third-party services where the analysis software runs on the service provider's computer. Typically, you must install a small application on your web server which transfers the log files automatically to the service provider once per day. Reports are available via a special web site provided by the third party. Currently, this method is the only way to obtain independently audited traffic statistics, which is important to advertising-supported sites.

STANDALONE DESKTOP ANALYSIS Several prominent analysis vendors offer products which must be installed onto a standard desktop computer running Windows 95. These applications are not automatic. When you want a report, you manually transfer log files

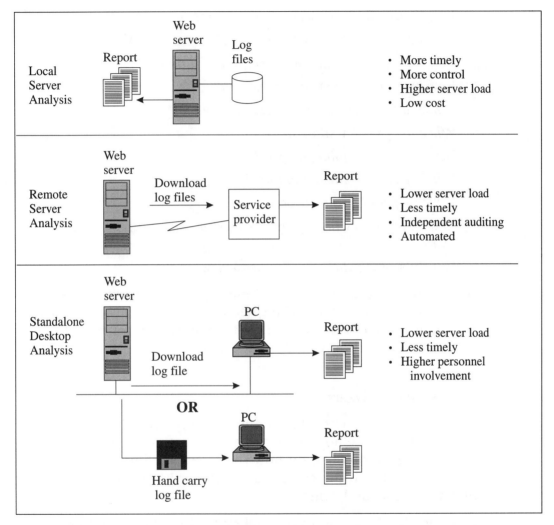

Figure 7.1 Three categories of server log analysis in the marketplace today.

from the web server to the desktop computer. Depending on the size of the log files, you may have a long wait while the computer processes the files. Reports may then be printed or manually transferred back to the web server for viewing by others.

All these approaches try to answer a common set of questions about how a site is doing by extracting data from the site logs that answer the following questions:

What pages are being viewed most often?

Has my site been getting busier lately?

How have the access trends been for a certain page?

How many bytes are being transferred?

Which directories are being accessed the most?

When are people visiting my site?

How are people finding my site?

Which pages are linking to mine?

Which types of errors are occurring?

How many times have people requested something that returned an error?

Which browsers are people using to view my site?

The real differentiator between these approaches is where the analysis program runs. The following sections discuss the pros and cons of each approach in more detail. We'll also review some of the leading solutions, including features and cost.

Local Server Analyzers

Local server analysis packages are probably most heavily used by third-party web site hosting services. The customers of these companies want regular reports on how their sites are doing, but the hosting services have to invest in servers rather than staff. Local server analyzers are a good compromise.

Typically, the software is installed on the same computer as the web server itself. Depending on how much horsepower the server has, the analysis software will run anywhere from once per day to once per hour. When each analysis run is finished, the results are stored at a "private" web site that can be accessed by the hosting customer any time.

This approach is also appropriate for internal IS organizations managing intranet sites. These organizations often face the same challenge as a hosting service. The departments who are their customers want regular reports on their sites, while the IS staff has many other existing commitments. This makes an automated analysis solution ideal.

The advantages of this approach include:

❏ *Instant Availability*: Site measurements are always available on a moment's notice. There is no waiting for reports to process as with the standalone desktop approach. If your server has enough capacity to run measurements hourly or even every few hours, you will get more up-to-date information than from the remote server approach.

❏ *Time Savings*: Since a local server tool is totally automated, there is no staff time required to prepare reports.

❏ *Free or low-cost*: Most local server analysis packages are written for UNIX servers. As is often the case in that community, these packages are generally in the public domain or are shareware with only a modest fee.

❏ *Easy Backup and Restore*: Backups are a breeze because the web server, the server logs, and the analysis reports are all on the same computer. This provides protection in the event of a system failure.

Disadvantages of this approach include:

❏ *Server Load*: Processing log files can tax your web server hardware. Since every line of the log file must be analyzed individually, disk accesses increase significantly during processing. This is fine if you have just a handful of web servers running on a single computer (also known as *virtual servers*). However, some third-party hosting providers have so many virtual servers per machine that the load gets out of hand. In this situation, they may only process the log files once per day, actually often in the middle of the night.

❏ *Platform Support:* Most local server analysis systems have been developed for UNIX servers. Only a handful, such as *e*Watch ClickTrack, are available for Windows NT and NetWare.

❏ *Installation:* Some of the public domain packages assume an experienced administrator is handling the installation. Part of the reason that these systems are inexpensive is that the cost of sophisticated help systems and technical support is borne by the user.

Two excellent examples of local server analysis are reviewed in the following sections. One is a commercial package while the other is shareware. Links to all of the packages covered in this section can be found at our web site (http://www.siteimpact.com).

eWatch ClickTrack

ClickTrack is the newest member of the *e*Watch family of Internet monitoring and analysis services. It is designed primarily for advertising and public relations managers who need a nontechnical view of site data to make ongoing decisions. But, it also reports technical measures, such as browser type—as shown in Figure 7.2—which may impact audience acceptance of the site. ClickTrack has also become popular on intranets because department heads want simple and fast information.

*e*Watch ClickTrack is one of the first commercial web site analysis tools that runs in real-time along with a web site. In addition to measuring standard items like page views, point of origination, and browser types, ClickTrack features reports on session duration and average pages viewed per session. According to Jim Wallace, marketing manager at the Toro Company and longtime ClickTrack user,

> This software lets me understand the business impact our site is having. Knowing that the average visitor spends seven minutes lets

---

Browser Platforms

Unidentifiable Platform (5729)Windows 95 (5156)Macintosh 68K (733)Macintosh PPC (393)Unix (384)Windows NT (285)Text Only (57)NonBrowsers (Spiders, Robots, etc) (11)Amiga (5)OS/2 (1)

Browser Types

Netscape 2.0 (7038)Netscape 3.0 (2268)Netscape 1.0 (2049)Unclassified Browsers (267)AOL (199)SPRY Mosaic (178)Prodigy (154)IBM WebExplorer (114)Explorer (112)NCSA Mosaic (84) Netscape 0.0 (70)NetCruiser (67)Lynx (Text) (57)Enhanced Mosaic (20)Spyglass Mosaic (15)AIR Mosaic (12)Spiders (11)MacWeb (10)Quarterdeck Mosaic (10)Charlotte (8)Lotus Notes (6)AWeb (5)

Figure 7.2 "Browsers hitting the site" report.

me do an apples-to-apples comparison with the cost of 30 seconds of network television.

A clicktrack depth report, shown in Figure 7.3, illustrates how average time spent at the site is measured.

Interestingly, ClickTrack reports only page views, not hits. According to James Alexander, managing partner of *e*Works! which developed the software,

> Hits may be important to systems administrators to do capacity planning, but they are meaningless to a non-technical person. They can also be misleading since sites with higher graphic content will report many more hits than a simple site even though a visitor may look at the same number of pages.

Beyond reporting page views, the ClickTrack package offers some reports that we haven't seen on any other package as of this writing, including:

❑ *Session Analysis*: The system is able to show how long visitors stayed at the site and how many pages they viewed before leaving.

❑ *Most Common Entry Page*: All packages will tell you what the top-requested pages are at your site. But, ClickTrack is the only package we reviewed that can show you the top *entry pages—*

Depth Report
Using a user session time of **30 minutes**
- User Sessions: **83295**
- Average Session Length (in seconds, excluding 1 page sessions): **302**
- Maximum Depth in 1 session: **60**
- Average Depth in 1 session (excluding 1 page sessions): **4**

74173
1657
2261
1552
1201
812
542

Figure 7.3 Depth and most common entry page report.

where visitors start. This tells you which pages are being book-marked and can be useful for deciding what areas should be expanded.

❑ *Most Common Exit Page*: ClickTrack will also tell you what are the most common pages last viewed by visitors before exiting the site. This is useful if you think you may have a compatibility problem that is causing visitors to quit or, in general, if you are trying to make visitors stay longer.

Additional features of ClickTrack include:

❑ *Online Graphical Reports*: ClickTrack reports are stored at a special web site which can be password-protected, making access a snap. All of the reports use easy-to-read charts to convey usage information. These are done with a quick-loading method that makes them transmit very quickly over the web.

❑ *Nontechnical Titles*: ClickTrack substitutes actual document titles in place of complicated filenames on its reports, which takes a lot of the technical complexity out of reading them. The software also reports the full name of Internet domain holders which helps you analyze the origins of visitors.

❑ *Online Help*: All reports have an integrated help screen which explains how to read them. There is also a glossary of terms that can be accessed from every individual page at the report web site.

❑ *Supports All Major Web Servers*: The ClickTrack engine works with log files from all major server packages and can be customized if necessary.

❑ *Fast Processing*: By storing previously analyzed data in a compressed form, ClickTrack is able to provide reports all the way back to the origin of your site. The compression system means that only those accesses since the last ClickTrack report must be analyzed. This dramatically reduces processing time and associated system load.

❑ *Large Log Files*: Unlike some shareware packages such as MK-Stats which are commonly written in PERL and therefore are too slow to handle large logs, ClickTrack is written entirely in C++ for speed.

A future version promises to provide an API that allows a web site to report custom statistics on the same report. For instance, if you wanted to show how many e-mails were received by a site or how many people had ordered particular items in a catalog, *e*Works! promises that you will be able to easily track this information.

Pricing for ClickTrack starts at under $100 and is based on the number of virtual web servers running on the actual computer. As of this writing, *e*Works! is shipping versions for Sun Solaris, Silicon Graphics Irix, Windows NT, and NetWare.

A downloadable demo of ClickTrack is available via our web site at (www.siteimpact.com) or surf directly to (http://www.clicktrack. com). You may call *e*Works! for more information (612–288–0000) or send e-mail to (info@clicktrack.com).

MKStats

If you prefer shareware, one tool that has become popular is MK-Stats, by Matt Kruse. As with ClickTrack, we liked the graphical approach versus the purely text reports that are common with many public domain utilities. As stated at the web site for MKStats:

> The goal was not to create a program that extracts a lot of statistics from the logs and just prints it out. Instead, the goal is to answer the questions you want answered about your web site and present the information in a useful, meaningful way.

According to the supporting documentation at its web site, MK-Stats tries to answer the following questions:

What pages are being viewed most often?

Has my site been getting busier lately?

How about the last 14 days?

How have the access trends been for a certain page?

How many bytes are being transferred?

Which directories are being accessed the most?

When are people visiting my site?

On which days of the week and month? On which hours of the day?

Which weeks have been the busiest?

How are people finding my site?

Which pages are linking to mine?

Have people bookmarked my page?

Which types of errors are occurring?

How many times have people requested something that returned an error?

Which browsers are people using to view my site?

Figure 7.4 shows the various report selections available with this program. The report formats are mainly text-oriented, as shown in Figure 7.5 which illustrates a report on referring sites.

We tested MKStats on a UNIX-based server. The author claims to have personally tested it on Windows 95 and Windows NT as well. Because MKStats is written in PERL, your system must have PERL preinstalled in order to use MKStats. PERL is not supplied with MK-Stats, which means that installation requires you to have an experienced administrator. Skills needed to successfully install the program include decompressing the software, configuring the PERL 5.0 programming language, setting up *shell variables* and modifying the UNIX scheduling system *cron*.

Summary Information
 Information from various places pulled together to summarize activity.
Visitor Information
 Who is visiting your site and where they are coming from.
Page Information
 Which pages are getting accessed and in what ways.
Times and Dates
 When people are coming to your site, and what kinds of trends can be seen over time.
Referring Sites
 Information about how people are finding your pages, using links, bookmarks, etc.
Browsers Used
 The browsers people are using when visiting your site.
Errors
 The problems your server encountered while trying to fulfill requests.
Misc.
 Miscellaneous information that does not fit into other categories.

Figure 7.4 Reports available with MKStats.

```
7199  /~mkruse/www/scripts/index.html
5327  /~mkruse/mkstats/index.html
4148  /~mkruse/isca/index.html
2601  /~mkruse/www/info/ssi.html
1421  /~mkruse/www/scripts/access3.html
 873  /~mkruse/www/scripts/counter.html
 812  /~mkruse/mk3/mk3.html
 589  /~mkruse/index.html
 288  /~mkruse/www/scripts/indexer.html
 250  /~mkruse/www/scripts/table.html
 245  /~mkruse/pov3/index.html
 241  /~mkruse/raytracing.html
 206  /~mkruse/www/scripts/index2.html
 205  /~mkruse/experiment/index.html
 199  /~mkruse/www/scripts/mailer.html
 124  /~mkruse/www/scripts/counter/counter.txt
```

Figure 7.5 Report on referring sites available with MKStats.

The author requests a shareware fee ranging from $50 to $300, depending on your nonprofit status and whether you are an Internet service provider. A link to a downloadable demo of MKStats is available via our web site at (www.siteimpact.com) or surf directly to (http://www.mkstats.com). For more information, you may also send e-mail to (mkruse@mkstats.com).

Other Shareware Tools

There are many other shareware tools of varying quality available online. If you have the time and interest, addresses of web sites for several more tools are listed in Figure 7.6.

Also, try visiting Yahoo! for a more complete list. The Yahoo! category for these software packages is:

http://www.yahoo.com/
    Computers_and_Internet/
      Internet/
        World_Wide_Web/
          Servers/
            Log_Analysis_Tools

Package Name	Web Site Address
3Dstats	http://www.netstore.de/Supply/3DStats
AccessWatch	http://www.netpressence.com/accesswatch
CreateStats	http://www-bprc.mps.ohio-state.edu/usage/
Getstats	http://www.eit.com/software/getstats
VB-Stats	http://home.city.net/win-httpd

Figure 7.6 Web site addresses for local server analyzers available through shareware.

Remote Server Analyzers

The local server analyzers we've just examined are the most convenient and affordable way to obtain ongoing measurement of your web site. However, there may be situations where doing it yourself doesn't make sense. In this case, you may wish to turn to a third party to do the work for you. Given the cost of these services, the only situation where remote analysis makes obvious sense is for advertising-supported sites. Potential sponsors want independently audited usage results in order to justify spending precious advertising dollars. In the future, price changes and new applications may expand the market for remote analysis providers.

Conceptually speaking, remote server analysis is virtually identical to local server analysis. The difference is that the analysis software runs on the service provider's computer located elsewhere on the Internet. The provider installs a small program on your web server which automatically transfers the log files at preset times.

Most of the advantages of local server analyzers apply here, too. Additional advantages of this approach include:

❑ *Reduced server load*: Since the log processing is not done on your web server, server overhead—particularly CPU load—will be lower. There will be an increase in communications load when the logs are transferred to the processing site, but generally this should not impact web site performance, if the transfer is done during off-hours.

- *Automated*: In theory, using a third-party to analyze log files means you don't have to do any work. For some organizations, this feature alone is worth the investment. If you do not have an experienced systems administration staff for your web servers, remote analysis may be your only option for ongoing measurement.

- *Credibility*: Because the results are compiled by someone else, they have an "aura" of trustworthiness. You do not necessarily have to purchase audited results just because you use a third party. For instance, Internet Profiles offers both a compilation and an auditing service.

- *Norming*: Advertisers and market research executives may be interested in the detailed demographic data available from a remote analysis provider. Since these companies compile data on many web sites, they can show you how your results compare to norms for your industry or the Web as a whole.

- *Lower Storage Requirements*: These services claim that another benefit of remote analysis is that you don't have to keep log files around, which frees up disk space. In practice, we haven't found any web site administrators willing to completely erase this data. However, your situation may be different.

The disadvantages include:

- *Cost*: As alluded to already, Remote Analysis can be very expensive. Prices range from $250 to $6,000 for unaudited service. Audited reports can cost up to $20,000.

- *Frequency*: Remote analysis reports are typically offered on a daily basis because they have so many customers to process. If you need more frequent information, local analysis may be a better choice.

Two major remote server analysis providers are discussed in the following sections. Links to all of the services covered can be found at our web site at (www.siteimpact.com).

Internet Profiles Corporation

One of the first real Internet measurement companies, Internet Profiles (also known as I/Pro) enjoys strong support in the advertising community. A.C. Nielsen, the well-known provider of television ratings, is a major investor in the company. I/Pro offers three basic services.

I/Count: Essentially, this is a basic site statistics report run for you on a remote computer system. I/Pro provides additional value by including industry benchmarks using its database of site performance. According to its marketing materials:

> Site usage can be analyzed whenever convenient, by generating I/Count reports using I/Pro's web site. A selection of popular preformatted reports are available or you can create your own custom reports. Once a report is created, I/Count allows you to see it online or receive it via e-mail. Reports can also run automatically on a regular basis. I/Count is installed on your web server. Each night, usage data is securely transmitted from your site to I/Pro where it is processed, encoded and indexed for maximum performance, and loaded into a fully relational database.

I/Audit: Nielsen I/Audit provides independent, verified, and comparable reports of web site usage in a standard and easily understandable printed report format. I/Audit reports are used by web sites for external verification of traffic and by advertisers and media buyers for comparative purposes. For nonadvertising-supported sites, I/Audit provides a standard set of usage information. For sites with advertiser inserts or ad banners, I/Audit can also report the following:

❑ AdViews by day

❑ AdClicks by day

❑ AdClick rate by day

❑ Ad comparisons that do not compromise advertiser confidentiality

❑ Advertiser summary statistics by page

Note that I/Audit has an essential manual step, where the audit reports are checked for accuracy before being delivered. For this reason, delivery of reports can take up to several weeks. I/Audit reports are available on a monthly or single-use basis. If you have Acrobat

Reader, you can view sample reports at their web site. An overview of the I/Audit methodology is also available online.

I/Code: This ambitious service is designed solely to provide you with extensive demographic data on the people visiting your web site. I/Code has two parts. The first is a registration system which all I/Code customers must implement at their sites. The registration system poses demographic questions to visitors and assigns them a code number. This code is good at any other participating site; this means that a visitor only needs to go through the process once. The second part is demographic reports. I/Code customers receive detailed reports on site visitors, including such data as household income, age, education, and so on.

The marketing materials for I/Code indicate that you will be able to answer the following types of questions with the service:

How does income distribution affect which part of my site visitors return to over time?

What type of professionals are the most frequent repeat visitors to certain pages on my site?

What is the gender breakdown of visitors to my site who view a particular file?

What is the marital status of visitors accessing my site from commercial organizations?

All of these services can be combined. For instance, the combination of I/Code with I/Audit can provide you with usage data enhanced by demographic data about your users to provide to advertisers or potential advertisers. Instead of just telling advertisers the number of visits to your site, an I/Code-enhanced I/Audit will also tell the advertisers about the demographics of the visitors.

This service provides audience information by various criteria, such as by state as shown in Figure 7.7. It also provides information on site usage by month or other timeframe, as illustrated in Figure 7.8.

Internet Profiles is promising real-time delivery of demographic data in the near future. This means that your site can be customized on-the-fly for a visitor based on who he or she is. We anticipate that

```
State    Yesterday  1 Wk Ago 1 Mtn Ago  1 Qtr Ago
-------- ---------- -------- ---------  ----------
  CA          0%        0%        0%         25%
  ??          0%        0%        0%         23%
  ??          0%        0%        0%         17%
  PA          0%        0%        0%          7%
  NY          0%        0%        0%          4%
  VA          0%        0%        0%          3%
  WA          0%        0%        0%          2%
  NJ          0%        0%        0%          2%
  MA          0%        0%        0%          2%
  TX          0%        0%        0%          2%
  MI          0%        0%        0%          1%
  IL          0%        0%        0%          1%
  CT          0%        0%        0%          1%
  MD          0%        0%        0%          1%
```

Figure 7.7 Web site percent usage by state.

such customization will become increasingly important for both advertising-supported and marketing-oriented sites.

Pricing for the Internet Profiles services ranges from a few hundred dollars per month (ongoing services such as I/Count and I/Code) to many thousands of dollars per individual audit. A link to Internet Profiles can be found at our web site at (www.

```
COMPANY: I/PRO Corporation (Guest Account) / I/PRO Corporation (Gu
DATE:    Sun Sep 22 15:41:40 PDT 1996

Usage Statistics - Monthly, Past 6 months


This unaudited report is based upon access information supplied to
for the I/COUNT Web Measurement and Analysis System.  This report
generated without human review and does not reflect the verificati
authentication of "audited" output.

Date             Visits     Pages
--------------- ---------- ----------
JUL 1996           4839      10398
JUN 1996          12207      27969
```

Figure 7.8 Web server percentage usage by month.

siteimpact.com). You can also point your browser directly to (http://
www.ipro.com) or for more information, call (415–975–5800).

Audit Bureau of Circulations

"Auditing your own counts is like students grading their own papers," thunders the home page for this service. The Audit Bureau of
Circulations (ABC) competes directly with Internet Profiles I/Audit
service, taking aim at the same market for independently audited
site usage data. As of this writing, ABC does not offer an unaudited,
statistics-only service.

Unlike I/Pro's marketing materials which assume you already
understand the importance of auditing, ABC explains some of the
risks if you don't:

> For the Web to be accepted as a reliable advertising vehicle, ad-
> vertisers need proof that activity claims have been audited by an
> independent third party. An audit provides assurance that a web
> site's activity counts have not been misrepresented (counted incor-
> rectly), manipulated (counts don't reflect actual activity), or re-
> ported in a format not universally recognized by the advertising
> community.

Like I/Pro, the ABC method installs a software program on your
web server which transmits log data to its system on a preset schedule. Once transferred to ABC, your data is incorporated into a rela-
tional database system so that draft reports can be created. These
reports are reviewed by auditors who look for unusual events,
strange traffic patterns, and the like. For instance, if your site sud-
denly shows up as a "Cool Site of the Day" you may experience sudden traffic increases. These must be identified and noted in the
audit report. Finally, the audit is sent to you online or via the mail.

Pricing is handled on a custom basis, determined by your web
site's average number of page views per month, number of HTML
pages, and number of log files.

A link to the ABC web site is available at our site on (www.
siteimpact.com). Additional information is available by calling
(847–605– 0909 x282) or by sending e-mail to (hepnerea@accessabc.
com).

Standalone Desktop Analyzers

We call the final category of web server analysis tools standalone analyzers because they are run by hand on a desktop PC that is separate from the web site. The PC may be connected on the same Local Area Network (LAN) as the site, connected through a communications line, or it may be completely independent of the site. Some of the best-known packages include Intersé Market Focus and net.Genesis' net.Analysis.

The approach taken by these packages has several steps. First, the log files must be transferred from your web server to the machine that is running the analysis software. At this writing, this is a manual process. Second, you must fire up the application and configure it for the reports you want to produce. Third, you wait while the system processes all of the log file data. Process duration can be many hours, depending on the size of your log files. Finally, you must output your report, either by transferring it by hand back to a web site, so that others can see it, or by printing it. This entire sequence must be repeated every time you want a report.

The authors are hard-pressed to explain why anyone would go through so much work, work that potentially requires great technical skill in case something goes wrong. In our opinion, such packages have appeal at this time only because local server analyzer systems are typically shareware and remote server analyzer providers are too expensive. We argue that the major companies in this area should adapt their products to run as local server applications.

Depending on your specific situation, advantages of such systems may include:

- ❏ *Runs Under Windows 95/NT*: All of the major offerings in this category run under Windows NT and/or Windows 95. If you're trying to avoid UNIX and don't want to pay for remote analysis, standalone analyzers may be the way to go. But with the release of *e*Watch ClickTrack there is now a credible local server implementation on these platforms.

- ❏ *Internet Domain Database*: These systems generally offer a way to look up more complete information about domain name holders. This makes the reports less "techy" and can save you having to do your own research on a domain name you don't recognize.

Disadvantages of this approach include:

- ❏ *Time Requirements*: The time necessary to perform all the steps previously described can be extremely high. Most of us already have a shortage of free time; so a manual system doesn't make sense.

- ❏ *Delayed Access*: Our interviews made clear that web site administrators expect to have access to measurements on a timely basis. They don't want to wait for processing.

- ❏ *Windows 95/NT Only*: The flip side to the Windows advantage is that if you're running a UNIX server, you have to have a separate Windows machine in order to process statistics. A local-server package that runs automatically is going to be superior.

- ❏ *Cost*: Based on pricing for ClickTrack, MKStats, and other local server approaches, the standalone analysis tools are dramatically more expensive.

- ❏ *Report Size*: Another problem we noted in our product review is the size of the reports which can be produced. These systems are oriented toward producing single documents, as opposed to the local server approach which splits report sections onto individual web pages. When we selected a complete set of reports, the length of the resulting document was so great that we ran out of memory trying to view it using a web browser. Standalone packages need a convenient way to create multiple output documents.

The following sections discuss two standalone desktop analyzers.

Market Focus

Perhaps the first and best-known offering in this category is Market Focus by Intersé. There are two versions of the product; a Standard Edition with a built-in database and a Developer's Edition which supports Microsoft Access or SQL Server. This package can basically

---

User demographics

User organizations

Organization name# of visits% of visits1. Microsoft Corporation3482.89%2. America Online, Inc.2642.19%3. NETCOM2482.06%4. CompuServe, Inc.1791.48%5. UUNET Technologies, Inc. 1581.31%6. 206.86.231531.27%7. Best Internet Communications, Inc.1050.87%8. On-Ramp Technologies, Inc.870.72%9. The Internet Access Company770.64%**Total:1,61913.43%**
User country of origin

Country# of visits% of visits1. United States7,87565.31%2. Unresolved IP address3,02825.11% 3. United Kingdom1571.30%4. Canada1531.27%5. Japan1170.97%6. Italy1100.91%7. Germany97 0.80%8. Finland650.54%9. Sweden620.51%10. Israel550.46%**Total:11,71997.19%**
User organization type

Figure 7.9 Portion of site measures executive summary provided by Market Focus.

consolidate information into a single executive summary, a portion of which is shown in Figure 7.9.

The marketing materials describe the Standard Edition this way:

Intersé Market Focus 2 Standard Edition (Microsoft Access compatible) web analysis software lets you conduct web site analyses at your place of business, protecting the confidentiality and privacy of your data. This easy-to-use software includes 14 pre-defined reports so you can learn about all aspects of your Internet site's activity—right away. This edition is ideal for analyzing one Internet site with log file sizes of 75 MB or less. You don't need Microsoft Access to use Intersé Market Focus 2 Standard Edition.

Compatible with most web server software, Intersé market focus software takes "hit"-based usage data and uses several inference-based algorithms to reconstruct the actual visits, users, and organizations that interact with the web site. Intersé market focus enables users to conduct in-depth analyses and produce a comprehensive suite of standard analysis reports, providing you with valuable insights for making more informed Internet business decisions.

The Developer Edition is explained as follows:

Intersé Market Focus 2 Developer's Edition (for use with Microsoft SQL Server) web analysis software is ideal for enterprises with large or multiple web sites. This developer's edition delivers maximum scalability and flexibility for advanced design of complex analyses, including the ability to aggregate, cross reference, and combine properties of many sites for analysis. You must have Microsoft SQL Server to use this developer's edition.

At this writing, pricing for the Standard Edition is $695. Pricing for the Developer Edition is $3,495 for the Access-compatible version and $6,995 for the Microsoft SQL Server version. Support contracts are also available on an annual basis. We have a link to the Intersé web site at our site on (www.siteimpact.com) or you may go directly to (http://www.interse.com). You can contact Intersé at (408–732–0932) or send e-mail to (info@interse.com).

net.Analysis

Another well-known offering in the standalone category is net.Analysis. In our opinion, net.Analysis differs from Market Focus primarily by providing more onscreen interactive reports, whereas Market Focus is geared to producing "static" reports in a Microsoft Word or HTML format. net.Analysis is also available for the Sun Solaris UNIX platform at additional cost. net.Genesis describes the product this way:

> net.Analysis Desktop for Windows NT/95 is an easy-to-use, low-cost tool for analyzing and viewing web site usage information. Filling the reporting needs of Internet or intranet web sites with low to moderate traffic, net.Analysis Desktop offers state-of-the-art features like detailed browser and geographic reports and the ability to build your own queries. A standalone solution, with a built-in FoxPro relational database, net.Analysis Desktop makes it easy to view long-term trends in site usage reporting across multiple log files.

Like Market Focus, net.Analysis comes with numerous predefined reports, including visits per unit of time, hits per unit of time, bytes per unit of time, top domains, top hostnames, top referrals,

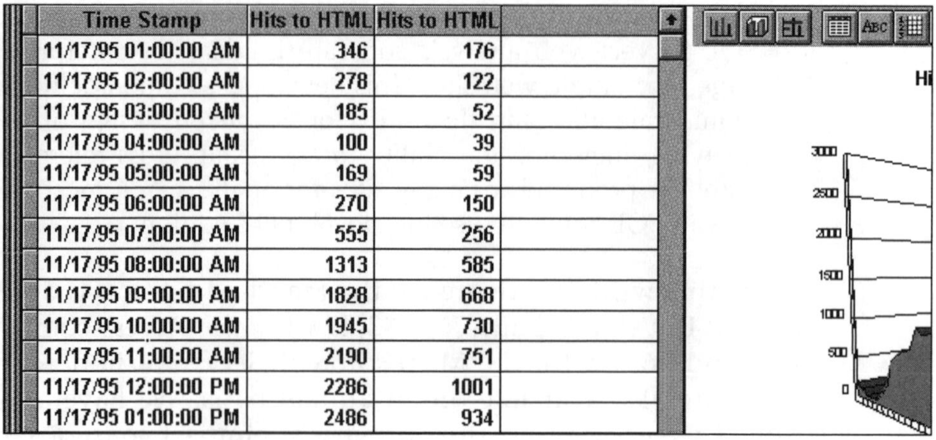

Time Stamp	Hits to HTML	Hits to HTML	
11/17/95 01:00:00 AM	346	176	
11/17/95 02:00:00 AM	278	122	
11/17/95 03:00:00 AM	185	52	
11/17/95 04:00:00 AM	100	39	
11/17/95 05:00:00 AM	169	59	
11/17/95 06:00:00 AM	270	150	
11/17/95 07:00:00 AM	555	256	
11/17/95 08:00:00 AM	1313	585	
11/17/95 09:00:00 AM	1828	668	
11/17/95 10:00:00 AM	1945	730	
11/17/95 11:00:00 AM	2190	751	
11/17/95 12:00:00 PM	2286	1001	
11/17/95 01:00:00 PM	2486	934	

Figure 7.10 Web site hits per unit time.

top browsers, and more. Figures 7.10 and 7.11 illustrate some of these report layouts.

Interestingly, net.Analysis also supports predefined *filters* to either select or exclude certain types of information. Examples include hits to pages, hits to images, hits to CGI scripts, hits to home page, hits from commercial, and others.

Pricing as of this writing is $495 for the Windows version. A Sun Solaris version is available for $2,995. Support contracts are also

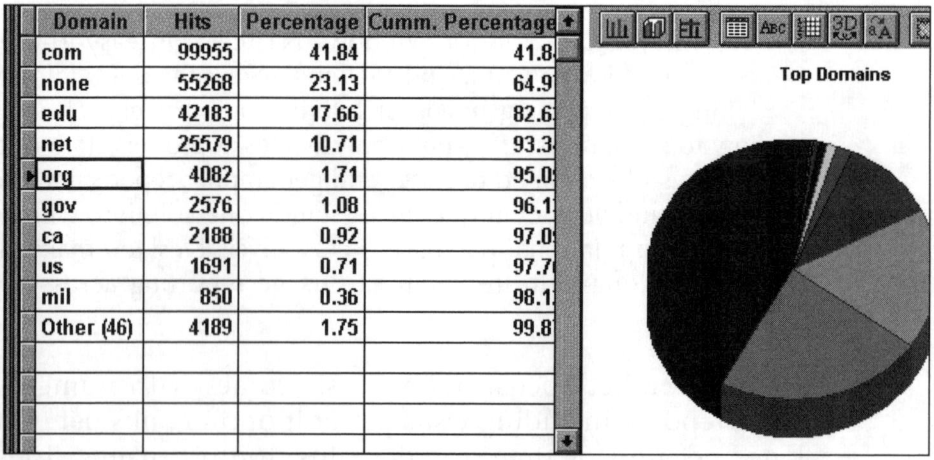

Domain	Hits	Percentage	Cumm. Percentage
com	99955	41.84	41.8
none	55268	23.13	64.9
edu	42183	17.66	82.6
net	25579	10.71	93.3
org	4082	1.71	95.0
gov	2576	1.08	96.1
ca	2188	0.92	97.0
us	1691	0.71	97.7
mil	850	0.36	98.1
Other (46)	4189	1.75	99.8

Figure 7.11 Web site top domains.

available on an annual basis. We have a link to the net.Genesis web site at our site on (www.siteimpact.com) or you may go directly to (http://www.netgen.com). You can contact them at (617–577–9800) or send e-mail to (info@netgen.com).

Other Commercial Packages

The preceding product discussion is only a sampling of what is available for log and site analysis. Given the rate at which new products appear in the Internet marketspace, it would be a good idea for you to drop by our web site to get the most up-to-date list of products. You can also check out Yahoo! as previously described.

All site log analysis tools scan the log files and extract Raw Measures from which the program consolidates and interpolates the information presented in the reports. Often the report contents and other Raw Measures discussed in the next section are needed to generate the Consolidated and Impact Measures against which site success can be measured.

Definition and Sources of Key Raw Measures

The following list is not all-inclusive, but it does identify most of the major Raw Measures and at least one source for each. You should use this as a guideline and add additional measures particular to your site and needs.

Annual Maintenance Agreements

Definition: The total cost of all annual hardware and software maintenance agreements related to operating the web site.

Primary Sources: MIS manager or the purchasing department.

Average Call Duration

Definition: The length of time, on average, of a long-distance telephone call for a particular application.

Primary Sources: Telecommunications department.

Average Cost Per Minute

Definition: The cost your company pays, on average, for one minute of long-distance.

Primary Sources: Telecommunications department.

Base Salary Midpoint

Definition: For a particular position, the halfway point between the minimum salary and maximum salary defined by human resources.

Primary Sources: Human resources.

Benefits Percentage

Definition: A multiplier which adds in the out-of-pocket cost paid by an employer to provide a defined set of benefits to an employee. Typical benefits include health care, tuition reimbursement, vacation, and so on.

Primary Sources: Human resources or finance departments.

Bonus Potential

Definition: The amount of money eligible to be earned by a particular position during a calendar year, if certain conditions are met. Conditions may include gross sales revenue, company profitability, completing a course of study, achieving a target level of quality, or customer satisfaction.

Primary Sources: Human resources.

Browser Type

Definition: The specific web browser manufacturer and version being used by a particular visitor to access a web site.

Primary Sources: Web site access log (when browser type capturing is turned on).

Call Frequency

Definition: The average number of calls per period of time for a specific purpose, such as support calls to a help desk. Used for calculating cost savings due to a web site.

Primary Sources: Telecommunications or IS help desk

Cost of Capital

Definition: The interest rate paid by your organization to borrow money. Typically factored into capital equipment purchases to arrive at a true investment cost.

Primary Sources: Finance department or management team.

Depreciation Period (Months)

Definition: The number of months required to depreciate or amortize a capital equipment investment. This has important tax consequences and applies across an organization.

Primary Sources: Finance department.

Downloads

Definition: The number of times a particular file is requested to be sent to a web site visitor.

Primary Sources: Web site access log.

E-mail Complaints

Definition: The number of e-mails received via a web site of a negative nature during a specified period of time.

Primary Sources: The webmaster.

E-mail Praise

Definition: The number of e-mails received via a web site of a positive nature during a specified period of time.

Primary Sources: The webmaster.

E-mail Resolutions

Definition: The number of e-mail complaints or other problems received via a web site that are resolved in a particular period of time. Resolutions are measured by a follow-up affirmative e-mail or a logged telephone call or letter.

Primary Sources: The webmaster.

E-mail Frequency

Definition: The number of e-mails received from a web site per specific period of time.

Primary Sources: The webmaster.

E-mail Senders

Definition: The number of individuals who send e-mail via a web site in a specified period of time. Will always be the same as or less than the total number of e-mails.

Primary Sources: The webmaster.

Employer Tax Percentage

Definition: The percentage of out-of-pocket cost paid by an employer to state, federal, and local governments for a given position. Typically, this includes a matching Social Security payment and unemployment tax.

Primary Sources: Human resources or finance departments.

Facilities Allocation

Definition: An amount spent per employee per year to cover the physical environment, including office/cube cost, telephone, computer, air conditioning, and other expenses.

Primary Sources: Finance department.

Hits

Definition: The number of requests for a file to be transferred from a web server to a browser.

Primary Sources: Web server access log.

Hit Frequency

Definition: The number of hits in a specified period of time.

Primary Sources: Web server access log (make sure that time stamping is enabled for the log).

Monthly Hosting Fee

Definition: A fee charged by a third party to rent space on a web server that the party owns for one month. Typically, such a fee is all-inclusive, covering hardware, software, personnel, and Internet access charges.

Primary Sources: Vendors.

Monthly Internet Access Fee

Definition: The monthly cost from an Internet access provider for a dedicated circuit for your own connection.

Primary Sources: Internet access provider.

Monthly Local Loop Fee

Definition: The monthly fee from the telephone company to provide a dedicated circuit between you and your Internet access provider.

Primary Sources: Your local telephone company.

Network Address

Definition: The Internet Protocol (IP) address of the computer being used by a particular visitor. Passed with every hit from the browser to the web server.

Primary Sources: Web server access log.

Network Equipment Cost

Definition: The total cost for network hardware, software, and maintenance to provide access to a Web server and/or Internet link to the employees of an organization.

Primary Sources: MIS or purchasing department.

Number of Sessions with Only One Page Request

Definition: The number of times that a person connects to a web site, but only requests a single HTML document.

Primary Sources: Web server access log (be sure that time stamping is enabled).

Originating Domains

Definition: The domain name associated with the computer being used by a particular visitor to access your web site.

Primary Sources: Web server access log (be sure that domain name resolution is activated).

Originating Countries

Definition: The top-level domains of visitors to a web site when the top-level domain specifies a country instead of a type of organization (i.e., ".ca" for Canada instead of ".edu" for Educational Institution).

Primary Sources: Web server access log (be sure that domain name resolution is activated).

Page Views

Definition: The number of requests for the HTML source for a specific page or pages at a web site. Excludes requests for other items on a page, including artwork and multimedia elements.

Primary Sources: Web server access log.

Payment Methods

Definition: The list of methods chosen by web site visitors to pay for items purchased online.

Primary Sources: Transaction log file.

Per-Piece Shipping Cost

Definition: The average cost to mail, overnight, or fax a specific document.

Primary Sources: Shipping department or finance department.

Platform Type

Definition: The operating system and/or type of computer being used by a visitor to access a web site.

Primary Sources: Web server access log.

Purchase

Definition: The number of times that a purchase is made online via a web site.

Primary Sources: Transaction log.

Referring Links

Definition: The URL where a visitor to a web site was immediately prior to coming to that web site.

Primary Sources: Referring link log file (be sure that referring link tracking is activated).

Run Size

Definition: The number of pieces in a production run for collateral or some other document. Used for calculating the per-piece cost.

Primary Sources: Purchasing or marketing department.

Server Errors

Definition: The list of problems experienced by a web server, regardless of severity, over a period of time.

Primary Sources: Web server error log.

Server Hardware Cost

Definition: The total capital equipment budget for a web site if hosted on new equipment owned by the web site operator.

Primary Sources: MIS or purchasing department.

Server Software Cost

Definition: The total software expense budget for a web site if hosted on new equipment owned by the web site operator.

Primary Sources: MIS or purchasing department.

Sessions

Definition: The number of people who request pages from a web site, where all of the requests that occur within 30 minutes of one another count as a single session.

Primary Sources: Web server access log (be sure that time stamping is activated).

Session Time Limit

Definition: The total amount of time spent by a visitor in a single session, on average.

Primary Sources: Web server access log.

Site Annual Update Budget

Definition: The total annual expense budget for making content or other changes to a web site.

Primary Sources: MIS, purchasing, creative services, or finance departments.

Site Creative Fee

Definition: The fee charged internally by a creative services department or externally by an advertising or public relations agency to develop the content for a web site.

Primary Sources: Vendor or internal department.

Site Programming Fee

Definition: The fee charged internally by MIS or an outside web developer to write the software and/or HTML pages necessary to create a finished web site.

Primary Sources: Vendor or internal department.

Spider Visits

Definition: The number of times an automated search engine or other exploratory software has requested pages at a web site.

Primary Sources: Web server access log (be sure that browser type logging is activated).

Systems Administrator Salary

Definition: The annual base salary of the individual responsible for keeping a web server operating.

Primary Sources: MIS or finance departments.

Total Creative Cost

Definition: The total fee paid to an outside vendor or internal creative services department to construct a piece of print collateral.

Primary Sources: Vendor or internal department bid.

Total Production Cost for Collateral

Definition: The total fee paid to an outside vendor to print a desired number of copies of a print collateral piece.

Primary Sources: Vendor bid or past purchase orders.

Total Web Customers

Definition: The total count of visitors who have purchased one or more items from a web site during a particular period of time.

Primary Sources: Transaction log.

Total Web Item Revenue

Definition: The total gross revenue of all items sold through a web site during a particular period of time.

Primary Sources: Transaction log.

Total Web Items Sold

Definition: The total number of items sold via a web site in a specified period of time.

Primary Sources: Transaction log.

Unique Cookies

Definition: The number of unique browsers that have been assigned a permanent identifying code that can be detected by a web server on the next visit by that browser.

Primary Sources: Web server access log.

Visitors

Definition: The number of people who have requested pages from a web site in a specified period of time.

Primary Sources: A Cookie log; Web site access log with detailed analysis; or a Login log.

Volume Surcharges

Definition: The monthly variable fee charged by an Internet access provider if your circuit is not on a flat-fee price.

Primary Sources: MIS or telecommunications department.

Part III

Analysis and Actions

CHAPTER 8

How Often Should You Evaluate Measures?

Simple as it may seem, the question of how often one should evaluate a particular web site measure came up frequently in our interviews. In talking with many web site operators, it became clear that some measures must be checked daily while others are only valuable on a weekly or monthly basis. This is similar to driving a car and checking the speedometer more often than the gas gauge. We found that *frequency* of measurement changed over the life of the site. Also, depending on the span of time covered, the same measurement might have very different meaning. Though everything in this chapter is firmly rooted in common sense, the role of time in site measurement is so important that it is worth covering in depth.

The simplest answer to "How often should you evaluate measures?" is "As often as necessary to understand the success, operation, and audience acceptance of your site." But, how do you decide what is necessary?

Web sites are like many other business activities. The newer they are, the more visibility they have within the organization and the more powerful the microscope used to examine their results. Most managers we spoke to originally examined every measure daily. Part of this was to get a feel for the site's operation, and in part, honestly, because a new site is like a new toy. After a short time, the daily measure check was shifted to a weekly or monthly review.

Measurement Triggers

Between the case studies and our own experience, it is clear that there are two basic *triggers* that cause an evaluation of one or more site measures: events and calendars. The most common trigger by far is events. Events that make a web site manager pay attention to the numbers may include:

Business events (acquisition, sale, budget cycle, quarterly earnings, annual report, downsizing).

Sales or promotional events (major new business, new hires, product announcement, award).

Site events (launch, new feature, new ad campaign, personality visit to chat room, award).

It is safe to say that the vast majority of web operators we spoke with are event-driven. Most people seem to lack either the time or the discipline to use a calendar-triggered approach. While all seem to check their hit rates on a near-daily basis out of sheer curiosity, the kind of very thorough analysis needed to make informed choices about the future is done around key events.

Measurement Depth

In addition to deciding how often to evaluate measures, you must consider two other time-related issues:

❑ What granularity to use in collecting, consolidating, evaluating, and presenting measures.

❑ What measures are most valuable for trendlines and historical archiving for your site.

Granularity means the level of detail you select for your reports. Depending on your particular goals or the event for which you are preparing, you may be able to use simple roll-ups of measures like visits, downloads, and errors. On the other hand, you may need to break down specific metrics in detail to use them effectively. For instance, suppose you had to answer the question, "How many downloads of our demonstration software happen daily?" You would simply total the requests and report the number. However, if you were expected to answer the question, "How many *people* download our demonstration software daily," you would need considerably different data.

The other component of measurement depth is *history*. Some web site measures only need to be totaled, such as the distribution of visits by day of the week (see Figure 8.1). In this case, time only improves the accuracy of the measurement and there is no need to look at how it has changed over time. Conversely, some measures need to be looked at on a per-month, per-week, or per-day basis. An example of this is shown in Figure 8.2, which shows average visitor time spent at the site as a function of visitor depth (pages accessed). In this case, a site that doesn't keep visitors very long made a change to its splash page and wanted to see if retention improved. Totals are useless because they would mask the change. In Figure 8.2 you can see that the number of visitors staying past one page increased in the months following the change.

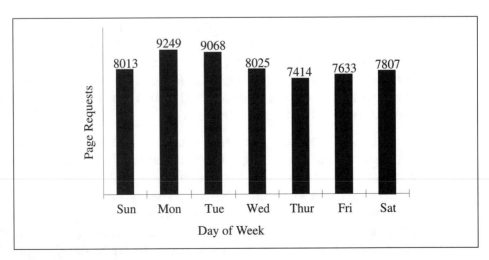

Figure 8.1 Visits by day of the week.

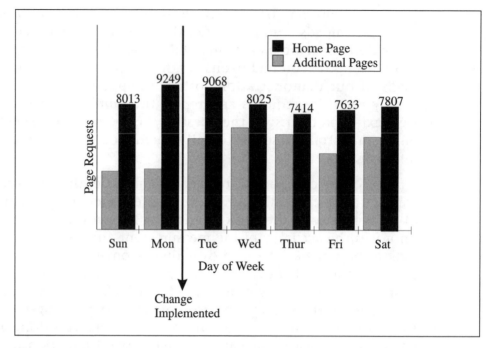

Figure 8.2 Average visitor time spent at the site as a function of pages accessed.

Consolidation versus Evaluation

While *evaluation* of site measures may often be event-triggered, you should carefully determine whether *consolidation* of site measures needs to be done on a calendar basis. Consolidation refers to the process of breaking a large web server log file down into specific measures of interest. This is critically important and often over-looked until it is too late. Here's why.

Let's say that your web site is taking 100,000 hits per day. Every hit results in a line being added to the log file describing what was requested. If the average log file entry is 100 characters, that equals 1 MB of growth every day. Now let's say your hard drive had 60 MB free when you finished your site (and you felt pretty good about having enough space). Just under 60 days later your log file would stop because there was no more room to write data. Depending on what server software you use, you may or may not be notified of the problem. If you only check statistics monthly and the drive runs out the day after you look at it in month two (as it inevitably will), you stand to lose up to 29 days of information for month three. Or, worse, the server may crash when free disk space reaches 0 MB.

This brings to mind a story which illustrates some of the previous points and puts data collection and evaluation in perspective.

EXAMPLE: TELEPHONE CALL TRACKING IS LIKE INTERNET SESSION TRACKING

The telephone call management system had been in place and running for about six months. The organization used the information generated by the system for its billing at the end of each month. Therefore, it did not need information from the system during the month and ignored the measures (call data) and measure consolidation (call costing).

At the end of each month, the call management program would scan the telephone call logs generated by the public business exchange (PBX) and extract call details, such as originating number, destination number, duration, and call routing (whether WATs, SPRINT, etc.). The activity entries for an individual call were scattered throughout the log, entered sequentially by time, as they occurred in the PBX. See Figure 8.3 for an example of a call log format.

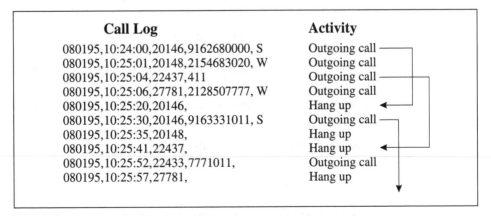

Figure 8.3 Call tracking is composed of individual activity entries, much like a web site access tracking log.

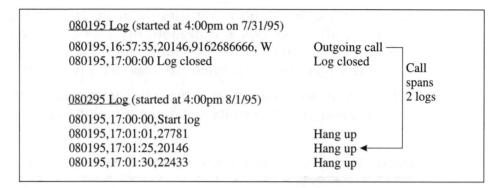

Figure 8.4 Call activity can span multiple logs based on call origin and duration, and the time when new logs are created.

Each month about 23 call logs were generated, one per workday, when the system was backed up daily at 5:00 PM before the office manager went home.

Based on the call log entries, the call management system consolidated the raw measures into a call record and calculated the cost for each call. The system was working great until one month one call log could not be recovered from the backup tape they were routinely stored on. Because raw measures (log entries) for a single call could be recorded across two log files, see Figure 8.4, the single missing daily log impacted call details entered in the prior log as well as the next log. The company lost one full day and portions of two other days, or 5 to 10 percent of its monthly billing for telephone use. Naturally, company personnel kept personal logs and much of the call information was recreated from their notes, but this took a lot of time away from servicing clients and delayed invoicing.

The moral of this story is collect and consolidate incrementally. Do not assume that you will always have required raw measures for future consolidation.

One easy method of averting the problem described in the example, is to divide the measurement process into two schedules—a

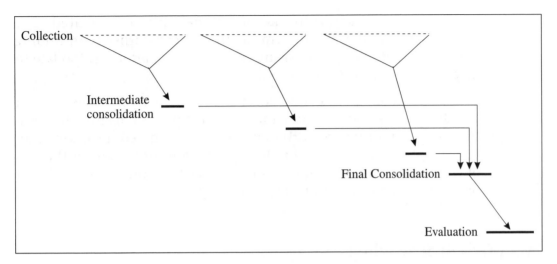

Figure 8.5 Overlapping schedules for measure collection, consolidation, and evaluation.

collection and consolidation schedule, and an evaluation schedule. The first schedule outlines when raw measures are extracted to produce interim consolidated measures and the second schedule defines when consolidated measures are used to calculate Impact Measures, as shown in Figure 8.5.

This process is facilitated by many of today's off-the-shelf web site analysis tools, which basically require you to download your log files to your PC in order to process them. More sophisticated tools are capable of *caching* old log information in a compressed format. This eliminates the need to constantly reprocess old log data and keeps hard drive space free. Chapter 7 outlines different approaches and tools for log data analysis.

For Microsoft's Internet Information Server (IIS) the first schedule could be done daily or weekly, when a new activity log is started, while the second schedule may be done monthly for site activity reporting purposes. If the dual schedule process had been used in the previous example, where consolidated calls were calculated on a daily basis for that day before the backup, all calls, except for those few that spanned the lost log and the previous or proceeding log, would have been saved. This approach ensures that you collect and process key information at the time it is created. The process also highlights problems as they occur, rather than finding a problem that prevents measure consolidation, after it is too late to do anything about it.

Unlike people, web sites don't maintain personal logs, so lost data is truly lost information and you must protect against that possibility. Maintaining both the raw and consolidated measures is an additional precaution, so that losing one does not result in the loss of the Impact Measure, and losing both at the same time is a lower probability with this built-in redundancy.

Event-Driven Scheduling

The following sections discuss scheduling Impact Measure evaluations and insuring that Raw and Consolidated Measures are available to allow you to calculate the required Impact Measures. No matter when you evaluate measures, the objective should be actionable results that:

> justify the ongoing operation of the site, as discussed in Chapter 9, or
>
> evolve site content, as discussed in Chapter 10, or
>
> evolve site strategy or promotion, as discussed in Chapter 11.

Think of these events as externally focused activities where Impact Measures are communicated to audiences who may not typically see site measures on a regular basis.

Business Events

The first category of event-driven scheduling is oriented around business events, such as

- ❏ Budgeting
- ❏ Quarterly or yearly company planning meetings
- ❏ Informal off-site planning meetings
- ❏ Press and analyst meetings or tours

Usually, the measures presented will be at a very high level of consolidation; also, they are:

- ❑ Selected to achieve ongoing justification, such as in budgeting
- ❑ Used as input for business planning
- ❑ Employed to drive home a point, such as in a press interview

Luckily, most events that fall into this category are scheduled with adequate lead-time or are repetitive in nature, such as annual or semi-annual budgeting events.

Virtually any of the Impact Measures identified in Chapter 5 may be used, based on site justification, or in response to specific questions from management. In preparation for such questions and as part of your planning and site operating procedures, you should collect and evaluate information which you predict may be of interest. For example, even if site justification is based on product promotion and niche marketing, such as for Toro, it is very reasonable that someone should ask about the site's impact on customer satisfaction or service. Prior to such events, you may want to expand your data collection and evaluation to cover areas which you do not normally track, but which may be of interest to the audience during these meetings or events.

Data collection is only as valuable as the relevancy of the data collected. If, for example, you collect lots of data, but miss data points during the highest site loading or don't collect a complete set of data, the data you have collected does not provide an accurate representation of site activity. There are four key aspects, as shown in Figure 8.6, that you must consider in your data collection process:

- ❑ **Periodicity:** Time-duration required in order to collect significantly relative data.
- ❑ **Period:** Time over which the data collection is activated. It could be for a day, week, month, or year.
- ❑ **Interval:** Time between data points. It can be a second, minute, part of a second, or any duration you believe is significant. The interval must be sufficiently small to ensure no critical measurement is missed, as shown in Figure 8.7.

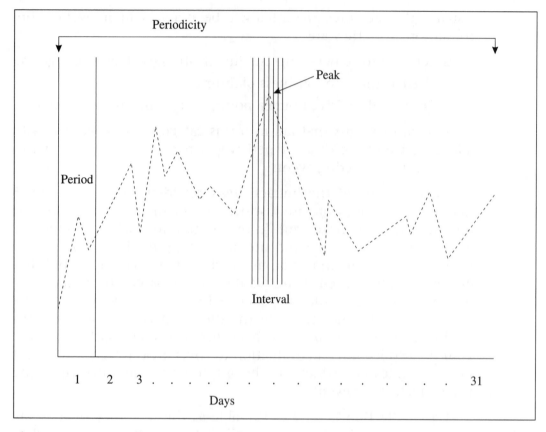

Figure 8.6 Data collection nomenclature.

❑ **Peak:** Highest measured value either for the period or the periodicity. For example, you may measure daily and monthly peaks for the data collected.

To illustrate the importance of data collection, consider an example we are all familiar with—monthly and quarterly financials. Based on the previous definitions:

❑ Periodicity is one month and three months.

❑ Period of collection is 30 days (end of month closing) and three sets of 30 days (quarterly report).

❑ Interval is event-based, rather than time-based, and is per invoice.

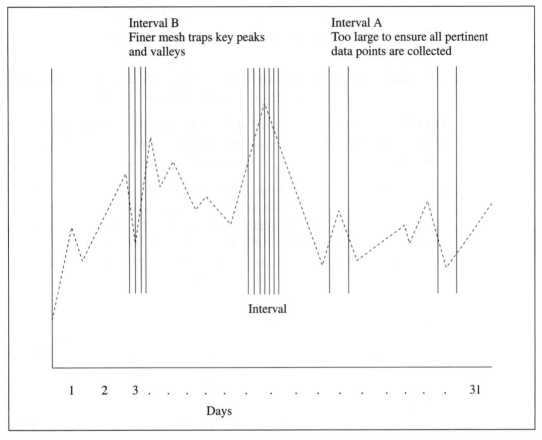

Figure 8.7 Data collection time interval must ensure no critical data is missed.

❑ Peaks can be equated to largest single invoice, highest daily total, and highest monthly total.

For example, if the collection mechanism misses one invoice, the totals will be off. If data is only collected for the first two months, the quarterly results will be off. If every second invoice is processed, and the results are doubled to get estimated totals, a large invoice (the peak) may be missed. The same issues are true for site measures, as explained later.

For statistically significant data, you should try to determine site periodicity and peaks, and collect data over one complete period of site activity and at peak intervals. For example:

❑ Toro's web site tends to have seasonal periodicity.

❑ The *Star Tribune*'s web site does not have an explicit periodicity.

❑ FedEx's web site does not have periodicity, but does have two or three peak periods, such as Christmas and Easter.

Therefore, to collect relevant data that provides a true picture of a site's impact, you must measure the site during normal periods, peak periods, and over one complete cycle. For example:

❑ Toro needs to collect data during a typical period, such as winter or spring, where the site's audience may be significantly different and have different needs. It should also recognize that the different seasonal measures may not be comparable; therefore, forecasting yearly activity based only on one season's measures may not be accurate.

❑ The *Star Tribune* needs to collect data for at least one month, including weekdays and weekends.

❑ FedEx needs to collect data over a typical month, probably not July or August when vacations slow business activity, or during a peak period, such as Christmas or Easter.

As you can see, evaluating a measure for an event may require preplanning, collecting, and consolidating raw data months prior to the event's actual date. Figure 8.8 illustrates how schedules for measure collection and consolidation, and evaluation could be coordinated for Toro's site. Note that while the primary evaluation is scheduled for just after the Spring sales season, intermediate evaluations are conducted to ensure that the collection and consolidation process is producing relevant results from the site.

Sales and Promotional Events

Because sales and promotional events are often discrete activities and may not be directly related to the basic site justification measures, evaluating these events often requires the following, as shown in Figure 8.9:

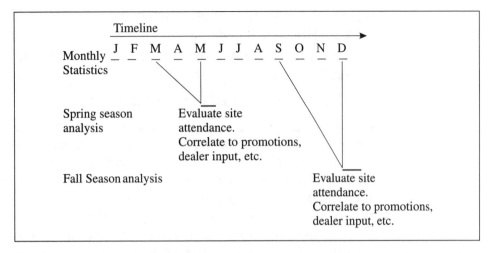

Figure 8.8 Scheduling measure collection, consolidation, and evaluation requires up-front planning.

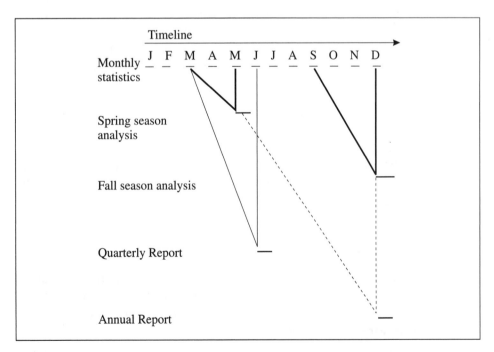

Figure 8.9 Modifying both measure collection and evaluation procedures to meet event needs.

❏ Modifying collection and consolidation of Raw Measures to track specific Impact Measures

❏ Evaluating the Impact Measures during and after the activity or event

Simple examples of this scheduling include:

❏ Measuring the increase in site activity based on a promotion campaign featuring the web site. This probably would not require a change in Raw Measure collection, as the basic measure would be site or page hits. To measure the increase requires existing trendlines of site activity. To get an accurate picture of how this promotion impacts the site, you may want to back previous promotion-related peaks out of the ongoing trendline. This ensures that previous promotions don't inadvertently diminish the significance of future ones.

❏ Tracking the sales of a product or service based on ordering availability through the site. If the order can be placed through the site, the Raw Measure would be the number of units ordered. Or, the raw measure may be non-site-oriented, such as the number of units sold through telesales where the site is mentioned as the customer's information source.

Once the event is completed, you may not have to, or want to, continue collecting the Raw Measures. The collection and evaluation of the measures may change from the individual event to a more generic event, such as advertising planning or sales meetings, where the Success Measures are evaluated not as individual data, but as part of a larger picture.

Site Events

These events typically have to do with planning for a site change or measuring the effect of an implemented site change. Therefore, these events basically require a combination of pre- and/or post-measure evaluation.

For example, if you are planning on upgrading the site, you may first want to do an audience survey to evaluate what percentage of the audience will potentially use the new features; then do post-implementation measures to track page hits on the new features and compare actual to survey results.

Often measure evaluations based on site events are related to trendlines which track how a site has changed over a specified period. This information is used to help evolve site contents, as discussed in Chapter 10.

A good rule of thumb for trend analysis is that data collection should cover at least two periods or a minimum of six months. For post-implementation measure evaluation, you should collect data over at least one period or three months minimum. Since both pre- and post-implementation data collection span relatively long times, it is very important that you:

❑ Conduct periodic consolidation of the Raw Measures to ensure no loss of data.

❑ Make preliminary evaluations of the Impact or Success Measures to verify that you are getting meaningful results on which to base further evaluation and decision making.

Calendar-Driven Scheduling

Calendar-driven evaluation tends to be used for internal tracking and site management, more so than for external communication. Though often, portions of these measures are used as input to event-driven evaluations. These evaluations are excellent to monitor:

❑ How the site is growing (hits, visits, and people)
❑ How visitors are using the site (how deep are they going, how long they stay, what is the most popular, what is the least popular, what are common search terms, etc.)
❑ Where visitors originate from
❑ What browsers and operating systems visitors are using
❑ How the site is performing
❑ Errors the site is experiencing
❑ Peak and average site use

You could look at every measure everyday, but you are not going to see much change in many of them and you will waste precious time that could be used for other tasks. The key is to understand when and what to look for as explained in the following sections.

Daily Evaluation

Measures that affect the health and viability of the site should be evaluated daily. These may include:

- ❏ Errors per day
- ❏ Average and maximum hits, visits, and people per hour
- ❏ Megabytes transferred per hour
- ❏ Average number of simultaneous users (i.e., server processes)
- ❏ Average CPU load
- ❏ Average memory consumption
- ❏ Remaining disk space
- ❏ Total number of hits per 24-hour period
- ❏ Number of sales per day
- ❏ Dollar volume of sales per day
- ❏ Number of failed login attempts per day

Evaluating the technical measures in this list will tell you if your site is experiencing problems, performance degradation, or exceeding capacity. You also want to monitor for security violations. While one day's measurements may not signal a problem, looking at the measures on a regular basis will allow you to track how the site is routinely operating and spot problems or problem indications. Daily measurement is important to the *Star Tribune*.

CASE STUDY

The *Star Tribune* is focused on daily news and, therefore, daily results of site activity are important to see how each story is received and accessed. It measures site activity daily with the intent of tracking usage of sections of the site and the number of hits per advertisement. For example, the *Star Tribune* wants to measure how many visitors look at metro news versus employment ads. As the paper provides extensive *niche* content, the type of stories viewed is also important to assess the demand for particular types of information.

Weekly Evaluation

Weekly evaluation should focus on those measures that create a mini-trendline of site usage for the week. Often, the measures include summarized daily measures for the week so that you can see trends that may not be apparent at the daily level and page hits by type per day and total per week. One example of summarized daily measures could be a slow growth in errors per week that is not evident from the day-to-day measures and signals a worsening problem at the site. Another example would be analyzing the days of the week and the hours of a day that tend to have the most traffic. Some sites are primarily hit from 8:00 A.M. to 5:00 P.M. Monday through Friday, while others get weekend and evening traffic. Obviously, daily information will not allow for such analysis.

While daily measures track the site's health, weekly measures are used to track the site's audience activity.

CASE STUDY

TORO Wallace originally monitored web site measurements daily, but now he tends to look at the data weekly. The measurements showed an initial spike when the site was first opened, then access dropped off slightly. After being online for about six months, visits are now growing at a healthy five to ten percent per month.

Monthly Evaluation

Impact Measures tend to be evaluated monthly or even quarterly. They provide general information on site usage and progress towards achieving site objectives. These measures provide information beyond the immediate health and activity of the site, such as:

❑ Revenue generated by site

❑ Maintenance cost per month

❑ Number of names added to e-mail list

❑ Number of surveys completed

❑ Number of free stuff items sent out

Certain *technical* measures are also generally consulted only on a monthly schedule. They include:

❑ Visitor point of origin (also called the originating domain)

❑ Most popular and least popular pages

❑ Average visit depth and duration

These measures can, for instance, help you determine the origins of your audience, or how a visitor navigates through the site. They may help you to:

❑ Verify assumptions

❑ Cross-check audience surveys

❑ Improve navigation through the site

CHAPTER 9

What Do Your Measures Mean?

The key to making good decisions from measurement data is in the interpretation process or methodology. History is full of examples where people have drawn wrong conclusions from accurate and relevant data. Of course, some people have a knack for getting to the right answer with nothing to go on. But, for most of us, to steer correctly between misinterpretation and instinct we need a roadmap to show the way. This chapter is that guide.

Part II discussed the various measures that apply to web sites and how they relate to one another. Chapter 8 described the important role of time in these measurements. This chapter and the remainder of the book address the final questions:

What do the measures tell you?

What actions should you take based on the measures?

How have others fared?

One of the best things about new technology and business opportunities is that you very rarely end up where you think you are headed. This is the thrill and adventure that drives most entrepreneurs. The key to most entrepreneurs and successful emerging businesses is adaptation. The key to successful web sites is also adaptation. Web site adaptation is driven by measuring and responding to audience feedback. Therefore, site justification is one reason for measuring and evaluating Impact Measures, but successful sites have quickly learned that these measures also provide excellent market and audience research. At the sites we interviewed, Impact Measures are actually being used more to evolve and improve the site, than for ongoing site justification.

Both site-specific and external organization Impact Measures provide hard data needed to:

❏ Support or refute your original justification strategy

❏ Determine if your site is improving or declining

❏ Select between competing ideas for improving the site

❏ Tell you when to promote your site

❏ Tell you when to discontinue a specific promotional strategy

❏ Identify if your site is providing unexpected benefits

❏ Explain a decision to shut the site down

Based on our research, the best way of analyzing your site is through the five-step *self-audit* process that we call the *Site Success Self-Test*. Each step uses Impact Measures to determine how previous actions affected the site and what actions you should take based on the latest measurements. This methodology ensures that you don't overlook either important problems or new opportunities for the site. The self-test follows the flowchart shown in Figure 9.1.

Of the five basic steps, the first three document where you've come from and the last two help you decide where you ought to be going.

❏ **Step 1:** Evaluate progress relative to justification objective

❏ **Step 2:** Rate the current status of the site

❏ **Step 3:** Identify unexpected results

❏ **Step 4:** Make evolutionary content changes, and/or

❏ **Step 5:** Revise site or promotion strategies

The steps are presented in a particular sequence because the results of a previous step can significantly impact the decisions and actions

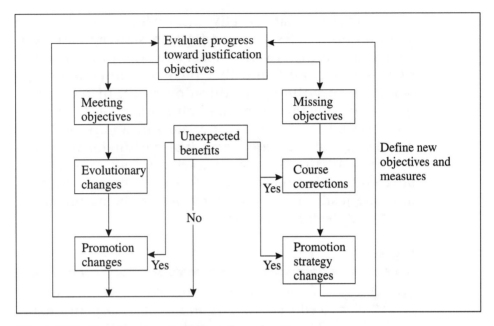

Figure 9.1 Site Success Self-Test flowchart.

formulated in subsequent steps. For example, if the site is not meeting its justification objectives, it may still be providing unexpected results in other areas. Our research clearly demonstrated that these other benefits can sometimes overshadow the original objectives for the site. Therefore, revised promotion strategies should perhaps focus on the unexpected benefits to encourage them further. On the other hand, some sites simply need minor changes to better target their original objectives. Because many times you don't have the resources or bandwidth to take both paths, herein lies the need for tough decision making. Measures can help you formulate those decisions using the self-test process discussed in detail throughout the remainder of this chapter.

Step 1: Site Justification Objectives

The basic question that should always be answered first is whether the site is meeting its initial justification objectives. If the site has a focused single objective, it is generally easier to tell if the site is hitting or missing that objective. If, for instance, the site is focused around online sales, the justification strategy based on increased sales is a straightforward Impact Measure to calculate. With most sites, however, we found that there are either several justification objectives or no initial justification at all. In the former case, the site will usually meet some and miss others. In the latter case, since there was no goal, you can only measure and record how the site is progressing. In this case, the initial measurements form a de facto baseline. All the sites we interviewed use measures to evaluate progress toward critical success factors. Following are case studies of how site justification and objectives are being measured and analyzed by different organizations.

CASE STUDY

FedEx Surveys and research have been used to get customer feedback. Results show that site performance rating is in the high 90s, which is as high as overall customer satisfaction with FedEx. Also, financial savings for the site are significant, as discussed in the next section.

CASE STUDY

The *Star Tribune* is tracking very closely to its R&D budget, therefore the feeling is that the financial objective is being met. Additionally, the paper is happy with the level of site usage and the ratio of page views to users (also known as average visit depth). Currently, the ratio is about 10 to 1 which indicates that visitors are spending significant time looking at various stories, sports, weather, and so forth on the site.

Most justification objectives are not precise, since they are based on a combination of hard data, estimates, and often assumptions. Therefore interpreting whether the objective has been achieved likewise has some latitude for interpretation.

CASE STUDY

Like the intranet sites that were interviewed, especially Silicon Graphics (SGI) discussed in Chapter 12, the Senate site has a large collective "ownership" of site content, where different entities have different criteria for measuring site success. At the most basic level, the Senate computer center considers the site a success because it provides Internet presence to the Senate. Individual Senators feel that the site has varying degrees of success, just as individual departments on an intranet rate the site based on how well their individual needs are being met.

Today the site provides a single external Internet identity for the Senate, has a growing attendance, and is within budget. All these measures point to a successful first implementation of an Internet site.

CASE STUDY

According to Wallace, "Toro is very pleased with the reception of the site. I doubt that we would ever shut down or obsolete it." The only reason he could foresee that would precipitate shutdown is Internet gridlock. Toro views the site as a proven marketing and advertising tool, and will make it available as long as people expect it to be on the Internet. The four major values that Toro believes it is receiving from its Internet presence are:

❑ Brand image

❑ Communication of product knowledge to potential customers, which reduces the sales cycle

❑ Heavy access of the dealer locator database, which helps get potential customers into the dealer showroom

❑ Heavy access of the *hot deals* page, which generates a database of visitor names and demographic data via a *free stuff* area and other features

Toro had a "soft" objective of achieving 50,000 people visits (as opposed to hits or page views) for the first year of site operation.

This equated to about $1.00 per person based on implementation costs. Currently, Toro believes the site is on target. But, what if at the end of one year the visits measured 45,454 with an equivalent cost of $1.10 per person? Does this difference mean that the company missed the objective? The original objective was a "gut feel" estimate and, though unspecified, there were certainly other implicit aspects to the objective which may or may not have been enumerated. These were that:

- Site use would show growth month-to-month.
- Critical pages relating to certain site features would have a high visit rate as a percentage of overall site traffic.
- Investments in promoting the site would result in demonstrated traffic increases.

If Toro achieved these three implicit objectives as well as 90 percent or more of its hit rate objective, the intent, if not the actual measures, of the objective was certainly met. If on the other hand, Toro achieved the target hit rate for the year, but hits per month had fallen over the last quarter and the percentage of critical page access versus overall traffic was low, then it is reasonable to say that "the operation was a success, but that the patient is dying."

A good rule of thumb for determining if an objective has been met is to list the explicit objective, any implicit objectives, and evaluate each objective to determine how well the actual measures meet the intent of the explicit objective. Based on this analysis, there are four possible cases, as mapped in Figure 9.2:

1. The hard data is 80 percent or more of the primary objective, and the implicit objectives are being met. This is the best of all possibilities. You should consider the objective as having been met.

2. The hard data is 80 percent or more of the primary objective, but the implicit objectives are not being met. This is the most difficult of the four possible scenarios. It may indicate that the site is doing as well as could be expected and that the target is just too high to reach. Or, it may indicate that the site is really headed toward major problems.

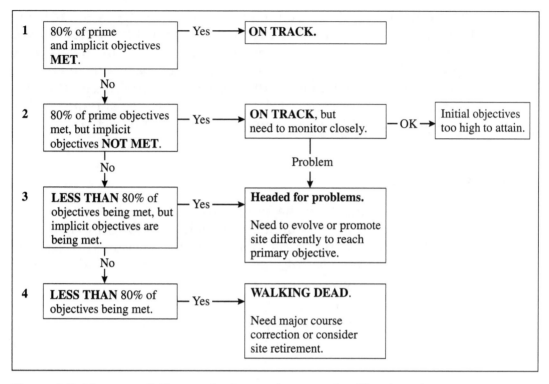

Figure 9.2 How to tell if your site is meeting your justification objectives.

3. The hard data is less than 80 percent of the primary objective, but the implicit objectives are being met. You should consider the objective as not having been met. There are potentially ways that you can use the measures to help evolve or promote the site to reach the primary objective, as discussed in Chapters 10 and 11.

4. The hard data is less than 80 percent of the primary objective and the implicit objectives are not being met. This is the worst possible case. It probably indicates that the original objective was flawed or completely unobtainable. You should consider the objective as not having been met, and consider the need for a major change in the objective and/or site, as discussed in Chapter 11.

Except for case four, the following discussion can help you determine if the site is on track, headed for major problems, or one of the "walking dead." For case four, site performance is so far below target and expectations that the measures probably cannot tell you what went wrong. Instead of spending time evaluating details when the overall site is in trouble, you should step back and re-visit the planning process. Chapter 11 discusses how to re-evaluate the site's strategy and promotion to determine if the site should be shut down, overhauled, or operate under a new set of objectives.

Step 2: Site Status

To best understand how the site is progressing you should rely on trendlines. Trendlines, examples of which are shown in Figures 9.3 and 9.4, provide an historical look at specific measures. This allows you to see how the measures have changed over time and to predict how they are likely to change in the future.

In Figure 9.3, the page views trendline shows growing 1996 month-to-month page requests volume over 1995. However, Figure 9.4's trendline for the same site shows that the view rate on *critical*

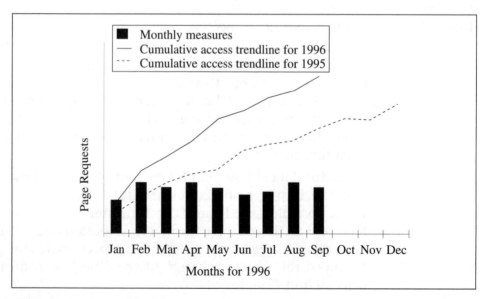

Figure 9.3 Trendline of page views for two periods, 1995 and 1996 year-to-date.

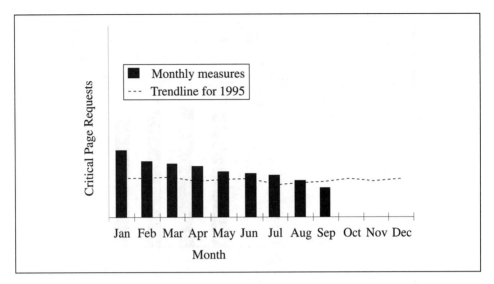

Figure 9.4 Trendline of critical page hits for 12-month period.

pages is dropping each quarter over the last nine months and is below the 1995 trend. This may indicate that, based on Figure 9.4, people visiting the site

Comprise a less-qualified audience

Represent more "looky loos" than potential prospects or customers

Find the site but, when considered with Figure 9.3, are unhappy with the site and don't stay long

Trendlines can also be used to compare:

Quantitative measures, as illustrated in the previous figures

Qualitative measures, such as level of customer satisfaction or site acceptance, as illustrated in Figure 9.5

Your site can also be compared against trendlines for competitors or industry averages, as shown in Figure 9.6. There is a whole industry starting for companies that provide independent compilation and/or auditing of site statistics. Often times, these companies can benchmark your type of organization relative to others. Generally, this is not detailed data because sources must be concealed, nor

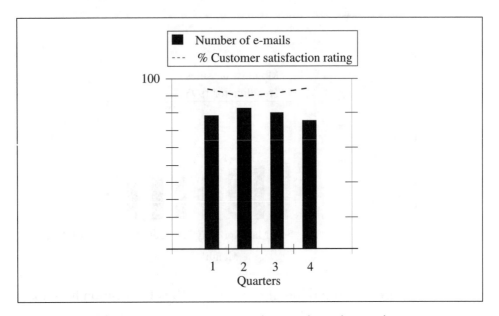

Figure 9.5 Trendline of customer satisfaction based on subjective rating (1-10) of customer e-mails.

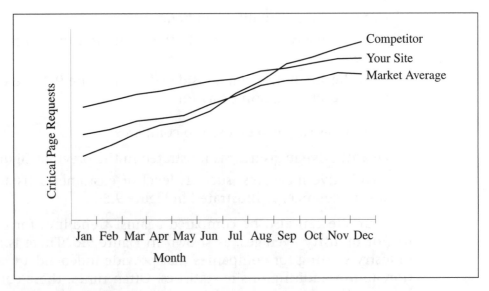

Figure 9.6 Trendline of your site activity compared to market averages and competitive sites.

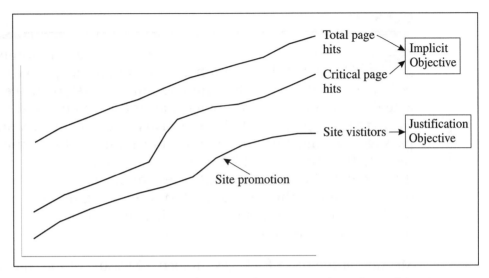

Figure 9.7 Trendline of justification objective and implicit objectives.

is such information inexpensive. However, the general measures shown in Figure 9.6 indicate that the market is catching up with your site and that potentially one competitor has surpassed your site. As with most market research, this is often a good way to checkpoint your progress.

If we apply the use of trendlines further, the primary and implicit objectives can be graphed, as shown in Figure 9.7. The trendlines show cumulative views year-to-date (YTD), customer satisfaction, and time per visitor spent at the site. These trends show that as attendance increased, the level of site satisfaction and time spent at the site decreased. This may indicate performance problems that are frustrating users or it may indicate that promotion is drawing "crowds," but the visitors don't find the site interesting enough to stay around.

Improving Site

Generally, if trendlines are all going up from left to right, you are making progress toward your goals. Following are case studies of the growth of web site use for the target companies.

CASE STUDY

FedEx Independent research and initial assumptions antici-
Federal Express pated that a significant portion of the people using the
web site would have called the 800-number. As you'll see shortly,
actual measures are much higher than initial estimates. Results also
show that 75 percent of the site visits also include a visit to the
package tracking page. In three to four months of operation, more
than 1,000 customers and 20,000 packages were being handled per
day through the web site. While these numbers are small relative to
overall business, the Web is the fastest-growing method of support
for FedEx. With these measures FedEx has reached one important
point of the larger strategy:

Measure of the site = Packages shipped = Measure of the company.

Just to give you some actual measures, site activity in mid-1996 is
250,000 visitors per month and 375,000 packages tracked per
month.

CASE STUDY

 Between March 12 and August 24, 1996, the service has
TRAVELOCITY provided to its consumers:

Total registered members of 248,948 with 63,601 per month

Total site visits of 2,424,375 with 679,013 per month

Total page views of 29,045,510 with 8,332,535 per month

Total hits of 95,846,750 with 27,707,729 per month

The site is on a very steep growth curve and the Internet is proving to be a very viable commercial media. Figure 9.8 lists the
breadth of services offered by the site that generate the very impres-
sive numbers previously listed.

Figure 9.8 Listing of Travelocity services offered to a visitor.

CASE STUDY

There has been a steady growth of visitors over the last year, which may be attributed largely to the overall growth of the Internet. Additionally, most visitors, based on time of access, appear to be from the East coast. Tracking originating domains indicates that many visitors are from educational sites.

Besides a new Senator home page drawing more visitors, several activities have generated site attendance peaks, including:

Internet protect day held in Spring 1996

Senator Ashcroft's online survey concerning term limits for Senators.

Site measures are reported using Excel spreadsheets and graphs based on Raw Measures collected from the UNIX software the site is running. The Senate site is one of the few which shows measures online, as illustrated in Figure 9.9

Senate site measures are available at (http://www.senate.gov/others/stats.html), and the sample graph of daily Senate web server requests is available at (http://www.senate.gov/others/daily.gif).

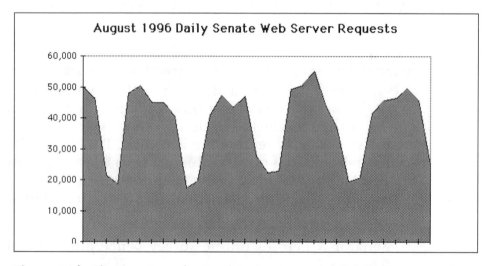

> ▲ **The United States Senate**
>
> ## Senate Web Usage Statistics
>
> * Last Month's Daily Requests (Chart)
> * Last Month's Hourly Requests (Chart)
> * Monthly Requests Comparison (Chart)
>
> Return to the United States Senate Home Page
> Send comments to webmaster@scc.senate.gov
> Last modified September 3, 1996

Figure 9.9a The Senate web site showing web usage statistics.

Figure 9.9b The Senate web site showing a graph of daily Senate web server requests.

Site Is Improving, but Needs Work

If some of the trendlines are going up while others are flat or going down, as shown in Figure 9.10, you need to analyze the trends. Unfortunately, there may not be sufficient historical information to really analyze the trends; therefore you may have to guess at the reasons that may be causing the trend. In Figure 9.10 you can read-

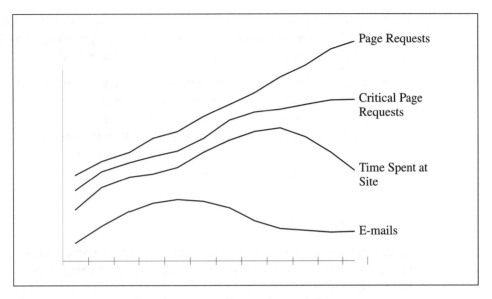

Figure 9.10 Example where trendlines show different patterns.

ily see that people are not spending time at the site (viewing more pages), but you don't have sufficient data to tell you why. You would have to use site-specific feature measures, as discussed in Chapter 4, to get further information to help evolve the site and increase audience longevity.

If no increase in site visits was measured after a site promotional effort, the reason may be:

- ❑ The promotion did not reach the target audience.
- ❑ The promotion reached the audience, but did not stimulate the audience to visit the site more often.
- ❑ The promotion reached the audience, but they could not reach you due to technical problems, server load, or incompatibilities with their browsers.
- ❑ The target audience is *saturated*; to increase site activity will require reaching other secondary audiences.

After listing the reasons that may have caused the lack of response or other poor trend response, put together a plan to address the most likely cause. For instance, if you are using direct mail with a list you trust and come to find out only five percent of your customer base visited the site, then the most likely cause of the problem was the message. It did not motivate a call to action to visit the site.

You can apply this simple process to any trendline which does not appear to be growing or not growing as fast as you would like it to be. It is even important to perform the same analysis on "good" trendlines so that you understand precisely why things are working. This will prepare you for future downturns and for tough managers who pose tough questions about both success and failure.

"Walking Dead" Site

If all the trendlines show flat or decreasing site attendance, then the site is effectively one of the "walking dead." As the saying goes, "Either you are progressing or falling behind. You are never standing still."

When this happens, you should immediately follow these steps to arrive at a plan of action:

- ❑ Examine the promotional strategies to determine if the site URL is being communicated effectively to the target audience.
- ❑ Re-evaluate the original solution and justification process to determine why the site is not providing the expected value and benefits.

Let's examine these issues more closely.

Analyze Measures

Analyzing the measures may point out that most site visitors are simply "passing through" and few get to the important pages. Therefore, they won't realize the value of the site which may mean that few return for a second visit. Or, the measures may indicate that the visitors originate from domains that you didn't expect and few come from domains that you did expect. For instance, most visitors could be international, when you expected at least 50 percent to be domestic. Another problem could be site-responsiveness, where slow speed access coupled with excessive graphics frustrates the visitors. Typically, this is reflected by a large drop between the number of visitors who request one page and those requesting two or more pages.

Examining the measures will tell you how the site is being used. Next you have to compare that with what you expected, planned for, and implemented.

Site Promotion

Based on our interviews and case studies, it appears that many Internet users are beginning to use the system as an online library or Yellow Pages. When they need information, they go looking for it. When they want information on a company, they search for its web page. This means that getting your site registered with many search engines such as Yahoo!, Infoseek, and Excite is very important. However, this alone is probably not sufficient to attract a large attendance. If it was, companies wouldn't be using other forms of traditional advertising to get name recognition. Companies, like the *Star Tribune*, who own or can purchase space in a traditional media vehicle in which to publish their URL repetitively have a high probability of reaching their target audiences. But, companies without large advertising budgets need to find other ways of distributing their URL. If you haven't promoted the site, try one or two approaches. If you have been promoting the site, try a few new approaches. Remeasure attendance and see if promotion, or the lack of it, is your problem.

Back-to-Basics

The last step is to restart at the beginning and re-examine the original need, proposed solution, and justification for the site. It may be that actual hard data has proven the solution or justification flawed. You may also have overestimated the need. Maybe, the Internet technology enamored everyone into trying to apply it to a problem when another solution was actually better. If re-examination does not develop any plans that seem reasonable for improving or evolving the site, then you may have to consider shutting down the site and cutting your loses. Before making such a decision, read Chapter 11 on evolving site strategy and promotion.

Step 3: Looking for and Evaluating Unexpected Benefits

The second most gratifying outcome of evaluating site measures is the discovery and quantification of unexpected benefits. (The first is meeting the original objectives.) Two of the best examples that we have discovered are from FedEx and the *Star Tribune*.

CASE STUDY

FedEx
Federal Express
Two anticipated cost savings, that were not used as justification strategies, but none-the-less are important to note and probably were much better than expected are discussed herewith.

We can't disclose the exact savings on 800-number calls, but a research study commissioned by FedEx has shown that well in excess of 50 percent of the 20,000 packages tracked per day through the site would have been 800-number calls to the call center. At $2.00 to $5.00 per call, that is a significant dollar savings.

The average cost in the software industry to distribute a diskette is about $6.00. There have been over 140,000 copies of FedEx Ship and other shipping document preparation software distributed through the web site as downloads. This represents over a half-million dollar savings in approximately one year.

CASE STUDY

Online Star Tribune MINNEAPOLIS/ST. PAUL
The *Star Tribune* reduced the amount of horse racing coverage in its newspaper because of lack of perceived reader interest. Then, the paper realized that for information-hungry sports fans this gave them an opportunity for online readership. It found that Internet users, predominately male audi-

ence, were very willing to use the web site to gets detailed sports information, particularly on Canterbury Park, the local race track.

Unexpected site benefits are usually discovered in one of two ways:

- Collecting and evaluating a broad range of raw measures which leads to the discovery or quantification of the benefit, such as in the FedEx case.

- Informal remarks or an unexpected occurrence, such as increased visitor traffic at Toro's site during the East coast blizzard. The site provided essentially mail-order product ordering for customers outside the Northeast where the local dealers were sold out of winter type products, specifically snow blowers. Other national dealers who had product on hand to sell were located by site visitors through the dealer locator. Northeast dealers, other dealers, and Toro all benefited from the site and the process resulted in many sales which, in previous years, would not have been made. Best of all, Toro managed to do this without going into the direct sales business, which would have caused difficulties with their dealers.

The lesson learned in talking with site managers was don't be too focused on a single objective. Expect the site to be a learning experience and actively look for new ideas, value, and benefits. Watch and listen to how the audience uses the site and always be willing to evolve the site. There is no "right" approach to a site at this time—the medium is too new and user preferences are evolving too quickly. As a colleague is fond of saying, "It's 1960 and no one knows what the game show is yet."

CASE STUDY

TORO By studying the average session duration of visitors, Toro knows that the typical visitor stays for nearly seven minutes. When compared with the cost of a 30-second broadcast commercial, the web site has proven to provide extremely inexpensive niche marketing. It also provides far more trustworthy measurement data, as the site provides the capability to measure the exact number of views. Running a TV commercial does not guarantee that the target audience will see it or allow you to measure exactly how many saw it.

Step 4: Making Evolutionary Content Changes

If your site is meeting its objectives, growing, and perhaps even providing some unexpected benefits, you will want to continue measuring and fine-tuning the site, but you shouldn't have to plan on any revolutionary changes in content, strategy, or promotion.

If the site is doing well, the following rules provide guidelines for making incremental, controlled changes to the site that will improve it without disrupting its reliability, interoperability, content, audience acceptance, or performance.

Rule 1

The first rule of thumb is don't try to evolve the site's core technology too often. Core technology includes the server platform, operating system, web server software, and communication interfaces, such as modems, lines, and firewalls. Every time core technology is changed you run the risk of reliability, performance, and interoperability problems. Bundle changes of this nature into one or two per year and test them thoroughly before releasing the changes into production.

Rule 2

The second rule of thumb is fix problems as you find them. Since most sites have multiple issues, encompassing browser compatibility, server load, database glitches, and many other problems, it is important to prioritize them. If you have limited resources, a suggested prioritization order is:

❑ **Priority 1:** Changes that improve data accuracy
❑ **Priority 2:** Changes that make navigation work better

❑ **Priority 3:** Changes in compatibility

❑ **Priority 4:** Changes in look

Rule 3

The third rule of thumb is there are two ways of evolving a site. The first method is by adding or changing major content or navigation. For example, Travelocity plans to upgrade its entire site to use Java in order to provide new levels of service to its customers. Toro created a complete parallel site that was compatible with AOL.

The second method is to make small incremental changes to content or navigation aspects of the site. An example would be adding new product-line information, updating pricing, or previewing new pages on corporate background information.

For major content or navigational changes, you should plan on no more than two per year. This is important because visitors learn *how* to move around your site and don't want to have to re-learn the process, unless it provides significant advantages to them.

Incremental changes can be rolled into the site on a periodic basis or on an as-needed basis in direct response to audience feedback or to fix a problem. The *Star Tribune*, as described later, makes one type of incremental change almost hourly (weather forecasts) and has made other incremental changes to format and navigation based on audience feedback. Other changes can be directed toward resolving specific problems or perceptions of the site.

Rule 4

The only required changes are those that:

❑ Fix bugs

❑ Keep the site responsive

❑ Grow capacity to meet demand

Discretionary changes can improve and expand the site, but

❑ Make them in a controlled fashion,

❑ Test them well before release, and

❑ Don't impact or replace existing capabilities.

Even if your site measures indicate that the site is successful, you will probably have requirements that dictate changes in site content to better meet your audience's needs. Chapter 10 discusses in more detail the four basic content changes you should consider:

- ❑ Mix
- ❑ Presentation
- ❑ Navigation
- ❑ Transmission

Step 5: Revising Site or Promotion Strategies

If your site is not meeting its objectives, then simply remodeling its content as previously discussed and further elaborated on in Chapter 10 won't be enough to solve your problems. You will have to re-evaluate your site strategy and promotion plan to determine your site's problems.

A Methodology for Evaluating Strategy and Promotion Choices

For the following discussion, you may wish to first revisit the web site life cycle presented in Chapter 1. The following discussion of strategy and promotion uses the key life cycle phases to analyze, based on your measurements, why your site is failing. Specifically, you must answer a sequence of questions in order to determine where the site is failing. These questions include:

Is the site achieving its objectives? (Objective-Setting)

Is the site drawing the desired visitor demographic? (Audience Analysis)

Having arrived, do visitors find the content of value and use it? (Content Selection)

Do the current methods of communicating the site's existence succeed in drawing desired levels of traffic? (Promotion Planning)

A decision tree describing the major points of this methodology is shown in Figure 9.11. Our research suggests that it is best to tackle strategy issues in the same order in which you originally decided them. Just as your choice of objective fed your choice of audi-

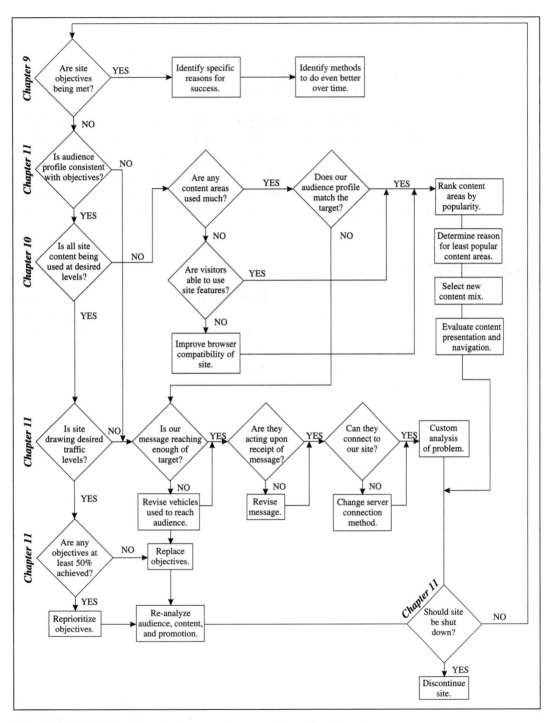

Figure 9.11 Web site strategy and promotion decision tree.

ence, then content, so, too, will a change in objective require a new audience and content definition. By retracing your steps, it is easier to accurately assess the cause of your problem.

Actually, the flowchart in Figure 9.11 applies equally well to a successful as an unsuccessful site. It is often as important to analyze a successful site to understand why it has been successful, as it is to analyze an unsuccessful site. Chapter 11 discusses in detail how to analyze your measures and use the acquired information to modify site strategy and promotion or, when appropriate, to retire the site.

Measures Make the Site

Measures provide much more than justification for the site. As previously shown, they can be used as input to evolve and improve the site, as well as to determine if the site should be shut down. This chapter discussed how to use measures to determine the *health* of the site while Chapters 10 and 11 discuss how to use measures to evolve and change the site.

10

Content Evolution Choices

Y ou've analyzed the impact of your web site using the methodologies described earlier and you know that the site content needs to change. What are your options? This chapter looks at the central issues of web site content, as documented by our research and our own experience. To make your choices simpler, we have organized these issues into four overall categories:

- ❏ Content mix
- ❏ Content presentation
- ❏ Content navigation
- ❏ Content transmission

Recall from Chapter 9 that there is a pivotal difference between content evolution and strategy evolution for web sites. Broadly speaking, strategy addresses the contribution of the site back to the organization and the method by which you attract visitors. Strategy evolution choices are considered in Chapter 11. Content means the tools or tactics you use to achieve the strategy. Put differently, if you wanted to build a house, the blueprints and choice of lot are your strategy, while the specific choice of carpet, fixtures, paint color, and cabinets used for the finished house is the content. Over time, the content of a web site is evolved or modified to:

1. Better meet basic audience needs, thereby providing better value and benefits.

2. Maintain audience interest and increase the return rate of visitors.

3. Attract new audience.

4. Implement new features.

5. Maintain server performance, reliability, and interoperability with user systems.

The first four changes require information about the audience. You need to understand their likes and dislikes, needs, and perception of the existing site. If you are selling through the site, you also need to understand product mix, price points, and promotional impact on your sales. The fifth change is not audience-specific, and requires monitoring generic site measures, such as hit rates, response time, and browser types used by the audience.

One critical prerequisite for making good content evolution choices is to have good visitor feedback. Never lose sight of the fact that you may have built your web "house," but you don't live there; the visitors do. Therefore, it is imperative that you provide clear methods throughout your site for every visitor to tell you what he or she thinks. Encourage their use. Respond to them as much as possible. Content decisions made in a vacuum can only result in a failed site.

Some of the most interesting lessons from our case studies appear in this chapter; each example helps drive home these points. Frankly speaking, most web sites aren't old enough to really warrant a serious look at strategy yet. But many sites are remodeling and building additions. We'll look at some eye-opening issues confronted by Federal Express, the Minneapolis *Star Tribune*, and others over the next several pages.

As in Part II, each time a measure appears, it is followed by a letter in parenthesis which denotes its level in the hierarchy:

Impact Measures are shown with an (I).

Approximated Measures are shown with an (A).

Consolidated Measures are shown with a (C).

Raw Measures are shown with an (R).

Content Mix

In any web site, the *mix* of different kinds of content is a deliberate choice designed to achieve the objective(s) of the site. In our view, content mix is very different from content navigation (which we will study later in this chapter). Specifically, we use the term *mix* to refer to distinct types of content, regardless of location at the site. We use the term *navigation* for travel between locations.

Examples of Content Mix

Just because you have five different icons or hyperlinks to choose from on a home page doesn't mean that there are five types of content. Three of the five could be (and often are) information on different product lines. In this case, if the other two choices are an e-mail response page and a free stuff page, you have only three content types.

In Figure 10.1, we have identified each type of information, entertainment, or other feature at the site regardless of depth and complexity. Most sites will have a mix of custom content and common features. Custom content is usually specific to the purpose of the site itself, such as the online catalog at an online store. Common features were presented at length in Chapter 4 and include things like e-mail response pages, online quizzes, chat rooms, and many other similar features.

Measures Affecting Content Mix

Specific Raw and Consolidated Measures should be consulted as you evaluate your content mix. Consolidated Measures include the following:

Average annual per-customer purchases (C) and percentage of buying visitors (C): If one objective of your site is to sell products or services,

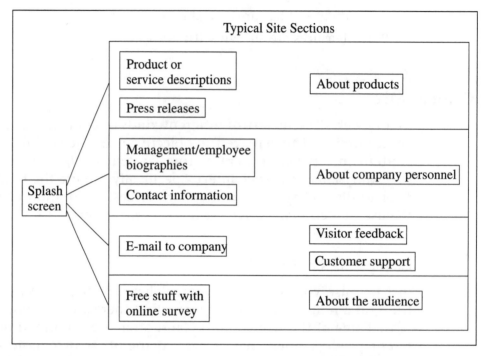

Figure 10.1a Common content mixes found on the public Internet—typical site sections.

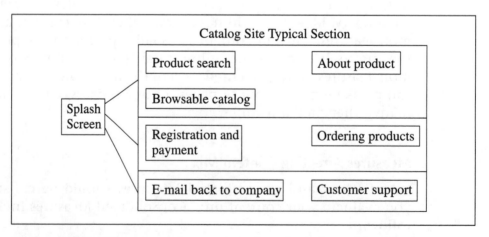

Figure 10.1b Common content mixes found on the public Internet—catalog site sections.

then you should be closely monitoring how much each visitor spends with you. If the figure is below your expectations, altering the content mix could improve results. Some possible analyses include:

❑ The products or services you are selling may not be matching the interests of the visitors you are attracting. Look at the demographics returned by survey forms and e-mails to see if there is a close match. If not, your content mix and/or promotional activities are not drawing the right crowd.

❑ You may be making shopping too hard. If you are emphasizing browsing, but customers want to quickly search for items, then visitors may leave without buying. Conversely, you may only have a search feature but your visitors want to window-shop.

❑ Your content mix may be less compelling than a competitor's site.

Top visit-generating promotions (C): A sure way to tell what appeals to visitors is to look at the roll-ups of page views (R) to see which promotion methods resulted in visits to various parts of your site. Ineffective promotions tied to specific types of content should be discontinued, as should the content.

Raw Measures that affect the content mix include the following:

Downloads(R): This is a particular type of content. If you offer material for download, compare your actual counts with your targets. Low or high performance may indicate that a change is due.

E-mail categories: Pay close and constant attention to e-mail complaints (R), e-mail praise (R), and e-mail resolutions (R). Your visitors are your best intelligence on how the site is doing.

E-mail frequency (R): If you're not getting much e-mail, you should be concerned. Our research conclusively demonstrates that visitors often exercise their first amendment rights. A good rule of thumb is that total monthly e-mails should be at least one-half of one percent of the total page view count for that month. If you can track sessions (as opposed to page views), you should aim for at least a 3 percent response rate. Many sites do significantly better than this. If yours isn't, go back to see how strongly you emphasize e-mail response.

Number of sessions with only one page request (R): This could mean that the visitors couldn't see your page (see Content Transmission later). Or, it could mean that they saw it, but weren't swept off their feet.

Page views (R): Look closely at which parts of your site draw the most and least traffic. High-traffic areas should be emphasized. You may want to rethink low-traffic spots.

Platform type (R): On the off chance that you offer content specific to one type of computer (Windows, Macintosh, UNIX, etc.) you should keep an eye on the platform type (R). If your visitors differ substantially in the platform they are using, you could be turning off perfectly good visitors.

Referring links (R): This is an incredibly valuable tool. A referring link tells you the URL a visitor was last at *before coming to your page*. This can provide useful intelligence about thinking patterns. For instance, let's say (hypothetically) that Toro noticed that many people linked to its site from the Home Decorating list on Yahoo!. Toro might want to increase its emphasis on outdoor lighting products as a result.

Session time limit (R): Knowing how long people stay at your site is a good way to decide if your content is really captivating. Good sites capture people for at least five minutes per visit.

Total web customers (C), total web item revenue (C), and total web items sold (C): See the comments under average annual per-customer purchases (C) previously presented.

Evolving Your Content Mix

Of the five content issues looked at in this chapter, mix is the most directly tied to strategy. Therefore, content mix usually changes under two circumstances:

The strategy associated with a given site changes.

The strategy is not being achieved with the current mix.

Both situations are common. In the Toro, Federal Express, and *Star Tribune* case studies presented here, the strategy of the site expanded which, in turn, required additions to the content mix. Toro's strategic decision to include custom dealer presence under its web umbrella necessitated adding both new user features as well as a way for dealers to periodically update their listings. The *Star Tribune*, on the other hand, found that content requirements changed in two significant ways as explained in the *Star Tribune* case study below.

CASE STUDY

Like many companies, Toro tries to maintain a certain brand image. Toro has found that the Internet brings new dimensions and issues to controlling your brand image, which are not directly related to nor dependent on having or not having a web site. For example, historically a dealer that wanted to run an advertisement or a short TV commercial was limited in the audience it could reach because of cost considerations. However, on the Internet the cost of creating a web page is relatively low and potential distribution or access is virtually unlimited. Therefore, for only a few dollars dealers can reach a large audience. And, if the dealer's presentation is not professionally done, it can reflect negatively on Toro's brand recognition. This new development was a surprise to management. As a side effect of the web site, Toro believes that, in retrospect, its Internet presence provides more brand image control. First it establishes a site that most users will see if they are searching for Toro information; second, with the site, dealers are more inclined to integrate with or leverage the Toro site rather than create their own.

CASE STUDY

The *Star Tribune* discovered that many visitors use the site as a reference library. They remember reading an article and want to see it again or show it to someone. Therefore, site and story aging become a significant issue. Some site content is aged based on contractual requirements, such as AP stories which are deleted after 14 days, while other content is at the discretion of the *Star Tribune*. Currently, most items are maintained for three weeks, but this is an area that may change.

Another area that is affecting site content and evolution relates to changing objectives for the site. For instance, some advertisers have told the *Star Tribune* they are getting customer traffic driven to them from the web site. These early measures indicate that web advertising may be paying off, which may lead to the next step of content-specific advertising, something that is easy to do electronically, but impossible to do in a newspaper.

The *Star Tribune* is also using online commerce in the form of classified ads for both auto and home sales. Initially this just involved republishing classified ads that had previously appeared in the newspaper. Now, in the areas of real estate and automotive ads, the *Star Tribune*'s web site includes databases that go significantly beyond the classified ads that appear in the daily newspaper and the site is focused on attracting the consumer.

On the other hand, there are an awful lot of sites that aren't coming anywhere close to achieving their objectives. Sometimes this is a result of the business strategy being wrong. Classic examples of this outcome include the *USA Today* Online and the Utne Lens sites. In the case of the Utne Lens, projections for paid advertising at its web site never materialized. This forced a complete reconfiguration of the content mix to enable the company to produce a continuing online presence at the actual funding level. The Utne Lens case study is discussed in Chapter 11.

Sometimes the content mix is not adequate. We studied many web sites where visitors come expecting a specific kind of content based on their knowledge of the site sponsor, but fail to find it. Some well-known companies don't include all of their product lines due to time or budget constraints, but visitors who come expect to find everything. Another example is Toro's experience that many customers want online product manuals. No one knew this would be needed in the original site planning session. But a steady percentage of site e-mails request this feature. In this case, Toro is achieving its objective but could make the site even better for some visitors. Fortunately, visitors will be very frank with you about what they think you should have at your site.

Many companies evolve their sites to meet customer requirements for a complete capability comparable to non-web systems currently in place. FedEx is a good example of this type of content enhancement.

CASE STUDY

FedEx In the absence of any other justification, customer usage satisfaction is the key to keeping the site and is the criteria on which site evolution is based. For example, another function that has been added, as a direct result of customer requests, complements package airbill preparation, shipment scheduling, and tracking, is online invoice adjustment. This new feature completes the full cycle of package handling and billing that most customers need.

Another change which FedEx is considering isn't exactly content-related in the basic sense of what the audience will see, but more an extension of its site's services to other sites. With a "chip" now in the Internet game, FedEx believes that there may be ways to expand the site through electronic commerce, where products purchased through other sites are electronically scheduled for shipment through the FedEx site and shipped to the Internet customer (product fulfillment) without the supplier being involved in the scheduling process. This would extend the umbrella of financial benefits of the site. Successfully implementing such a system could result in even stronger customer loyalty and higher package counts.

Site evolution is not just external in nature. In many instances, substantial changes take place behind the scenes. These are often organizational or financial and are critical to maintaining the ongoing success of the site. Toro is a good example of how both external and internal evolution of the site occurred, and how often unexpected issues influence these changes.

TORO   As the site has moved into the operational phase, several significant changes have occurred in site content, measurement, justification, and funding. These include the following:

❑ On a monthly basis, new *hot deals* are offered through the site while major site content is usually changed seasonally by the product line managers. The hot deals have created a lot of interest and become one of the most active pages on the site.

❑ Product prices are not posted on the site, because they vary both regionally, and internationally. At first many visitors asked for pricing, but demand for product pricing is dropping off.

❑ Dealer URLs can be included in the dealer locator and, in August 1996, Toro announced that it will host dealer pages on its site beginning in 1997.

❑ Toro added a corporate section to the site (http://www.toro.com/corporate) which includes the Toro story and links to press releases and current stock prices.

❑ Budget responsibility for the site has been transferred to individual product lines which use the site. The costs for adding new product information and changes will now be allocated to individual product-line cost centers, much like other marketing costs are allocated.

Toro continues to analyze its measurements to determine:

How many more product lines to include on the site

Whether to include a financial relations section on the site

If a section on company history would increase sales

How and when the Internet may be a practical means for product ordering with local product fulfillment through their dealers

Visitor e-mails are an essential part of this process. Toro has learned that visitors are very candid about what they would like to see added. Toro management continues to follow the success and measurements of its Internet site; early success is beginning to fuel future plans for more sites and intranet projects.

The initial release of this site was characterized by a very close focus on the centralized information components concerning the Senate as an institution. In retrospect, the site developers feel the site would have benefited from more interaction and consultation with individual Senators' and committee offices. Such efforts are now under way as part of an ongoing office requirements assessment incorporating staff from member and committee offices. This effort will undoubtedly have significant influence over future site content and enhancements.

Content Presentation

Once you've tuned your content mix to the satisfaction of yourself and site visitors, you may wish to examine how you present that content. What we mean by "presentation" is the *style* and *organization* of individual pages at your site. We are not referring to any relationship *between* pages, which is covered in a few pages under Content Navigation.

Content Presentation Issues

Designing the look and functionality of a web page takes concentration and candor. To put yourself into the visitors' shoes and think critically from outside your organization is not easy. Broadly speaking, there are four overall components to how you present content, as shown in Figure 10.2: method, layout, style, and substance.

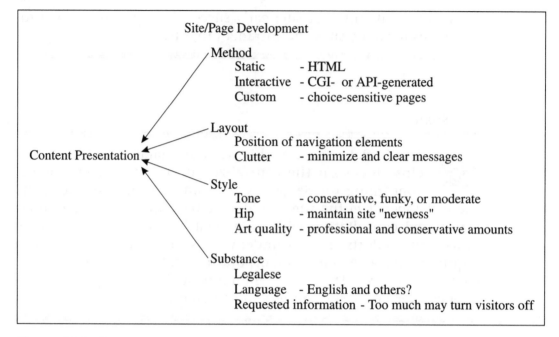

Figure 10.2 Content components.

Method

Should your page be the same for everyone or customized? Should it include a way for visitors to communicate back to you? The options are:

- ❑ *Static*: Nothing ever changes; all visitors see the same page.

- ❑ *Interactive*: Visitors must return information to you; all visitors get the same page.

- ❑ *Custom*: Visitors see different pages based on prior choices; interactive is an optional aspect of custom pages.

Layout

Where will you place individual page elements on the page or screen? There are two basic layout considerations:

❏ *Position of navigation elements*:   Where will they make the most sense to a visitor and consequently increase the average depth of site visits (C)? Poor placement of navigation aids makes people leave a site.

❏ *Clutter*: Use only as much content as necessary on each page. If your message is confusing because it's jumbled with too many other things, visitors will leave. Conversely, if you don't explain your message well enough, visitors won't get it either.

Style

What type of "look" are you striving for? Be sure that the look is consistent with the expectations of your visitors or you risk turning them off. Consider three key aspects of style at your site:

❏ *Tone*: This is the term used by design professionals to describe the *feel* of the page. Many web sites, even some corporate sites, have a *funky* tone: heavy use of black with in-your-face artwork. Mainstream sites such as online newspapers have a *conservative* tone, typically using solid white backgrounds and cheery illustration. Be sure your tone supports your content.

❏ *Hip*: It's amazing how many sites were put up in the early days of the Web in 1995 and have never been touched since. Many visitors see a flat gray background or other visual clue and get turned off because the site feels "old".

❏ *Art Quantity*: Are you using too much, too little, or just enough illustration? Besides the impact on download time (see Content Transmission on page 272), having too much art can cloud your message. As they say in print, "white space is good."

Substance

This is the actual content of the page. Independent of your particular message, you may wish to think about these general issues:

❏ *Legalese*: Will a lot of copyright or other intellectual property legal copy turn off your visitors? Corporate counsel is increasingly sensitive to asserting ownership, but this must be weighed with its impact on privacy-sensitive (and therefore legalese-sensitive) visitors.

❏ *Language*: Do you need to provide content in more than one language? If so, does your layout need to change to accommodate the *size* of the page taken up by the same point?

❏ *Requested information*: Are you asking for too much information from privacy-conscious visitors? Ask for only what you *must* have, and even then decide what is mandatory and what is optional.

Consolidated and Raw Measures that Indicate You Have a Problem

The most relevant Consolidated Measure is average depth of site visits (C), discussed in Chapter 6, because it tells you how far people venture into your site. In general, the further visitors go, the more satisfied and/or captivated they are. While you can't always infer that low average depth (C) is caused by problems with presentation, high average depth (C) tends to indicate that all four external content factors (mix, presentation, navigation, and transmission) are on target.

Raw Measures that may provide important clues are the following:

E-mail categories: As with mix, keep a close eye on e-mail complaints (R), e-mail praise (R), and e-mail resolutions (R). Your visitors will tell you what they think of the presentation.

Number of sessions with only one page request (R): This could indicate that the presentation of the splash page was disappointing.

Page views (R): Compare tone and substance between the parts of your site that draw the most and least traffic. What you did in the high-traffic areas should be replicated throughout the site.

Platform type (R): Remember that different platforms can display differing amounts of information. Also, some visitors may have large monitors while others have small ones. Layout is directly impacted by platform type.

Session time limit (R): Knowing how long people stay at your site is a good way to decide if your content is really captivating. Good sites capture people for at least five minutes per visit.

Case Studies in Content Presentation

The following case studies show how the *Star Tribune*, the Senate, and Travelocity dealt with content presentation.

CASE STUDY

Originally, the *Star Tribune* tried different methods of presenting feature content on its Interchange service. However, through audience feedback the paper found that most visitors thought of the site as a "newspaper" and looked for feature content in the "usual" format. It was decided not to try to change visitor perception and now present the news in sections or pages of the site that correspond to the newspaper's sections.

The *Star Tribune* example shows the overlap between content presentation and navigational issues. Often you cannot consider content-related issues independently, but must analyze how presentation may impact navigation or vice versa.

CASE STUDY

The Senate has a somewhat unique issue because of the large number of contributors, Senators and committees, to the site. Some organizations have a technical capability to maintain their own pages, while others rely completely on the computer center. This led to the decision that the posting process for getting new content and pages on the site must be made easier. This requires a simpler way of creating HTML files from WordPerfect text files or a forms-based system for entry and posting of new page content. As more sites evolve this, we believe, will become a common requirement at many locations.

Travelocity is hard at work on the next release of its site which will incorporate many of the latest web technologies. In particular, the company is moving from an HTML-based environment to a Java-based environment. This is important for the Travelocity application because it has virtually no static content at the site. Java will enable the company to offer even more features. Site personalization is also on the horizon, where individual visitors will be recognized and the visit experience tailored to their particular tastes.

Content Navigation

Audience use of your site can be measured by charting the navigation of a typical user through the site. Good navigation is as important to retaining visitors as the content mix and presentation. As you saw in the *Star Tribune* case study on page 269, and will see in the case study for Toro on page 271, many sites have evolved their initial navigation models based on specific audience feedback.

The Navigation Problem

Finding a good navigation model for your content mix means that you must successfully balance content presentation, mix, and transmission. The mix determines how much content you have to communicate, while presentation and transmission affect how much can effectively go on one page. Mix often determines how many *signposts* appear on the home page and subsequent navigation aids.

Making a site too deep means that a user must click too many times to get to the information he or she wants. In this case, the visitor often leaves. "Too many" is subjective—but you can study page views (R) and average depth (C) reports to determine if you are experiencing attrition. Sometimes visitors will tell you through e-mail complaints (R) or e-mail praise (R) how they feel about your navigation.

With the advent of *frames* to divide a screen into two or more smaller areas, many sites have effectively flattened themselves by one click. This is because a navigation button in one frame will typically trigger new content to appear in another frame. Since the original navigation button is still in the same place, it has the practical effect of saving the user from clicking the *back* button when finished with an area.

Case Studies in Navigation Change

The following example illustrates how Toro handled navigation of its site.

CASE STUDY

TORO Based on qualitative feedback, Toro has learned that if visitors don't find what they want fast, they are very likely to leave. The more casual the visitor, the more important is the site access speed. Therefore, as the site evolves, Toro plans on reducing the amount of initial graphics. As the company puts it, "drop art for words." This will speed page downloading and provide more key words (content) for the search engines to find. Also, it wants to reduce the number of clicks or selections (site navigation) that the visitor must traverse to get to *real* (product) information. The company intends to provide more product listings to select from, rather than making the visitor navigate through multiple screens to reveal product details.

One poignant example of this occurred in the first month of site operation. The site was originally designed to be compatible with the Netscape browser, which meant that major online services like AOL and Prodigy could not correctly view the site. After several weeks it was clear that these visitors made up nearly 30 percent of the traffic and they were leaving after just one page. Toro quickly created an alternative site that displayed correctly on those services. It uses an *autosensor* to detect the browser type and automatically send the visitor to the right version for him or her. Since then, online service traffic has remained strong, proving the value of this investment.

Content Transmission

Today, most content transmission issues center around two areas: performance and browser capability. Performance can be further broken down into *server throughput* and *access throughput*. None of the web sites we interviewed had major concerns or issues with server performance. This, however, may not be indicative of the future. As more complex web sites evolve, using products such as Netscape SuiteSpot which provides multiple integrated services distributed across many computers, server configuration, tuning, and capacity will undoubtedly become a more important issue. Today, most sites use static HTML (HyperText Markup Language) or simple CGI (Common Gateway Interface) pages which are not terribly resource-intensive. As more complex operations, such as data base lookups, are developed, server capacity will become a more pressing problem. However, that is a complex topic for another book.

Transmission Speed

Today, most sites we spoke with were much more concerned with access throughput which directly impacts the user's time at the site and his or her perception of site responsiveness. In case you aren't familiar with some of the underlying technology of the Internet, the following short description explains why fast access is so important.

When visitors log onto the Internet and link to a web server, they typically operate through a modem connected to their PC. Typical modem rates vary from a low of 2,400 baud to roughly 28,800 baud (also called 28.8). The lower the number is, the slower the speed of transmission between the web server and the PC. When a web page contains text, the text characters are represented by codes that are sent across the link. The total amount of data transferred for a text-only screen is fairly low. However, when a web page contains complex graphics, the amount of data that must be transmitted goes up significantly. This is why you often just sit waiting and waiting for something to display when you access a web page. Links of less than 28.8 do not provide great perceived performance for graphics transmission. According to the most recent Georgia Tech web survey, over one-quarter of the people who access the Internet using a modem are slower than 28.8.

Every case study we interviewed told us they were reducing graphic content in favor of text. Most sites initially included very nice graphics to create a sophisticated web page display. However, most also found that their audience didn't want to wait for the graphics to be communicated to the PC. The audience wanted speed (performance) over sophistication. Many sites are now scaling back on the graphics they use or providing two sites, one that is graphics-oriented and one that is not. As faster modems become the norm, we will see more graphics, but most sites now realize that content is more important.

More text also provides two additional unexpected benefits:

❑ It provides more content for search engines to reference, thereby giving the site more visibility on the Internet.

❑ Text-based pages work better with a wider range of browsers; this brings up the second key technical issue most sites are dealing with today—transmission compatibility.

Transmission Compatibility

There are hundreds of different browser versions available today. They each support a basic set of Internet standards for communication, but unfortunately they each contain other features of a proprietary nature. Therefore, a web page designed for one browser's special features probably won't work with another browser. At the same time, a web page designed around the lowest common denominator of features for all browsers doesn't offer good performance. These differences get even worse when graphics are involved.

To resolve the browser problem, sites have tried different approaches, including:

- ❏ Creating different page versions for each of several leading browsers

- ❏ Developing a *generic* page for the "lowest common denominator"

- ❏ Using browser-specific features and not worrying if not everyone can see the site

The *Star Tribune* has taken the approach of attempting to work with as many browsers as possible.

CASE STUDY

When the *Star Tribune* evolves or develops new site capabilities, it looks at designs that should work with most browsers. The paper doesn't try to optimize for many browsers. It tests with different browsers, but doesn't currently follow up by measuring visitor browser types at the site.

On the other hand, Travelocity is an interesting example of a site where technical decisions influenced target audience focus, rather than audience capabilities influencing the site.

CASE STUDY

Travelocity's statistics show that 95 percent of visitors are using a Netscape browser. At the time of this writing, it is important to remember that America Online's web browser did not support the HTML table feature. Virtually all of our other case studies found that AOL regularly accounted for up to one-third of their monthly traffic. But because Travelocity uses tables heavily, this may explain the high percentage of Netscape. "We simply had no choice," according to Goel, "because of the complexity of the information we had to present." In other words, Travelocity deliberately decided to trade off potential visitors for a limited time for a better product.

Consolidated and Raw Measures Affecting Transmission

The most important Consolidated Measure governing content transmission is average depth of site visits (C). If this number is consistently low or if there is an extreme fall-off between visitors who look at one page versus multiple pages, you could have a transmission problem. Note that there is an inverse relationship between web site cost (C) and transmission; the more compatible you make a site, the more expensive it gets.

There are several Raw Measures worth noting.

Browser type (R): As with platform type (R) that follows, be certain that the browsers being used by real visitors are supported by your site. As a general rule, be sure that your site *fully* supports the top five browsers in use, or the browsers that account for at least 80 percent of your traffic, whichever is more.

E-mail categories: You have heard over and over that e-mail is your best feedback. It's as true here as with other content issues.

Hits (R): Unlike other content issues, hits (R) offer a way to determine transmission problems. The page view (R) measure only tells you how many requests there were for a given HTML page. By contrast, hits (R) should record every request, including artwork and multimedia elements. If you suspect a compatibility problem that is keeping people from viewing your graphics, verify that the number of hits (R) is correct for each individual page at the site. If people are loading only the HTML document and there are no hits (R) for images, you may have stumbled onto a problem.

Number of sessions with only one page request (R): Another form of average depth (C), where a high number here spells trouble.

Page views (R): As with hits, low values on a site you would intuitively expect to do well are a pretty good indication of a transmission problem.

Platform type (R): This information can tell you what are the most common PCs and operating systems accessing your site. This information should be checked against your original decisions at the time the site was created to make sure you're not turning away large numbers.

Server errors (R): Older browsers or browsers which lack features you use at your site can result in error messages being recorded on the server. Be sure to monitor all error messages and take appropriate action.

Session time limit (R): As with content mix, low session times (R) mean people aren't staying long. This could be because your site isn't compatible with their browser. They might also not like your presentation or navigation.

Since site objectives, content, and audience are extremely diverse, we cannot tell you exactly how to best evolve your site. The lessons learned, and for which you should be prepared, all point to the fact that you will have ongoing site changes, as you better understand the nature of your audience, identify new features, and address new technologies for the Web.

11

Strategy and Promotion Choices

Remodeling the content of your web site was the subject of the last chapter. But, what do you do when remodeling isn't the right approach or wouldn't be enough to solve a problem, as discussed in Chapter 9? This chapter considers how you should adjust your overall site strategy and promotion plan based on site measurements.

Referring to the web site strategy and promotion evaluation decision tree introduced in Chapter 9 and reshown in Figure 11.1, this chapter follows the flow of the decision tree in dealing with:

- ❑ Adjusting the target audience
- ❑ Revising promotional activities
- ❑ Modifying objectives
- ❑ Shutting down a web site

Adjusting to the Audience

If your objectives are not being met, the very first place to start investigating is the composition of the audience. This is because sites can draw a lot of traffic and have great content, but still miss their

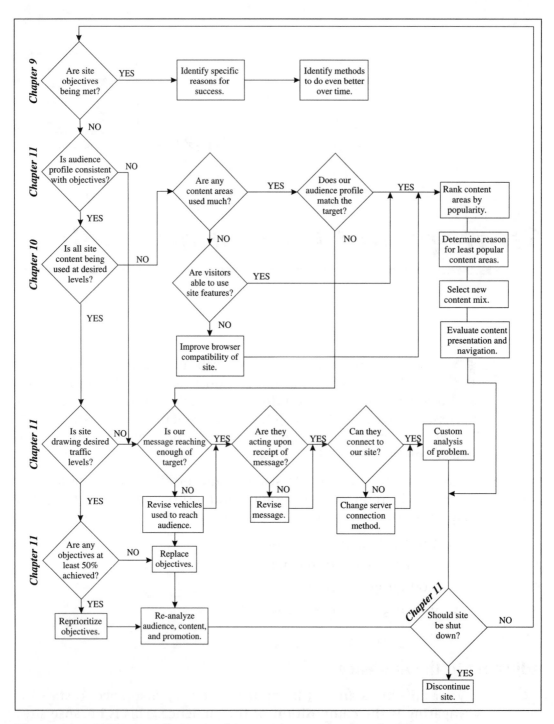

Figure 11.1 Web site strategy and promotion evaluation decision tree.

intended target. For example, Yahoo! recently created completely separate versions of its service for both children and certain cities, including San Francisco. Its core objective of revenue generation wasn't being fully met in spite of the unbelievable amount of traffic the site receives every day. Why? Because advertisers want to know precisely who they will reach and a purely traffic-focused strategy didn't provide enough quality to attract advertisers.

Attracting the right audience is really a promotional issue. If your promotion is effective in driving lots of the wrong kind of traffic, you may still have good use of your content. Make no mistake—your content must be *attractive* to your desired audience. But it is promotion that does the attracting. Therefore, if your research shows you are not drawing the kind of people you want, the following promotion section can help you improve audience draw.

How do you know if the audience is on target? As discussed in Chapters 4 and 9, you should plan to use e-mail and online surveys extensively to obtain this very qualitative information. Outside survey firms can also be valuable if you have sufficient traffic that telephone-based surveys will produce enough responses.

Updating the Promotion Plan

A web site that is not promoted will have little or no traffic. Common sense requires that this be true, yet it's impossible to count the number of sites where no thought or budget has been committed to getting visitors there. There is a true *Field of Dreams* mentality that promises, "If you build it, they will come." You may very well have purchased this book because your own site is suffering from poor promotion.

If you're not convinced, think about two popular network television shows. Most everyone knows "Seinfeld" and "ER" now, but when they first aired people didn't care much. In this case, NBC invested its own airtime and production money to create advertisements for the shows. It took out ads in *TV Guide* and placed articles on the shows and their stars. It persuaded the critics. And over time these shows became huge hits.

But does that mean that if the network switches nights for the shows or has to cancel a show for a week that it can trust viewers to follow? Not at all. Even the best-known, highest-rated shows will produce commercials and print ads to alert viewers of a schedule change. They do this primarily to ensure that viewers catch the new time or date, protecting the ratings from large fluctuations. They also regularly promote the current week's show even when it doesn't change time. If famous shows with famous stars have to go to so much trouble, think about your web site!

Of course, investing time and money on promoting your site won't guarantee traffic either. That's the subject of this chapter. But you certainly won't get much traffic without promoting it.

Assessing Promotion Effectiveness

A famous marketing executive once pointed out, "I know that half of my advertising budget is going to be wasted. I'm just not sure which half." For the first time, the Internet may change that. While some site-related promotions using traditional means operate under traditional measurement limits, it is possible to gauge the effectiveness of a given campaign far more easily on the Web.

When evaluating effectiveness, you should consider two dimensions of the promotion effort. First, what is the aggregate impact on the site as measured by overall traffic levels? As you study the strategy and promotion evaluation decision tree, you should ask key questions at this high level:

Is our message reaching enough of the target?

Are they acting upon receipt of the message?

Can they connect to the site?

The initial question is important because it forces you to prove that the promotional vehicles you selected are actually getting to your target audience. The second question makes you prove your response rate. Finally, you should always be aware of connectivity or technology problems that inhibit access to your site. The best promotion is wasted if people can't visit you.

The second dimension is to evaluate the individual promotional tactics you have selected by themselves. Understanding which vehicles provide the highest response rates at the lowest cost allows you to stretch your dollar while achieving your objectives. For each individual tactic, answer the following questions:

What is the actual circulation / views of the vehicle?

What was our total cost including creative and production?

How many visits did we receive from the vehicle?

What is the cost per person (per impression)?

What is our response rate as a percentage of circulation?

How many of the visits were a target audience member?

What is our response rate for targeted audiences?

How long did it take for a visitor to act on the promotion?

If you can answer these questions, you should be able to quickly arrange the answers into a table for comparison. Low-yielding and/or expensive tactics should be eliminated in favor of high-yielding and inexpensive approaches. As discussed in Chapter 4, you can measure promotional program success by:

❑ Measuring site access based on promotion-specific URLs

❑ Measuring site access based on last prior domain visited

Promotion-specific URLs can be used in any form of traditional or online promotion, while last prior domain visited provides success measures for ad banners and click-through from other web pages and sites.

While Travelocity's site is not undergoing major strategy changes, it is worth noting its experience with advertising and the future direction it is taking.

CASE STUDY

One interesting result is that both online advertising and traditional media placements have been very effective for Travelocity. Today, 43 percent of Travelocity members saw print ads about the Travelocity services. Also, promotional activities, such as the "T-shirt survey" on the home page, have been effective in signing up new members.

In measuring promotional success, you can equate many site promotions to more traditional promotional activities and, therefore, use comparable criteria for measuring success. Additionally, you can use promotion measures for evolving site content. Both of these uses are discussed in the next section.

Using Promotional Measures

Figure 11.2 shows how an Internet coupon program can actually provide a much finer measure of coupons "clipped," and can also

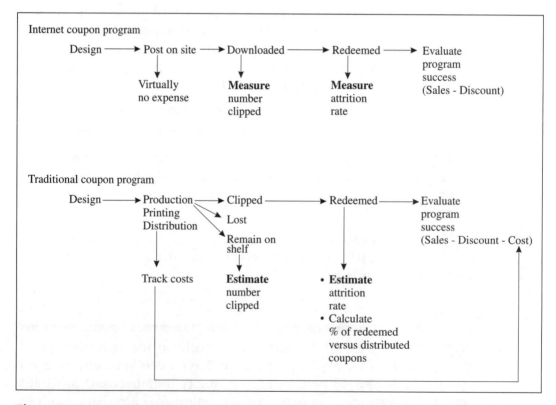

Figure 11.2 Internet coupon program can effectively measure coupons "clipped."

reduce program costs by eliminating printing and distribution. The down side is that fewer potential customers will probably see the Internet coupon than a coupon displayed in a store or some advertising media. Clipped and returned coupons can also be used to measure audience interest in specific site content or identify areas where there is audience interest that could help expand the site's coverage of specific products or services.

Ads on the Internet should include a *call-to-action*; responses can be measured similar to 800-number calls for traditional media advertising. Figure 11.3 compares the Internet to traditional advertising media. Again, Internet advertising can be less costly than traditional advertising, but will also generally reach less potential audience. Advertising measurements provide input on both site content and audience interest. You can calculate cost per response, cost per additional sale, measure which ad types or content are most successful, and use ad response to influence site content.

Click-throughs are unique to the Internet. In one way they are similar to a banner ad on another web site; in other ways, they are

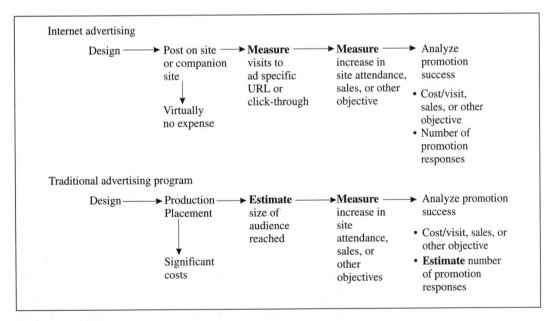

Figure 11.3 Comparing Internet to traditional advertising media.

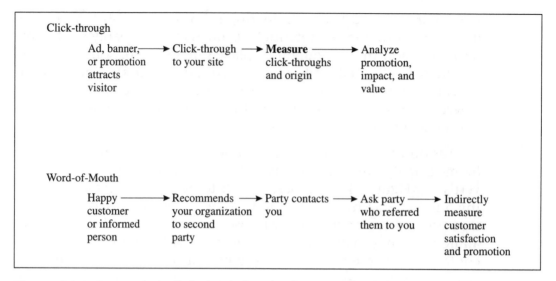

Figure 11.4 Comparing click-throughs to reference selling.

like word-of-mouth advertising or reference selling. Figure 11.4 compares click-throughs to reference selling. As in the other promotional forms, input from click-throughs can be used to identify audience interests and site content.

Revising Objectives

The first phase of the web site life cycle was to set an objective or objectives. It is fitting that the final phase (before starting all over again) is to assess how well the objective was met. At this point in the decision tree, you have determined that your web site isn't fully meeting its objectives. However, you've also shown that the audience, content, and promotion are fine. In this situation (which is increasingly common) you have two choices: modify the objectives to conform to what is working or shut down the site.

As you will see in the discussion on site shutdowns, most of our case study participants do not consider missed objectives strong justification for shutting down a site. They do believe that by measuring, enhancing, improving, and measuring the site they can get closer to meeting original or modified objectives. This illustrates their unanimous belief in the importance of the Internet and their universal lack of a track record. We believe that because the Web is very new, this is indicative of how many organizations view the Internet. They don't know what good objectives or measures are, so they are willing to continue trying and learning for the near future.

One well-publicized site which failed to meet significant financial objectives was the Utne Lens, an online companion to the popular *Utne Reader* magazine. However, the company didn't shut down the site, but used the lessons learned to evolve it along a different path which is in keeping with its strategic perspective on the long-term importance of the Internet.

EXAMPLE: THE UTNE READER SITE EVOLUTION

The *Utne Reader* is an important bimonthly cultural journal that was attracted to the Internet because it appeared to offer opportunities for:

- ❑ Providing current-event and original content on a more timely basis
- ❑ Multimedia content, specifically graphics and sound
- ❑ Interactive conversation capabilities for readers to discuss current topics

The web site project was a proactive business decision to create a biweekly electronic publication with all new content (compared to the company's printed bimonthly magazine). This addressed the first two opportunities, but the publication delayed implementing the third objective because the Utne staff believed there was no adequate web software in early 1995 for interactive conferencing. Project justification in mid-1995 was based on:

- ❑ Standard business and financial planning which required a first-year budget of approximately $400,000.
- ❑ An advertising-based model for ongoing funding of the publication based on guesses for subscriber growth, market pricing of banner ads, and the size of the field of willing sponsors.

❑ Existing readership as the target audience. While analysis showed the Internet was a younger audience than the magazine's traditional audience, it was felt that the online site could attract existing readership first, then perhaps expand to a larger audience.

Part of getting the green light from management was to have an advertising base signed up prior to starting the project that represented 20 to 30 percent of the project's first-year budget. While ad agencies liked the site prototype, gave lots of positive feedback, and predicted attendance of up to 100,000 visits per month, only one major advertiser was signed up by August 1995. Believing that other advertisers would soon follow, management gave the go-ahead for implementing the site.

Between August and October 1995 site attendance averaged 25,000 page views per month and no new advertisers were signed up. The Utne Lens was typical of other magazine sites during late 1995. All were experiencing:

❑ Lower readership than predicted

❑ Lower advertising revenues than needed

❑ Higher production costs than forecast

❑ The need to cut back on expenses or close the site

In late 1995, rather than closing the site, it was scaled back. The staff of six full-time and three field editors was reduced to just two full-time personnel. While the site structure was not changed, the frequency of new content additions was reduced. More importantly, the company's Internet focus shifted from the first two objectives to the third, with the objective of providing interactive conversation through a new companion site.

The seeds of Utne's new success were sown in the final days of the full-blown Lens site. Sensing that conversation technology had improved, Utne invested in one of the first major online conferencing systems. This capability has now moved to a new site called the Utne Cafe. This new site has proved very popular and expansion plans are near.

The Utne's Cafe web site opened the last week of October 1995. Today, Cafe is the largest conferencing system on the Internet with about 48,000 visitors per month. The advertising-based revenue model is still a problem as there is difficulty attracting large advertisers. The company has had to rely on a variety of revenue sources, such as smaller advertisers, memberships, magazine subscriptions, book sales, and CD sales.

While the Utne Lens was never officially retired, it is certainly an example of a site that failed to meet its objectives. It is one of the first examples where a hard decision had to be made to dramatically cut back. As we were told, the publishing paradigm is:

"Readers expect online content to be free, so publishers must make their revenue through other means." Or, in the language of publications, the Internet is going to become a paid medium.

If your site isn't meeting its objectives and it doesn't make sense to shut it down, you have only two options:

- ❏ Reprioritize original objectives.
- ❏ Replace original objectives with new ones.

Let's look briefly at each choice.

Reprioritizing Objectives

The Utne Lens is a good example of a site that could have been shut down because it was not achieving its two most important objectives. Instead, the company reprioritized its objectives based on real-world experience and is now getting back on track. In fact, several of our case studies illustrate how site measures and results from earlier online trial systems influenced how the site looks today. Since the Internet is new, organizations do not have historical reference points on which to base Internet objectives. This makes initial objective-setting very difficult and virtually guarantees that most sites will miss one or more key objectives.

In order for reprioritizing to be possible, one of your original objectives must be at least 50 percent achieved. Only you can translate this guideline into your objectives, but it makes common sense. Cynics might call this the "throw-it-against-the-wall-and-see-what-sticks" concept. Since the Internet is so new, there is little alternative. In all cases, lessons learned through our case studies indicate that site measures helped the organizations understand which objectives were being met, which were being missed, and how to evolve the site to better meet their objectives and audience needs.

Replace Original Objectives

If none of your objectives are at least 50 percent achieved and you do not intend to throw in the towel, you'll need a new set of objectives. In this case, the best technique for finding a winner is *category elimination*. Category elimination means that if you picked "printing and postage savings" as your Impact Measure but there are no savings to be found, then you should switch to a different Impact Measure.

This technique will save you a great deal of time experimenting. It is based on the assumption that if a specific Impact Measure can't be proven, minor variations will also fail. Some goals just can't be met through a web site and its useless to keep trying if your first attempts don't succeed. Imagine that Federal Express had put up its package tracking feature and no one was interested? Experimenting with different user interfaces, promotional methods, and perks would have had no effect if the audience didn't care about the feature.

A real recent example is the site of a major national realty organization which was substantially justified on revenue growth. After finding out that charging a fee to list a home didn't work, the organization switched to a sponsored model and still couldn't make money. At the time this book goes to press, the site is widely reported to be near shutting down when free home-listing sites are springing up all over the Net. What happened? The organization's objective turned out to be incompatible with its content. All the experimenting in the world would not make that site succeed.

In this and similar situations, *replacing* the objective is the only possible course of action short of shutting the site down. In the realty example, successful justifications range from cost-cutting to customer satisfaction. Some newspapers even offer free listings at their web sites to protect their classified ads from attack by online competitors. At this time, few if any people make money on pure Internet home listings.

Promoting Your "New" Site

Generally, site promotion falls into three categories:

- Rollout
- New releases
- Ongoing *block-and-tackling*

These are discussed more fully in the following sections.

Rollout Promotion

Several of the sites we interviewed were brought online without fanfare or promotion for the first several months. This is a good strategy for ensuring that the site is solid before attracting significant visitors. In all cases, however, the sites were finally promoted to their target audiences on an active basis using a mix of tactics.

It is vital to understand that if you build it, they won't automatically come. Therefore, you must do some level of initial and ongoing site promotion, but the level of promotion can vary widely. The minimum level recommended, and also done by the organizations we interviewed, is:

- Register your URL with search engines. Also, make use of new features such as Infoseek's ability to let you specify your own keywords by embedding them in the site.
- Include the site address in company and product materials and collateral.
- Inform your organization, sales, and distribution channels.

Beyond the minimum, the rest is up to you based on the site objectives, your advertising and promotional budget, and the breadth of audience you are targeting. Basically, treat the site as you would any new product or service rollout and you can use most traditional strategies to promote the new site. See Chapter 2 for more information on possible site promotional activities.

Organizations are constantly coming up with creative ways to get an address out:

- ❑ Paint the address on your trucks.
- ❑ Make up buttons, T-shirts, or umbrellas. Abercrombie & Fitch even displays its web address on cash register screens while clerks ring up your sale.
- ❑ License a web browser such as Netscape or Internet Explorer and distribute free copies with your product or brochure. The browser can be personalized for an additional fee so it has your logo and points directly to your site when it starts up.
- ❑ Toro used an electronic press kit that was sent to all the media for its site launch.

New Releases

Again, you can apply many of the traditional methods for funding and promoting new features and so forth of the site as you would for promoting new products and services. The time and cost involved using traditional methods means that only major new features or bundled minor changes can be promoted cost-effectively in this manner.

Sites can be their own best promotional vehicle. As attendance grows, the site's home page can be effectively used to announce new site features and direct the visitor to the appropriate page. One nice advantage is that with site self-promotion you can easily change the home page to promote incremental additions.

Ongoing Activities

One of the worst mistakes that many organizations and people make with traditional marketing is the *big bash* fallacy. Often at roll-out, a product or service is heavily promoted for a short period, then no more is heard of it. A big bash is great for getting initial market attention, but it is ongoing, day-to-day, product-in-your-face marketing that creates customer demand and closes sales.

Web sites aren't any different. If you spend time and money on a big bash, you will probably get initial attention and visitors, but in reality you will only reach a small portion of the potential audience. If you don't reinforce the site's message, many of those who heard about the site will quickly forget about it. The *Star Tribune* and many television stations are great examples of providing ongoing promotion because everyday you see their URLs either in print or as footers across the TV screen.

Travelocity presents a good example of a company that is expanding its site promotion to encourage further visitor traffic.

CASE STUDY

While Travelocity is not changing its site strategy, it is changing its site promotion; these changes and reasons fit into the previous discussion. Online advertising and public relations efforts for the site have been very extensive during the initial introduction of the site. Travelocity, however, believes that visitors do not get online initially to use the service, but rather "find" the service and access it because they are online.

Also, advertising is now expanding through deliverables, such as ticket jackets, and so forth. This is effective word-of-mouth advertising, and may be one of the best ways of reaching and maintaining repeat business.

Other forms of ongoing promotion used by many sites are:

- ❑ Including URLs on all materials, press announcements, etc. from your organization
- ❑ Adding site content (text) that generates more search engine *hits* for your site
- ❑ Doing traditional activities to promote the site, such as mailings or telemarketing

❏ Negotiating reciprocal links with related sites or industry advocacy groups

❏ Periodic e-mails to those who have registered at your site

❏ Targeted announcements in Internet newsgroups and online service forums

❏ Running a contest, such as CompuServe's $1 million scavenger hunt

❏ Purchasing hotlinks at high-traffic sites

Should You Shut Down Your Site?

Any time your site poses questions serious enough to warrant thinking about this strategy, you need to candidly answer this question.

Generally, the answer is no. Every organization we spoke with, whether its site was formally or informally justified, seemed very reluctant to consider the possibility of shutting down the site. Even the Utne Lens site, which was launched with specific revenue targets and later fell short, has simply changed its format and is now regularly producing web content. But you should always leave yourself open to all possible options. As Colin Powell is fond of saying, "Don't let adverse facts stand in the way of a good decision."

Case Study Learnings

Two themes emerged when we asked our case study participants about the circumstances that would make them shut down their sites.

First, all the organizations seemed to have an inherent belief that the Internet was a critical long-term aspect of communicating to their audiences which they needed to be part of. Several are using their site as a learning tool, with the intent of proceeding slowly. Others are using it as a new revenue opportunity. Some are using it to improve customer service and support. In all cases, the organizations believe that the Internet offers new opportunities for their companies which they cannot ignore.

Second, the organizations we interviewed, except one, believed that their sites were meeting their initial objectives. Most of these sites, however, are fairly new and still do not have a track record of success. Only time will tell if these sites can continue to meet objectives and attract more audience. Since this is true of most other web sites, chances are good that you feel this way, too, regardless of how your site is performing.

We also learned that web sites, as is true of other business activities, take on a life of their own. Once the activity is started, the inclination is to preserve the activity—even if it is not meeting objectives—by spending money to modify or enhance it, rather than making the difficult decision of discontinuing it. Rightly or wrongly, the success or failure of a web site becomes an extension of someone's credibility. However, given the rapidly escalating costs of site construction and maintenance, this may not be in the best interest of the organization.

Criteria for A "No-Go" Decision

Our interviews revealed a specific set of criteria for making a shutdown decision. If any one or more of these are true in your case, you may want to consider this option:

- ❑ The site had a temporary objective that was achieved.
- ❑ Internet activity increases to a point where significant gridlock makes the Web useless for most people.
- ❑ Customers or other audiences no longer expect the organization to have a web presence.
- ❑ Site activity decreases to a minimal level that indicates the audience has abandoned the site.
- ❑ The site misses financial objectives that exceed the ability of the organization to pay for the unbudgeted costs.

Interestingly, all but one of these criteria require solid measurement data to make a decision. Even temporary sites may require measurement depending on their specific objective.

Temporary versus Permanent Sites

Individual sites are not defined by hardware or web server configurations, but by unique URLs. Therefore, a single web server can support multiple sites (URLs), most of which may be permanent, but some of which may be temporary. While most Internet sites are designed to be permanent systems, organizations have used temporary sites for:

❑ Promotional activities

❑ Transitional activities, such as mergers

❑ Converting from existing online services to new Internet-based online services

Temporary Sites

Three representative examples of temporary or transitional site activity are:

❑ Promotional activity with a specific URL address for responses

❑ Silicon Graphics merger with Cray Computers

❑ *Star Tribune* conversion from the Interchange Network to the Internet

As discussed in Chapter 4, having a specific URL associated with a specific promotional activity allows you to directly measure response rates, originating domains, and other characteristics of the audience attracted through the promotion. Once the promotion is completed, there is no reason to maintain the site and the site should be shut down. An effective way of shutting down the site is by replacing the original content with a short paragraph explaining why the site is no longer available, then providing a click-through link to your permanent site's home page or other appropriate page. This URL and link should be measured to determine activity and eventually retired as activity decreases. Exactly how long the site should be maintained is dependent on your perspective of the site's value in bringing new users to the permanent site. A good rule-of-thumb is to retire the site when hits drop to 5 to 10 percent of the peak hit rate for the temporary site; certainly don't continue maintaining the temporary site once the hit rates drops below the 5 percent range.

During the merger between Silicon Graphics and Cray Computers, Silicon Graphics maintained a newsletter under a specific URL which kept employees in both companies informed of the merger's process and progress. This is a good example of a temporary site which was retired or shut down once the merger was complete.

Permanent Sites

At this time we do not know of a major permanent site that has been retired, except for older sites that were being transitioned to new online Internet services.

The *Star Tribune* started with an Interchange Network online service, but has now switched to the Internet as its long-term online focus. Its intent is to eventually shut down the Interchange Network services. During the interim, the paper has linked sections of the Interchange Network to corresponding Internet site sections as they become available on the new web site. This provides for a smooth, virtually transparent transition for users of the older service.

While the original plan did not include shutting down the Interchange Network site, the *Star Tribune* has developed a process by which it can effectively implement the rollover for both its external audience and internal organization. The audience continues to have access to the Interchange Network, but more and more of the content is provided through links to the web site. Eventually, the audience will be fully switched to the web site and the old site will be retired. Internally, the *Star Tribune* only needs to spend time developing content for the new site and can simply maintain the old site until the new site provides all its functionality.

Another approach to transitioning audience and shutting down a site was taken by the *Los Angeles Times*. Like the *Star Tribune*, the *Los Angeles Times* now has an Internet site, but previously developed a site on a different online service. The *Los Angeles Times* simply shut down the site it maintained under Prodigy and three months later opened a new Internet-based site. This appears as a more radical approach from the audience's perspective, but depending on the number of original subscribers and differences in site content and services, this is a method that works and one to consider.

As with any business activity or location that is being closed, such as a product division or branch store, one of the foremost issues is customer perception. If the closure is unexpected and misunderstood, then significant damage can be caused between the organization and the customer. Additionally, the impact internally on the organization cannot be overlooked. As in the Utne Lens example, even though the site was not closed, it was significantly reduced and refocused, which caused audience and internal issues to be considered.

In our experience, if the site does not contain time-sensitive information, there may be very little advantage to retiring a site, since most sites are heavily upfront loaded, both from a financial and resource perspective. Even if the site is not meeting its objectives, once users find the site, it may be more difficult and burdensome to retire it than to just maintain it at a minimal level.

Procedure for Shutting Down a Site

Once you make the decision to retire a site, it's a good idea to take all of the following steps:

- ❑ Provide prior notification to the site's audience and a brief explanation of why the site is being retired. Give details on when a new site may be available, if appropriate.

OR

- ❑ If you know the site is temporary when it goes up, state the date of retirement prominently so it is no surprise.
- ❑ Provide or reiterate alternative access, such as 800-numbers, to comparable information in your message.
- ❑ Provide links to other sites that may be useful to the audience.
- ❑ Archive a copy of the site in case you want to reuse all or part of it later.

❑ Archive a copy of the site log files in case you need to perform analysis later on.

❑ Cancel your listings on search engines. While not supported by everyone, editorial sites such as Yahoo! will often update their material accordingly.

12

Measuring Intranets

While the Internet is hot, the latest rage among trade publications and the market is intranets. Basically, intranets are internally focused Internets that serve the organization or a small select group of the organization's clients. Internets, on the other hand, serve a much broader and heterogeneous group of the organization's customers, prospects, investors, constituents, or news media. Most of the interviews and case studies conducted for this book revolved around Internet sites, because, in general, these are more established than intranet sites. However, several intranet sites were interviewed; from these interviews, it is clear that there are specific differences and similarities between Internet and intranet sites, as shown in Figure 12.1 and discussed in the following sections.

Internet versus Intranet Site Differences

There are three main differences between Internet and intranet sites:

- ❏ Functionality
- ❏ Topology
- ❏ Content

		Intranet	Internet
Differences	Functionality	• Replacing traditional network and client-server systems • Automating new applications	Provides external communication, distribution channel, and niche marketing
	Topology	High-speed network and some remote communication	Heterogeneous com lines of varying speeds
	Content	• Broader set of contributors • Broader set of applications and content	More focused site content and objectives
Similarities	Measurement	• Critical to site success • Informal collection	• Critical to site success • Requires formal collection
	Justification	• Formal for major projects • Informal to none for smaller projects	Varies by site but most have some level of justification
	Underlying technology	TCP/IP HTML HTTP Java . . .	TCP/IP HTML HTTP Java . . .

Figure 12.1 Internet versus intranet site differences and similarities.

But, there are also several strong similarities including measurement, justification, justification strategies, and underlying technologies.

Measurement: In most cases, measurement has been critical to overall site success. In the Internet case, the measures are often more formal, while intranets often use informal measures and audience (company personnel) feedback to determine site acceptance. Interview results indicate that for the most part Internets and intranets require the same type of measurements, analysis, and management to be successful and meet their audience needs.

Justification: Both intranets and Internets often require formal justification, particularly for mission-critical applications and revenue-generating business opportunities, respectively.

Justification Strategies: These are focused on many of the same objectives:

- Intranet justification is often based on productivity enhancements through improved personnel support and communication within the organization. This is comparable to an Internet's external focus for improved customer communication and support.

- Niche marketing is a major Internet justification, while improved communications is a primary intranet justification. In reality, both these goals are fundamentally trying to provide better contact with their respective targeted audiences.

- Expense reduction is the second most common intranet justification, while revenue growth is a growing Internet justification strategy. Both approaches target improving the organization's bottom line.

Underlying technology: The basic technology, software, and hardware platforms used on Internets and intranets is the same. It is centered around standards, including TCP/IP, HTTP, HTML, Java, and a host of others.

Since these similarities can be related to the discussion of Internets throughout the book, the following sections discuss the differences in more detail.

Functionality

Intranet sites provide new business applications or, more often, the implementation of existing business functions on a new technology, the intranet. Organizations we interviewed are using intranet sites to replace existing manual or automated systems with new intranet-based applications. Examples include:

❑ Automated purchase order systems

❑ Automated human resource systems for communicating employee benefit programs and vested hours for vacation, sick leave, etc.

❑ Project status tracking for internal use and major client communication

❑ Customer support problem tracking and problem resolution databases

Each of these examples could have been implemented on a traditional network using client-server technology, but instead each was implemented on an intranet platform. Brett Manilo, in the Silicon Graphics (SGI) example, outlines several reasons why SGI chose the intranet approach. We believe these reasons are typical of why others have also chosen intranet implementations.

One major distinction you will see, as shown in Figure 12.2, is that an intranet site is often more like an entire network rather than just a server or server cluster more typical of the Internets we interviewed.

As with Internet sites, intranet sites usually start small and grow. SGI's intranet started in December 1994, long before the market was hyping intranets. The site started as an employee communication vehicle, but during the first year localized department sites that provided information to other internal groups were added.

EXAMPLE: SILICON GRAPHICS' INTRANET EXPERIENCE

Silicon Graphic's Silicon Junction is one of the largest, if not the largest, intranet with over 200,000 URLs distributed across 2,500 web servers running on 1,200 server platforms. Until about a year ago, market focus was on Internet sites; there are still many more Internet sites than intranets. But today, the intranet is a fast-growing segment of the web market and Silicon Graphic's (SGI) site exemplifies the opportunities and benefits organizations can achieve with intranets.

In December 1996, a major change took place on the SGI intranet. According to Brett Manilo, Manager, Corporate Web Sys-

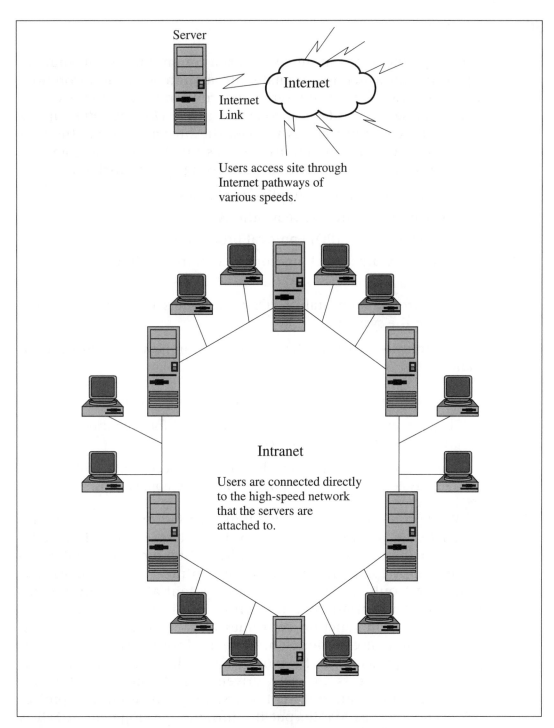

Figure 12.2 Comparing Internet (single server/cluster) to intranet configurations.

303

tems, "Intranet focus shifted from just a communication medium to a platform on which to automate information access and workflow. The objective was to create web-based front-end access to the corporate databases." The idea was to create a truly *electronic office*. In addition to a communications vehicle, the intranet became the host for critical company functions, such as purchasing. The company developed a complete electronic purchasing system, including:

- ❏ Online browsing of supplier catalogues
- ❏ Creation of purchase requisitions
- ❏ Purchase order (PO) approval processing
- ❏ Purchase order tracking from inception to fulfillment
- ❏ Purchasing
- ❏ Electronic submittal of POs to suppliers who are interlinked with the system

Manilo told us that the advantages the company sees with the intranet are:

There are no desktop client-server applications to maintain.

They can create a different user interface (UI) for each user which provides a more dialogue-based environment.

They feel they are getting much higher user acceptance of the intranet system than they did from client-server applications.

While other companies have implemented one or even several intranet sites, providing applications for systems such as Human Resources (HR) and project tracking, Silicon Graphics has literally permeated their company with a massive intranet. The benefits it is achieving would appear feasible and potential opportunities for many other organizations as they grow their intranet focus.

Today Silicon Junction continues to grow. For major projects, such as purchasing automation, there are formal justifications that precede the project. But, for most projects the justification is minimal and the projects are often driven more by need and the employee passion to succeed. As the system grows, each new project has been easier; as Manilo put it, "Intranet development at SGI is based on four basic fundamentals:

❑ SGI expects high employee achievement.

❑ Employees have good ideas.

❑ Development cycles for most projects are short, based on the expanding tool set.

❑ Most projects do not represent huge investments."

For example, many projects take only a few days; even large projects are measured in several person months (person months are *x* people working for *y* months).

Unlike Internets, where measurements are required to gain audience feedback, analyze site value, and evolve site content and navigation, Silicon Graphics does very little measurement of its intranet. Site feedback comes from a vocal, self-managing, candid workforce. This may not be true for all company cultures, but it appears to work quite well for SGI.

One important aspect of the intranet is the changing roll that IS must play in its development and support. Manilo offered these observations:

❑ The IS role shifts from development to leadership. IS must learn to manage through influence.

❑ IS must manage network infrastructure and define operational characteristics of a good intranet for the company.

❑ IS needs to help users create capabilities and applications for individual organizations, but organizations own the application content and evolution, not IS.

The bottom line is that IS must help to empower end users to create a broader source for intranet enhancement and value.

The SGI study also illustrates two other differences between Internets and intranets which are discussed in the next two sections.

Topology

Internet sites typically must support a large heterogeneous mixture of:

- ❑ Different browser types
- ❑ Different communication rates
- ❑ Difference audience interests
- ❑ Difference audience locations

Intranets, on the other hand:

- ❑ Have a much more homogeneous technology base, where most users are running similar hardware and software configurations.
- ❑ Are usually connected through high-speed network links rather than slower speed communication links.
- ❑ Service a more centralized audience which is usually distributed across the organization's headquarters and field locations, numbering in the hundreds of locations, versus supporting thousands or millions of locations which is typical of an Internet site.
- ❑ Support an organization where the audience has a more specific focus, a more defined and understood knowledge base, and similar cultural attributes.

These differences affect both the employment of the technology and the presentation of content in significant ways.

Since the technology base is more homogeneous and supported through higher speed communication links, an intranet can take advantage of specific browser and client platform features, provide more graphic content with the assurance of adequate performance, and eliminate the need for many of the security and firewall issues required for Internet sites. The net result is that with these advantages of intranet sites over Internet sites, intranet sites can actually provide many of the interactive user-related benefits that Internets would like to provide, but cannot effectively provide today because of interoperability and throughput constraints. Intranet sites can actually be more user-friendly and graphically oriented than Internet sites.

Additionally, intranet content is also easier to provide than Internet content as discussed in the following section. But, this also has a down side which organizations need to be aware of.

Content

Intranets tend to have a broader set of content contributors and features or capabilities, as indicated by the Silicon Graphics example previously presented. In effect, this means that an intranet is often a heterogeneous mixture of many different services and features, often supported across multiple servers. Some Internets have characteristics of an intranet, such as the Senate web site example, which includes many content contributors, each presenting individualized content to its audience.

Most Internet sites are developed by a small group of people who are very conscious of the need for a consistent look-and-feel. The broad content mix of an intranet, generated by many different entities within the organization, can have a downside because diverse look-and-feel can evolve, if the developers are not careful. One way to help alleviate this is to provide the developers with a tool set and guidelines for intranet site applications, as was done at SGI.

Unique Intranet Measurements

All the Internet Impact Measures and justification strategies, except for revenue growth, are appropriate for intranet sites. For some, such as cost reduction and customer satisfaction, the objective is the same, but the tactic for achieving it is different. For example, improved customer satisfaction, as discussed in Chapter 2, can be achieved through out-bound Internet services. Likewise, an intranet site focused around providing technical or customer support call tracking and response followup, is another way of improving customer satisfaction through an intranet implementation that improves organizational responsiveness to its customers.

Intranet sites often have a new justification strategy based on employee satisfaction, achieved through improved communications. As noted earlier, the intent here is very similar to improving customer satisfaction through an Internet site. Measuring employee satisfaction, at least at the organizations we interviewed, however, is much easier than measuring audience satisfaction. The many site feature collection methods outlined in Chapter 4 may not be needed on an intranet. Generally, employee feedback on intranet site features and benefits was easy to come by, and often very pointed and critical of intranet implementations that didn't meet their goals. Intranet audiences are more targeted, easier to evaluate, and often more vocal.

On the other hand, generic site measures using site logs are beneficial and required for both types of sites. Intranets, in the long run, will tend to exhibit usage and performance problems similar to today's networks. Intranet site Raw Measures should be tracked to determine performance, capacity, and use of various sites and applications on the intranet. As you find that it is very easy to bring up an intranet application, you may also find, in the long run, that there are many applications that aren't used very much. Therefore, it pays to monitor use and "thin out" intranet applications that have little use. We believe that intranet site shutdowns, or actually application or page retirement, will be much more numerous on intranets than on the Internet, for the following reasons.

First, intranet pages and sites will often be implemented with much less planning and audience analysis than Internet sites. Therefore, there will be a much higher percentage that miss their target and will have low audience attendance. An example could be the transportation group within an organization implementing a site to provide travel planning, when the audience would rather just pick up the phone and have the travel agency handle all the details.

Second, intranet sites, as communication vehicles, may often be event-focused and have a limited life expectancy. This means sites and pages will be implemented with the knowledge that they will be obsolete in a short period of time. A site oriented to a national sales campaign which tracks contest results for each sales person over a six-month period would probably be retired after the contest has finished and the top sales person is rewarded. Or, if not retired, it may be modified to provide ongoing tracking of sales status, but probably with less fanfare and perhaps more security so that different sales regions or individuals cannot view each other's status.

Critical Success Factors

For both Internet and intranet sites, success factors are always influenced heavily by audience acceptance. There is one key issue, database accuracy, we believe typically influences audience acceptance more heavily on an intranet site than on an Internet site. Nonbusiness features, that probably don't come into play on Internet sites, may have substantial impact on intranet sites.

Most Internet sites, except for a few like FedEx package tracking, tend to have fairly static content that may be changed on a regular basis (hourly, daily, monthly, or seasonably), but is not generated through database inquiries. Many intranet sites, particularly those that support mission-critical applications—such as SGI's order processing site—provide real-time data inquiry for their users. As with other systems, such as client-server applications, the accuracy and timeliness of the information is a critical success factor for the site. If the information is not accurate and timely, it is of little use to the audience and the site will quickly lose attendance.

Nonbusiness use of intranet sites is just another form of improving employee communication. In most organizations, the traditional cork bulletin board, sports pools for football and baseball, and social clubs are a way of life. As a communication vehicle, first electronic mail, now intranets are replacing the traditional communication of employees around the water cooler and bulletin board. Today's intranets have the unique ability to enhance how employees communicate with one another on nonbusiness matters. It is your challenge to both foster its use and avoid its misuse by your employees.

Fostering its use can be achieved by providing chat rooms, bulletin boards, and other capabilities that the employees feel are secure from "big brother" watching their every move. Avoiding its overuse can be achieved by limiting the number and length of time in the chat rooms, aging bulletin board contents, and creating an atmosphere throughout the organization that fosters use, but not abuse of the system. One additional way is to encourage off-hours access to the system, thereby expanding the time employees can use it and hopefully getting them to spend nonbusiness time on the system during non-prime-time hours.

Measuring the Impact of Your Web Site Online

Measuring the Impact of Your Web Site is online at **http://www. siteimpact.com**. The site is an essential companion to the book. Resources located there include:

- ❑ Downloadable originals for many of the forms and work-sheets shown in the book
- ❑ Links to many of the resources and sites described in the book
- ❑ Demo copies of some of the software discussed in Chapter 7
- ❑ Updates on our case studies
- ❑ Further information on services of eWorks! and Shiloh Associates, LLC
- ❑ Further additions based on your requests and feedback

Index